Longing for the Other

LONGING FOR THE OTHER

Levinas and Metaphysical Desire

DREW M. DALTON

DUQUESNE UNIVERSITY PRESS
PITTSBURGH, PENNSYLVANIA

Copyright © 2009 Duquesne University Press
All rights reserved

Published in the United States of America by
DUQUESNE UNIVERSITY PRESS
600 Forbes Avenue
Pittsburgh, Pennsylvania 15282

No part of this book may be used or reproduced,
in any manner or form whatsoever,
without written permission from the publisher,
except in the case of short quotations
in critical articles or reviews.

Library of Congress Cataloging-in-Publication Data

Dalton, Drew M., 1978–
    Longing for the other : Lévinas and metaphysical desire / Drew M. Dalton.
      p. cm.
    Includes bibliographical references (p.) and index.
    ISBN 978-0-8207-0425-8 (pbk. : alk. paper)
    1. Lévinas, Emmanuel. 2. Desire (Philosophy) 3. Other (Philosophy)
I. Title.
    B2430.L484.D35 2009
    194—dc22

                                                                                     2009023812

∞ Printed on acid-free paper.

for Robin and Thea

"[Longing] is never a possession, always a desire for something longer ago or further away or still 'about to be.'"
—C. S. Lewis, *Surprised by Joy*

"There is no past that we can bring back by longing for it. There is only an eternally new now that builds and creates itself out of the Best as the past withdraws."
—Goethe, *Maxims and Reflections*

Contents

Abbreviations	xi
Acknowledgments	xiii
Introduction: Levinas and the Problem of Human Longing	1
Levinas's Phenomenology of Metaphysical Desire	1
Defining Longing	4
The Unusual Grammar of Longing	11
Pursuing Levinas's Analysis of Human Longing	14

Part One: Human Longing

One • The Origins, Aim, and Ends of Human Longing: Levinas and Plato in Dialogue	19
Levinas on Longing	19
Levinas and Plato on Desire	24
Plato's Eros Reexamined	29
An Erotic Homecoming?	34
Longing, the Good, and the Other	36
Levinas and Plato on the Origins of Desire	43
Levinas on the Ends of Desire	49

Metaphysical Desire and Desire Proper	54
Plato's Account of Desire Reconsidered	60
Conclusions	65

Two • Longing and Striving for the Beyond: Levinas and Heidegger in Dialogue — 67

Levinas's Heideggerian Roots	67
Heidegger's Treatment of Plato and Eros	69
Heidegger on the Erotic Phenomenon	72
The Internal Inherence of Having and Striving in the Erotic Phenomenon	79
Authentic Eros and Primordial Longing	86
Heidegger and Levinas Reexamined	94
Heidegger's Being as "Beyond Being"?	98
Heidegger and Levinas on the Good Beyond Being	104
Conclusions	109

Part Two: Ethical Longing

Three • The Ethics of Longing: Levinas and Fichte in Dialogue — 113

Ethics: The Metaphysical Optics	113
The History of Idealism	114
Shame: An Introduction	121
Shame's First Revelation: Self-Consciousness	128
Shame, Responsibility, and Freedom	133
Shame and Longing	137
Idealism Reexamined: Fichte on Solicitation, Freedom, and Recognition	139
Strange Bedfellows: Fichte and Levinas on the Ethical and Longing	149
Levinas and Fichte Reconciled?	157
Conclusions	162

Part Three: Divine Longing

Four • The Metaphysics of Longing and Creature-Consciousness: Levinas and Schelling in Dialogue   *167*

    Through Shame to Creation   *167*
    Creation in Levinas: Creation as Contractio Dei   *171*
    Creation, the Trace, and Longing   *179*
    Creation in Levinas: Hypostasis as Contractio Hominis   *182*
    Creation through the Eyes of Schelling   *187*
    From Being to beings   *191*
    The Mutuality of Independence and Dependence   *200*
    Schelling and Levinas: A Missed Connection   *206*
    The Legacy of Creation: Ethics and Longing   *212*
    Conclusions   *221*

Five • Longing and the Numinous: Levinas and Otto in Dialogue   *224*

    Longing and the Beyond   *224*
    The Beyond and the Numinous   *229*
    Levinas and the Numinous: The Ambiguity of the Infinite   *236*
    Heidegger and Schelling on the Numinous: God in the Docks   *245*
    Longing and Evil   *250*
    Conclusions: Longing as the Vaccination of the Infinite   *257*

Notes   *263*
Bibliography   *293*
Index   *305*

ABBREVIATIONS

References to primary sources are abbreviated and cited in the body of the text. Full references are given in the bibliography.

WORKS BY FICHTE
FNR   *Foundations of Natural Right*
FTP   *Foundations of Transcendental Philosophy*
SK   *Science of Knowledge* (*Wissenschaftslehre*)

WORKS BY HEIDEGGER
Works by Heidegger are referenced by their *Gesamtausgabe* number followed by the German page number and the English page number separated by a slash.

GA 2	*Being and Time*
GA 5	*Off the Beaten Path* (*Holzewege*)
GA 6	*Nietzsche*, volume 1
GA 9	*Pathmarks* (*Wegmarken*)
GA 11	*Identity and Difference*
GA 14	*Time and Being*
GA 19	*Plato's Sophist*
GA 29/30	*The Fundamental Concepts of Metaphysics*
GA 34	*The Essence of Truth: On Plato's Cave Allegory and Theaetetus*

GA 40   *An Introduction to Metaphysics*
GA 42   *Schelling's Treatise on the Essence of Human Freedom*
GA 53   *Hölderlin's Hymn "The Ister"*
GA 54   *Parmenides*

WORKS BY LEVINAS

AT	*Alterity and Transcendence*
BPW	*Basic Philosophical Writings*
CPP	*Collected Philosophical Papers*
DF	*Difficult Freedom*
De	"Discussion d'ensemble," from *La Révélation*
EN	*Entre Nous: Thinking of the Other*
EI	*Ethics and Infinity*
EE	*Existence and Existents*
GDT	*God, Death, and Time*
NT	*Nine Talmudic Readings*
OE	*On Escape*
OB	*Otherwise Than Being or Beyond Essence*
TO	*Time and the Other*
TI	*Totality and Infinity*
Tr	"The Trace of the Other," in *Deconstruction in Context*

WORKS BY SCHELLING

AW	*The Ages of the World*
HF	*Of Human Freedom*
SS	"The Stuttgart Seminars," in *Idealist and the Endgame of Theory*

WORKS BY RUDOLF OTTO

IH	*The Idea of the Holy* (*Das Heilige*)

Acknowledgments

A work in progress now for a number of years, there are so many people who have contributed to the final completion of this project, both directly and indirectly, that the task of composing an acknowledgements complete enough to include them all becomes frankly impossible, something akin to constructing a map of a city on a 1:1 scale. Within this city of contributors, there are a few whose aid has been so essential that they deserve much more recognition than can be expressed by mere mention in these acknowledgments. Lacking any other means of conveying my gratitude to their foundational benefaction and promotion, however, my humble thanks will have to suffice.

Straight off, my deepest and most sincere thanks go to Professor Rudi Visker, my intellectual father, without whom neither this text nor my progress within philosophy would be possible. I should also like to thank everyone at the Katholieke Universiteit of Leuven whose guidance and support made the initial research into this project possible. I would especially like to thank Professors Paul Moyaert, Ignace Verhack, and Rudolf Bernet in whose classes the seeds to this project were first sewn. Of course, this list is incomplete without mention of Professor Jeffery Bloechl of Boston College who has championed my cause and this project since the beginning and whose friendship, hospitality, and scholarship guided me through the many drafts, dangers, and distractions encountered on the way to publication.

I would also like to acknowledge all of the hard work, patience and persistence of everyone at Duquesne University Press, especially Susan Wadsworth-Booth, without whose generosity and acumen the completion of this project is scarcely imaginable. My additional thanks goes out to my friends and colleagues at Saint Anslem College who have all put up with my long hours and bouts of moodiness along the way admirably; and, of course, my students, each of whom has most likely already familiarized themselves with the ends and outs of human longing from my countless tangents both in and out of class on the subject. Special mention must be made of Ryan Manley who helped me prepare one of the final drafts of this text.

Finally, I would like to thank all of my friends and family who have supported me in every way imaginable: my father, whose advice and strength I have drawn upon more times than I often care to admit; Robin and Thea, to whom this volume is dedicated and from whom I have learned more than I could ever teach. A special thanks also goes out to Professor Bruce Benson, of Wheaton College, whose classes first inspired my interest in philosophy and whose friendship in the years since has proved just as rich. And, finally, to all of the other scoundrels and scallywags who have put up with me: Rajiv Kaushik, Jeremy Hovda, David Hoffner, Rocky Clancy, Carla Pont, and Yongmi Schibel—thank you all.

Introduction

Levinas and the Problem of Human Longing

Levinas's Phenomenology of Metaphysical Desire

It is the aim of philosophy in general, and the special province of phenomenology in particular, to come to the aid of human experience by enlightening and informing through rigorous study and tireless pursuit those phenomena which constitute it. Considered in light of this charge, the work of Emmanuel Levinas stands out as one of the most fecund examples of philosophical and phenomenological investigation conducted in the twentieth century. Though often decried by its detractors as more prescriptive than descriptive, Levinas's work, when understood properly, proves to contain some of the most deeply revealing phenomenological descriptions of the human experience available, treating in its course such fundamental human phenomena as shame, birth and death, amongst others. On these topics his work proves not only gloriously profound, but deeply enriching as it provides for the reader a wellspring of insight into his or her own life. But there are other phenomena detailed by Levinas that are just as fundamentally a part of human experience, yet are not as easily identifiable by the reader — ones which seem to fall outside of or beyond our everyday subjective experience of the world. One such phenomenon is what Levinas terms *metaphysical desire.*

Metaphysical Desire, according to Levinas, is a desire unlike any of our other more quotidian desires — such as hunger and thirst, which he terms *needs*—in that it does not arise out of any determinate lack within us, nor aim at any particular object beyond us, much less promise any eventual satisfaction. Instead, he claims, metaphysical desire operates within the realm of the infinite where such distinctions as inside and outside or one and the other are blurred, if not entirely erased. It comes as no surprise then to note that very few readers have been able to identify or unpack precisely what Levinas is after in his descriptions of metaphysical desire and little to no scholarly research has been done upon the topic. After all, how is it possible that such an infinite phenomenon could make an appearance within the human subject who is, all else aside, decidedly finite? What we are presented with here, it seems, is a Zeno's paradox of sorts wherein an infinite phenomenon, if such a thing can even be conceived, is found within a finite container, human subjectivity. One would not be remiss for thinking then, at least at first glance, that Levinas strays here beyond his phenomenological and descriptive intentions and veers, perhaps irrevocably, into the realm of the firmly prescriptive, if not entirely imaginary. This conclusion has resulted in many declaring that at least in regards to his descriptions of metaphysical desire, and possibly elsewhere as well, Levinas appears to be less concerned with what one *does* experience than with what one *could* or *should* experience if desire were freed from the constraints of self-interest and bound to the ethical summons of the other. What is at stake in Levinas's analysis of metaphysical desire, they think, is not so much a picture of the way in which desire *actually* functions, but instead the way it could *ideally* function—that Levinas's account of metaphysical desire is essentially a hagiography of desire, an account of desire purified of the constraints of being and finitude. And yet it is Levinas's claim that metaphysical desire is not only an essential element of the *actual* experience of human subjectivity, it is, moreover, one of the most profound and poignant ways in which a subject becomes a subject and arises, on that basis, to its "true self" and hears the call that others place upon it.

The seemingly irreconcilable rift between our finite experiences and Levinas's phenomenological account of an infinite desire has partly resulted in a general misunderstanding within secondary literature concerning the role and nature of Levinas's account of metaphysical desire in particular and, as a result, his philosophical project as a whole. This is regrettable, but entirely understandable. What is even more regrettable, however, is that the seeming disconnect between Levinas's account and our own experience has made what is already a difficult task—that is, to read, understand, and see the application of the work of Emmanuel Levinas—even more difficult. The goal of the present work is an attempt to make this passage easier by filling in the valleys that separate our experience from Levinas's descriptions and reconnecting his thought with our own. To do this we must begin by attempting to identify the object of his inquiry—that is, we must endeavor to identify in our own language something which resembles his metaphysical desire. This, I propose, we find in the English verb *to long* or more specifically in its noun gerund form, *longing*. It is my contention then, that by examining Levinas's analysis of metaphysical desire as a human longing, something with which we are presumably more immediately familiar, we begin to glimpse what is really at stake in Levinas's account of metaphysical desire: namely, a phenomenology of human longing as an ethical, and ultimately, religious, phenomenon.

DEFINING LONGING

There are few experiences more poignant, enduring, or influential for the way in which we think about ourselves and the nature of our existence, than the experience of longing. Indeed, our longings function in many ways as one of the hidden foundations of our deepest and most secret identity—the one we are at pains to share or even identify ourselves. Nestled amongst the dark roots of our subjectivity, our longings serve to support many of our strongest hopes and dreams, providing support and underpinning for many of our actions and goals and yet strangely much more precious to us than what they may inspire us to achieve. Who among us would be willing to trade our most intimate longing for any amount of lucre or gain? Who among us would exchange the restless striving they inspire for any final ease or satisfaction? But though absolutely precious and priceless to us, their presence within us is by no means a source of pleasure. Quite the contrary, more often than not our longings inspire within us often unbearable feelings of dissatisfaction, melancholy, and pining.

As one of the subterranean underpinnings of our identity, our longings remain throughout our life a part of our being we think of as most us, and yet strangely, at the same time, few phenomena remain as elusive as our own longings—always removed at a distance from us, constantly evading our grasp or full understanding. Indeed, though we all may feel the poignant tug of our longings at our very core, few of us can truly give voice to them or declare forthrightly just what it is we are pining for. They seem, in a sense, too big for words—beyond the powers of ratiocination and language. And yet how is this possible? How is it that something we all identify as so much a part of our being can be so separate and other than us that we cannot speak it, much less fully understand it? Human longing thus appears to be a profoundly curious phenomenon, one which seemingly defies our modern understanding of ourselves.

In his work "The Buried Life," English poet and essayist Matthew Arnold seems to recognize the curious case of human longing referring to it as a kind of "unspeakable desire," one which pulses as the "deep" "unregarded river of our life," giving birth to the various streams and rivulets upon which our existence is buoyed.[1] For Arnold, this buried desire—this unspeakable desire—serves as the source of our drives, the impetus behind all our actions, informing and giving potency to all the more concrete objects or goals toward which we may endeavor in our conscious life. Ernest Hemingway, too, seemed to identify such an experience in his *A Moveable Feast* where he characterized human longing as a strange kind of hunger which cannot be satisfied by anything as simple as a good meal or sexual gratification and in fact functions to trouble the simple satisfactions such activities typically promise, keeping him awake at night, his vision drawn to the window and the distant hills.[2] Echoing the sentiments of both Arnold and Hemingway, C. S. Lewis describes his own experience of longing in his autobiography *Surprised by Joy* as a kind of "passionate, silent gazing at things *a long way off*," that seems always about things "*longer ago, further away or still 'about to be.'*"[3] Speaking almost directly to Hemingway's frustration at finding no end to his longing, Lewis suggests one "might as well offer a mutton chop to a man who is dying of thirst as offer sexual pleasure to the desire I am speaking of."[4] In recognition of the "unspeakable" nature of his longing Lewis writes that "it is difficult to find words strong enough for the sensation [of longing]. Milton's 'enormous bliss' of Eden (giving the full, ancient meaning to 'enormous') comes somewhere near it. It [is] a sensation, of course, of desire; but desire for what?"[5] Even Shakespeare found a place for longing in his work, recognizing its power therein to interrupt and disturb the complacency with which we typically enjoy the pleasures of the world. In *Anthony and Cleopatra,* Shakespeare has Cleopatra rise from her bed and declare "Give me my robe, put on my crown; I have immortal longings in me."[6] Cleopatra's longings are so great, Shakespeare seems to suggest, that they not only rise her from her repose and force her into action, but they also somehow exceed her, extending beyond her own mortality into the realm of the immortal and infinite. But how are we to understand the nature of these beautiful poetizations of our experience? What is the true nature of our longings? And, how do they function within us? Our first hint comes through an analysis of the historical definition of the word.

Longing is a very unusual word with a rich semantic history. A noun stemming from the intransitive verb *to long,* as we have already mentioned, *longing* has come to mean for us a kind of earnest or ardent, heartfelt desire "especially," as *The American Heritage Dictionary of the English Language* puts it, "for something beyond reach."[7] As such, it expresses a kind of "prolonged unfulfilled desire or need,"[8] what the *Oxford English Dictionary* refers to as a "yearning desire."[9] Etymologically, in its original verb form, *to long* is derived from the Old English word *langian* which comes from the Middle Dutch *langen,* meaning "to be or seem long; to 'think long,' desire; to extend, hold out, offer;" and from the Old High German *langên* and Middle High German *langen,* "to reach, extend, suffice."[10] All of these roots stress the passive nature of longing, the fact that it is not something which is done by someone, but is rather something which happens to someone. It is something which is aroused, extended, and held out to someone. Perhaps the oldest ancestor to the modern form of the word which still carries a resemblance to its contemporary meaning is the Old Norse *langa,* an impersonal verb meaning "to desire."[11]

These myriad old meanings are retained in the modern English form of the word giving rise to a constellation of contemporary usages all orbiting the same basic idea. As a result, the *Oxford English Dictionary* has more than four different entries for the word *to long,* the second of which, and the one that is of most pertinence to the investigation at hand, has eight different permutations. Firstly *to long* is defined as "to grow longer; to lengthen;" secondly, "to lengthen, prolong;" thirdly, "to put far away;" fourthly, "to cause to pass over a certain distance;" and fifth and sixthly, "to have a yearning desire; to wish earnestly," or "to be restless or impatient."[12] The *Oxford English Dictionary* consults us in its seventh permutation of the word that it can be used as an adverb only "with a verb of motion implied," as in the phrase, "to move longingly towards the bed." Finally, *to long* can mean "to grow weary."[13] This experience of growing weary through our longings is most commonly compared in both the *Oxford English Dictionary* and English literature to the experience of growing sick with desire. Even in our quotidian attempt to place a limit upon, or explain the genesis of our longings we will very often identify them as a kind of love-*sickness* or home*sickness*. When one declares him or herself to feel homesick or lovesick one attempts to give a name for the experience of having been overwhelmed and almost infected, as it were, with a deep longing that cannot be satisfied and which drives one into weariness.[14]

This latter reference to the sickness felt in the experience of human longing has been drawn upon extensively in the poetic employment of the word. A section entitled "Longing" in George Herbert's celebrated poem "The Temple" begins, "With sick and famisht eyes, / With doubling knees and weary bones, / To Thee my cries, / To Thee my grones, / To thee my sighs, my tears ascend: No end?"[15] Notice how Herbert simultaneously recognizes the protracted nature of human longing (that it has no end) and the weariness and sickness entailed in its ancient meaning. His poem is littered with such comparisons between longing and sickness referring to how his "soul is hoarse" as a throat can be with cough, and how in it he is moved toward death. He even names this longing a "curse" at one point, recognizing only at the end of his poem that his hope for cure and healing is held out beyond death through reunion with his God.

Shakespeare too drew upon the inexorable connection between sickness and longing in his famous 147th sonnet. There he writes:

> My love is as a fever, longing still
> For that which longer nurseth the disease;
> Feeding on that which doth preserve the ill,
> The uncertain sickly appetite to please.
> My reason, the physician to my love,
> Angry that his prescriptions are not kept,
> Hath left me, and I desperate now approve,
> Desire his death, which physic did expect
> Past cure I am, now reason is past care,
> And frantic-mad with evermore unrest;
> My thoughts and my discourse as madmen's are,
> At random from the truth vainly express'd
> For I have sworn thee fair, and thought thee bright
> Who art as black as hell, as dark as night.[16]

Notice how for Shakespeare longing is not merely a sickness which affects the heart, it is one which invades the mind, driving reason out and resulting in a kind of madness and mania. The connection between longing and sickness continues to this day. Even C. S. Lewis describes his own longings as a desire "with almost *sickening* intensity."[17]

It is interesting to note that the allusion to sickness present in the term longing is not exclusive to the English language. It is also maintained in the contemporary German translation of longing, namely *Sehnsucht*. The Wildhagen and Héraucourt German-English Dictionary rightly translates *Sehnsucht* as an "intense longing, ardent desire," and "yearning."[18] Growing from the verb root *sehnen* which is closest to the English "to long" and is translated as "to long, ache, hunger, languish,"[19] and the noun *Sucht* translated first as "disease," or "epilepsy, falling-sickness," and secondly as "mania, passion, rage" or "addiction."[20] This idea is supported by the Grimm brothers in their famous dictionary. There *Sehnsucht* is translated as a *"schmachtendes verlangen"* (languishing, yearning), as a kind of "*krankheit des schmerzlichen verlangens, liebeskrankheit, liebesbegierde*" (painful disease of yearning, lovesickness, loving-yearning).[21] Not only is the notion of disease or sickness the same there, even the reference to lovesickness is matched. To support this definition, the Grimm brothers go on to cite numerous uses and earlier definitions of the word, one of which is of particular note. By their citation, Johann Leonhard Frisch in his German lexicography the *Deutsch-Lateinisches Wörterbuch* (1741) defines *Sehnsucht*, dividing it into its two roots, *sehn-sucht*, as a "*desiderium quo quis quasi morbo laborat*" (An intense desire which labors almost to sickness).[22] Hence the Grimm translation of *Sucht* as "*morbus, passio, cupiditas.*"[23] Again, note the reference to morbidity, sickness, and disease, and to labor (*laborat*) and exhaustion.

While more contemporary Germans immediately associate the word *Sucht* with addiction, as in drug addiction, this is a more recent permutation in the meaning of the word resulting, perhaps, from its homonymous relationship to the verb *sucht* meaning "much sought after."[24] Originally, however, the *Sucht* present in *Sehnsucht* was derived from the verb *siechen*, "to be ailing, sickly, [or] in bad health," "to languish, to pine away," or, to reference the English cited above, "to grow weary."[25]

Human longing, *Sehnsucht*, is not all sickness and morbidity, of course. First and foremost, as a desire, it expresses a potency within human life to act and to move, specifically to move upward as it were, out beyond the immediate and toward that which seems to lie beyond our lives, in the immortality promised on the other side of life. Hence longing's close association with the concept of the holy. This is perfectly expressed in Goethe's poem "Selige Sehnsucht."

> *Sag es niemand, nur den Weisen,*
> *Weil die Menge gleich verhöhnet:*
> *Das Lebendge will ich preisen,*
> *Das nach Flammentod sich sehnet.*
> *In der Liebesnächte Kühlung,*

> *Die dich zeugte, wo du zeugtest,*
> *Überfällt dich fremde Fühlung,*
> *Wenn die stille Kerze leuchtet.*
> *Nicht mehr bleibest du umfangen*
> *In der Finsternis Beschattung,*
> *Und dich reisset neu Verlangen*
> *Auf zu höherer Begattung.*
> *Keine Ferne macht dich schwierig,*
> *Kommst geflogen und gebannt,*
> *Und zuletzt, des Lichts begierig,*
> *Bist du Schmetterling verbrannt.*
> *Und so lang du das nicht hast,*
> *Dieses: Stirb und Werde!*
> *Bist du nur ein trüber Gast*
> *Auf der dunklen Erde.*[26]

For Goethe, *Sehnsucht* seems to be a kind of impatience (*begierig*) for something amorphous and yet clearly beyond us, glimmering like the flicker of a flame in the darkness of our mortal understanding. Like the glow of candle, Goethe suggests, *Sehnsucht* calls us upward away from the terrestrial toward our death and that which lies beyond such that we may become (*Werde*) something other than we are here below. Clearly Goethe's thinking on the subject is fraught with metaphysical significance, the likes of which we can only imagine. But whatever its metaphysical meaning might be, his use of the word *Sehnsucht* to name this poem certainly works to confirm what we have already seen in the definition of the word; namely, that the kind of desire identified in *Sehnsucht* is one that seems to stretch beyond us, drawing us outside of our selves, inspiring us, but, simultaneously, draining us of our vital energy such that we grow weak and sick in its train. For even here we witness the appearance of a sort of morbidity, the link between longing and sickness and death. For, according to Goethe, to attain this beyond one must pass through death.

THE UNUSUAL GRAMMAR OF LONGING

To Long is not only an interesting verb semantically and etymologically, but also grammatically. In the English language a verb can be conjugated in the present tense in four different ways according to two intersecting possibilities: its relation to time and its mode, that is, the way in which it functions. In relation to time, a verb can be conjugated in the present tense either straightforwardly (*I write*) or perfectly (*I have written*); and, in relation to function, it can be conjugated either simply (see above) or progressively (*I am writing, I have been writing*, respectively). In regards to the first permutation the distinction is rather clear: when a verb is used to express something about the present in terms of the past, or to carry a past action into the present, it is placed in the present perfect. This indicates that though an action may have been completed at some time in the past, and is therefore *perfect* in the old/Latin sense (completed, fulfilled), it still carries a present significance. To recognize this we place the active verb in its past participle form alongside the verb *to have* conjugated in the present form, as in the phrase "I *have written* a number of pages." When, on the other hand, a verb participates solely in the present and bears no relation to the past it is conjugated in the straightforward present. This is relatively clear. The distinction between a verb's conjugation as either simple or progressive, however, is much more difficult.

Essentially this distinction concerns the way the verb functions within its designated time; if it refers to an action which is being actively engaged in *at the moment*—taken up by a subject—then it is placed in the present progressive. This conjugation is formed by placing the subject of the sentence alongside the copula *to be* conjugated accordingly and by attaching the suffix *ing* to the active verb. Thus the verb *to write* is conjugated progressively in the first person as "I *am* writ*ing*." This form indicates that now, actively, I *am* engaged in the act of *writing*. The copula ties the action of the sentence to the *being* of the subject, implying an intentionality in the subject's action.

The present simple, on the other hand, does not invoke the copula. Used to express actions that are true of the subject *in general,* the present simple does more than merely connote those actions which *are happening now*. Instead it indicates those actions which *generally* happen in and around the life of the subject. In this way the present simple does not relate so much *what* a subject *is doing,* but *who* the subject *is,* what actions generally distinguish or identify the subject, what his or her habits are. Thus when I say "I write," "I jog," or "I read," I am not telling you what it is that I am doing *now,* but what it is that I do *in general,* those actions which make up my identity, which express *how* or *who* it is that *I am*. Thus there is no need to invoke the copula here, as it is already implied in the action. "I write," renames in a more specific way my being, how "I am" in the world.

This is all well and good and generally understood by those who have studied English in any formal way. But there is something unusual worth noting here. In English there are certain words which are not normally conjugated in the progressive tense; and, when they are, their function in the sentence usually changes from that of a verb, to that of a noun gerund, nominating in some way the subject or his or her actions. Some of these verbs are *to believe, to love, to know, to belong, to remember,* and alternatively *to forget* and, not least among them *to long*. There is something which unites all of these verbs in that they express actions which, in a sense, can only be true *in general*. None of these actions can *actively* be taken up by a subject and engaged in the same way that a more simple action like writing can. They express something not about what the subject is concretely *doing* at any given time. *Belief* and *love* are not *actions* someone *does,* but are rather *states* in which someone can *be*. They thus define who a subject *is,* what actions designate the way in which a particular subject *is*. Thus, these sorts of actions are usually barred from conjugation in the present progressive. One would never say, for example "I am forgetting." The sentence does not make sense. One does not, or cannot, actively forget, despite Nietzsche's extortions to just such an action.[27] *Forgetting* is an action which comes over the subject. It is an action that a subject cannot have a volitional relation to. In this way these verbs resemble the nonvolitional verbs of other languages such as Tibetan and Teonaht, though they are not named such by English linguists. There is something about the meaning of these verbs which prohibits them from expressing an action actively engaged in or taken up by a subject. They seem to belong essentially and more directly to the realm of being. They need not and cannot be mediated by the copula as words conjugated into the progressive are. There is something special about these verbs which restrict them to that mode of conjugation which serves to rename the copula. Thus, these kinds of verbs appear to be tied in some special way to the being of a subject such that they cannot be split from it and placed alongside it as a specific action *happening now*, as it were. Whenever they are spoken or written, then, they must remain in being, conjugated simply in such a way that they rename and give shape to that being. The inexorable link between these words and being, then, seems to reveal something about what it means to be for subjects.

Since the verb under investigation here, *to long*, is counted among the ranks of this type of special verb, we should perhaps endeavor to pause momentarily and reflect on the significance of this fact. There seems to be something about the nature of longing which is tied intrinsically to our being so much that perhaps part of what it means to be is to long. Its nonvolitional relation to our being is supported by what we saw above of its old meaning. There we observed that the myriad etymological roots of the word *to long* somehow implied the passivity of the subject in relation to longing. (Longing was an extension of the subject, the subject being stretched beyond itself, *not* the subject's extension of itself. It seems to be in keeping with this old meaning that the contemporary word *to long* is grammatically restricted to conjugation in the simple.

It is an analysis of the meaning and significance of the remarkably rich and uncanny experience of human longing that Levinas's accounts of metaphysical desire aim at. In coming to understand this fact one has already plotted a route across the chasm of misunderstanding surrounding Levinas's account of metaphysical desire. The next step to this endeavor, the attempt to understand how Levinas's phenomenological analysis of metaphysical desire helps us to understand the nature and function of our longings, will form the lion's share of this work.

Pursuing Levinas's Analysis of Human Longing

Part of the confusion concerning Levinas's work is the result of a failure within contemporary scholarship to recognize those authors within the canon with whom Levinas interacts in the formation of his own thought. Indeed, there is a strange tendency within Levinasian scholarship to examine more closely Levinas's dependence upon the noncanonical texts than his interaction with the great thinkers of the Western tradition. Scores of texts have been written on Levinas's reliance upon the Torah and Talmud for inspiration, and especially the early Kabbalistic readings of those texts, his interest in the work of German thinker Franz Rosenzweig has equally been explored, as has the influence of French poetry upon his work, especially that of Arthur Rimbaud, Stéphane Mallarmé, and Paul Celan. In comparison relatively little has been written on Levinas's dialogue with the canonical thinkers of Western philosophy, though it is largely in response to an extensive study of their work that his own positions emerged. This is in part the fault of Levinas himself who only rarely mention in his major works any philosophical influence outside of Edmund Husserl and Martin Heidegger, not to mention of course his famous acknowledgment at the beginning of *Totality and Infinity* to Franz Rosenzweig which is left curiously undeveloped throughout the rest of the volume. It is also perhaps due to the fact that Levinas posits his work as a kind of critique of and attempt to escape from the excesses and missteps made within the history of Western philosophical thought. Indeed, Levinas forthrightly declares that the ethical account of the subject and the other who grounds it cannot fit within the traditional boundaries and interest expressed throughout the history of philosophy. Nevertheless, it is within this history, which could in itself be seen in some ways as Levinas's other, that the subject of his work is itself grounded and functions, and it is with this history that his work more often than not refers, lending credence to the claim that while Levinas does indeed seek to diverge from some of the tendencies established within the history of western philosophy, his work does not veer so far from that tradition as to be categorized outside of it.

In the end, though revolutionary in many ways, Levinas's work must still be understood as a part of that tradition. It is therefore essential to the study of Levinas's thought that his work be understood in relation to those thinkers from which it draws and against which it is directed. This is a difficult task, however, as we have mentioned, given Levinas's reluctance to interact directly within his major works, *Existence and Existents, Totality and Infinity, Otherwise than Being* with any of his influences outside of his former teachers, Husserl and Heidegger. Nevertheless, a good portion of his work is dedicated to refuting and/or expanding the ideas of a few key thinkers within the tradition, chief amongst them of course are Plato, Descartes, Husserl, and Heidegger who along with Franz Rosenzweig represent the main philosophical interlocutors with whom Levinas engages openly in his major works, and to a lesser extent Kierkegaard, Spinoza, and Martin Buber, who Levinas choose to address in smaller articles. But there are still other, silent partners, within the Levinasian oeuvre—partners who are much more seldom, if ever, acknowledged for example Fichte, Schelling, Hegel, and Rudolf Otto, who were profoundly influential on the development of both the major and more minor works. While not as obviously influential on Levinas, these thinkers nevertheless exert just as profound an influence on his work. This is especially the case, as will become more apparent, in the genesis of his thought on the nature of human longing. If it is in dialogue with these thinkers that Levinas's work develops, especially his account of metaphysical desire, then it must be through an excavation and exposition of this dialogue that his thought must be explored and interpreted. And so is born the chief aim of the work at hand: to follow the often obscured trail of Levinas's thought on the nature of human longing and the surrounding phenomena by revealing and reconstructing his sometimes occulted interaction with the other thinkers within the history of philosophy.

Given this task, what follows will at times take the form of a kind of philosophical detective story, following the clues left by Levinas's concerning his convergence with and divergence from other thinkers of the Western philosophical tradition in the hopes of solving the mystery concerning his understanding and our experience of human longing. In order to follow these clues sincerely, however, means that at times we may feel as if we are being led down a blind alley, or, conversely, pulling Levinas into realms he is loath to go, but it is only by following these seemingly twisted routes that we will ultimately arrive at our end: a deeper understanding of the uncanny phenomenon of human longing. Thus, though at times in this process we may glimpse a visage of Levinas we do not immediately recognize, as if reflected through a window darkly (our thinkers serving as such reflective surfaces), we must not fret, but instead trust that it is only by seeing him askance in this way, that we will ultimately be able to confront his account of longing face-to-face.

PART ONE
HUMAN LONGING

ONE

The Origins, Aim, and Ends of Human Longing

Levinas and Plato in Dialogue

LEVINAS ON LONGING

Levinas never uses the term "longing" in his work. This is not because, as we have already noted, he is not interested in it as a phenomenon, but rather because his native language does not provide him with a suitable equivalent. *Longing* is traditionally rendered in French merely as *désir,* though it is sometimes modified as being a particularly *grand, intense,* or *ardent désir.* It is alternatively translated as *nostalgie,* though as we will see Levinas goes to great pains to distinguish what he understands to be true longing from the experience of nostalgia. Indeed, it is precisely because of this perceived distinction that Levinas is forced to coin a new term for his analysis of human longing, namely: *metaphysical desire.*

To understand Levinas's notion of metaphysical desire one must first correctly accent the phrase. In this case, the accent should fall on the first word, *metaphysical,* and not, as one would initially think, on the latter. The notion of the metaphysical is in many ways the central theme in Levinas's works. It is in fact the subject of the first three lines of his most famous work *Totality and Infinity.* There he writes, quoting Rimbaud, that "'the true life is absent.' But we are in the world. Metaphysics arises and is maintained in this alibi" (*TI* 33). Metaphysics consists then for Levinas in what he terms the "'elsewhere' and the 'otherwise' and the 'other'" (33).

Given its metaphysical bend, then, Levinas identifies the desire we have termed longing as one which "tends toward something else entirely, toward the *absolutely other*" (*TI* 33). As a desire directed toward that which remains, by definition, always and forever something else and absolutely other, metaphysical desire must necessarily function within us as a kind of transcendence — that is, it will serve to perpetually draw us outward and onward, always further afield than ourselves and that which is present to us. But the transcendence initiated by Levinas's metaphysical desire results in more than merely noncoincidence with the self, although this too is part of it. Much more than this, it is primarily, Levinas thinks, a transcendence which is directed toward that which is "other than" and "exterior" to the subject (292). Indeed, the whole of *Totality and Infinity* is labeled an "essay on exteriority." As exterior, the metaphysical expresses that which is always *beyond* the subject.

But, the metaphysical for Levinas is still more than sheer exteriority. Its identity is not maintained in its relation to the subject as that which is simply exterior. Not everything which is outside the subject carries the weight of the metaphysical for Levinas, the desk at which we sit or the pen with which we write. Instead, he claims, the metaphysical proper bears a specific positive meaning and ethical value. It thus not only represents for him that which is "elsewhere" and "otherwise," but also that which is superior and above us. The metaphysical is, he claims, situated on a *height* (*TI* 34–35, 200, 297; *BPW* 12, 18). Metaphysical desire is thus directed, he claims, not merely outside, yet on the same level as, the subject, but rather it is directed toward that which is superior to the subject. Indeed, argues Levinas, the transcendence initiated in metaphysical desire is thus directed toward that which is *transcendent* proper. Hence Levinas's nomination of the movement which typifies metaphysical desire as trans*ascendence* (*TI* 35). In metaphysical desire one feels oneself ascendant, elevated, lifted up, over and beyond not only oneself, but everything which is horizontally immediate and available.

For this reason, Levinas not only avoids employing the French rendering of longing, *nostalgie,* but in fact pointedly distinguishes his metaphysical desire from it. Nostalgia, in stark contrast to the longing of metaphysical desire, is not oriented toward that which remains other, but remains forever solely on the level of the self—specifically that which the self has lost. As such, it is much more akin to what he terms a need (see *BPW* 51). Levinas writes, "As commonly interpreted need would be at the basis of desire; desire would characterize a being indigent and incomplete or fallen from it past grandeur. It would coincide with the consciousness of what has been lost." Residing as they do on the basis of need, all desires thus ordered become "essentially a nostalgia, a longing for return" (*TI* 33). What nostalgia aims at then is not that which is transcendent to it, but the restoration of a lost immanence.

Given its aim, Levinas characterizes need and nostalgia, as ultimately aimed at the consumption, absorption, and integration of some desired object such that "the forces that were in the other become *my* forces, become me" (*TI* 129).[1] Arising as it does from an absence in me or something lost to me, and venturing toward the renewal of me, need and nostalgia do not demonstrate movements which are motivated by or directed toward that which is other or properly transcendent. Instead, they are structured entirely around the interests of the present subject aiming ultimately at the subject's restoration and satisfaction. The only kind of transcendence expressed in such a movement arises from the temporary displeasure a subject feels with itself when it is lacking the object of some need—when it is hungry or thirsty, for example. This kind of transcendence stands in stark contrast to the kind of vertical transascendence occasioned by metaphysical desire, for herein, once the desired object is attained, the transcendence immediately ceases, and the subject is returned to a state of complacent equivalence with itself. This return is, of course, accompanied by enjoyment or pleasure, the satisfaction of the desire—hence Levinas's claims that need is essentially about the *enjoyment* of the subject (116).

There is no recognition or affirmation of the otherwise for its own sake within such an economy. To the contrary, nothing truly otherwise ever enters into the dynamic of need. Any determinate other encountered therein is immediately interpreted in terms of the subject's interests. As such its status is reduced solely to that of an object of possible consumption or use. Its otherness is not what is aimed for, as in metaphysical desire, instead it is an obstacle which must be overcome for its integration into the subject's life. The object of one's needs thus never arises to the status of the metaphysical proper, but remains always something which is merely at hand for the subject, a prop or episode, as it were, in the epic narrative of the subject's life.

Levinas thus compares the kind of movement expressed in the economy of need to the tale of Odysseus, the ultimate expression of nostalgia (*TI* 102, 176; Tr 346). Odysseus, by Levinas's read, though adrift in the otherwise and beset on all sides by alterity, never encounters anything truly transcendent to his own interests.[2] For, throughout his journeys Odysseus's sole intention is the return home. Any strange land or people he encounters along the way become merely an instrument for fulfilling this intention or an obstacle to be overcome. These temporary transcendences and others he encounters thus become little more than fodder for interesting anecdotes to be told later around the hearth fires of Ithaca. As a result, Odysseus's encounter with the foreign becomes nothing other than a temporary setback, a momentary delay in arriving back to himself and his own land, a suspension which is resolved through homecoming.[3] The result of all of these experiences and transcendences is not transformation, then, but gain; for not only does Odysseus have the pleasure of returning home, he returns home heaped with laud and wealth. For these reasons, Levinas sees Odysseus's story as essentially one recounting the movement of need and nostalgia: a subject is momentarily displaced from him or herself only to be eventually restored to immanence and end the day happier and healthier.

In contrast to this story, and to characterize the experience of metaphysical desire, Levinas proposes we read the story of Abraham "who leaves his fatherland forever for a yet unknown land, and forbids his servants to even bring back his son to the point of departure" as a kind of anti-Odysseus (Tr 348). Abraham's story of exile and peregrination seems much more suited to the dynamics of metaphysical desire. For metaphysical desire, argues Levinas, is not, like Odysseus's travels, directed toward "a lost fatherland or plenitude; it is not homesickness, is not nostalgia" (*CPP* 57). Instead, it is, "a desire that cannot be satisfied," that does not aim to return; nor does it arise out of some supposed loss (*TI* 34).

This is a radical distinction to make. Metaphysical desire is not merely the reassertion of an "unsatisfied need," (*TI* 179) as it seems to be for Spinoza, for example who defines human longing (*desiderium*) in book 3, proposition 36 of his *Ethics* as a "sorrow, in so far as it is related to the absence of what we love."[4] For Levinas, in contrast to Spinoza, human longing is not merely the result of an incomplete transcendence, one which, though striving for satisfaction is eternally denied or delayed its arrival. Rather, it is fundamentally and by nature *insatiable*. It is thus marked by a transcendence which is wholly otherwise than the one manifest by nostalgia.[5] There is no eventual unity promised between the desiring subject and the aim of metaphysical desire. Metaphysical desire ties the subject to an aim that is maintained at an insurmountable distance. Thus, though one may want to presume that metaphysical desire is directed toward some *end*, perhaps the metaphysical as such, whatever that would be, this end never becomes an *object* for the longing subject, never becomes a determinate aim categorized as a source of possible satisfaction (99). It is not the case, then, that were the subject of metaphysical desire to somehow reach the metaphysical itself, presuming such a thing can even be talked about in such a way, it would find itself placated. To the contrary, metaphysical desire only grows stronger as one pursues its presumed end. Thus, he argues that once one is caught up in the movement of metaphysical desire and pursuing the metaphysical in its own right, one does not find oneself in any way satiated, but instead even more desirous—even more restless (*CPP* 121). Metaphysical desire, it seems, is not a movement that once aroused can be bedded down, but one which instead grows increasingly intense the more it is pursued. It is transcendence which is forever, and by design, incomplete, and not merely because in our finitude we fail to attain it (*TI* 63). Instead, metaphysical longing is "situated beyond satisfaction and nonsatisfaction" (179).

LEVINAS AND PLATO ON DESIRE

Although Levinas's analysis of metaphysical desire is certainly interesting, and unfathomably profound, it is, as we have already noted, also a bit alienating to its reader. It is hard to get a grasp on precisely what it is that he is detailing therein. Though it is clear that he attempts to describe a phenomenon of human experience that had previously been covered over and forgotten as a result of being ordered under the form of desire rendered as need, it is nevertheless a struggle to identify precisely what the experience he details in metaphysical desire consists in. The experience as he describes it lacks any real tangibility or phenomenality. One is even left wondering whether his analysis is a description of a phenomenon at all. Or whether, as is so often accused, his program is much more prescriptive than descriptive—not the attempt to detail what one *does* experience, but rather what one *could or should* experience. Indeed, one is left with the feeling that perhaps in his pursuit of the "true life" which, for him, is "absent," he has forgotten that we, his readers, live here below in the world. To bridge this disconnect and to ground Levinas's analysis it is useful to bring his work into dialogue with another thinker. In this way we will be able to sharpen Levinas's blurry distinctions into something that can be perceived and grasped more clearly. Plato's work serves perfectly as the lens to bring this phenomenon into focus, not only because therein we find something correlate to Levinas's thought, but also because he is one of the thinkers with whom Levinas overtly interacts.[6]

Levinas's relationship to Plato is ambiguous, however. On the one hand, Levinas figures his work as a kind of return to Plato (*BPW* 58), and as little more than a repetition and clarification of the insights first glimpsed by Plato (*EN* 204). In Plato, Levinas finds an "affirmation of the human independent of culture and history," which is set against the way in which subsequent thinkers subsume the individual to universals and normative structures (*BPW* 58). Moreover, it is in Plato's conception of a "Good beyond Being" that Levinas finds a way out of the realm of ontology and into the realm of the otherwise and the ethical meaning grounded therein (*CPP* 175; *BPW* 21, 122–25; *OB* 12).[7]

But, on the other hand, much of Levinas's work is dedicated to a scathing condemnation of Platonic thought. Plato is in fact one of the few philosophers within the history of Western philosophy who is saddled with almost the entire list of Levinasian expletives. Plato's thought, he claims, establishes an economy of *need* (*TO* 64ff.) and *nostalgia* (*EN* 149) that favors *return* over exile (*BPW* 14; *CPP* 151). He is a proponent of *fusion* (*TO* 93–94; *EN* 112–13) over difference and his account of the "subject" verges into *solipsism* (*TO* 100–01; *BPW* 88; *CPP* 49). In a word, Plato's thought is seen by Levinas as supporting the *tyranny* of the subject over the world (*CPP* 16, 22–23), the same kind of *tyranny* expressed in the travels of Odysseus.[8]

This ambiguity in the Levinasian literature has led to sharp debate amongst readers of Levinas some whom, while acknowledging the ambiguity, insist that at the end of the day Levinas's thought diverges profoundly from the Platonic system while other authors insist that ultimately Levinas and Plato share much more in common than Levinas would be comfortable admitting.[9] Interestingly, one of the most apparent places where Levinas's troubled relationship to Plato can be seen, as is suggested by the language he uses to condemn him, is in his exploration of desire. To be clear, we are not asserting here that Levinas's account of desire differs entirely from Plato's. Quite to the contrary, as we have already noted, Levinas openly admits his dependence upon Platonic conceptions, especially, as we will see, with regard to desire.[10] Instead, it is suggested that, though drawing heavily upon Plato, Levinas must ultimately diverge from Platonic renderings of desire in order to assert his own phenomenological account of human longing *qua* metaphysical desire. In order to understand both his relationship to Plato and, through it, the singularity of his account of human longing, we must trace both his dependence and his divergence from Plato; and since the novelty of his account depends on the latter, we must proceed by trying to detail the precise nature of the way in which he seeks to take his distance from Plato.

As we have seen, the value of the metaphysical for Levinas is established in the fact that it is not only exterior to the subject, but situated on a height above the subject such that the subject is transported away from itself and toward the beyond. This is the crucial difference between his account of human longing and Plato's, where it is treated as a form of Eros. According to Levinas, Plato's treatment of the phenomenon reduces the singularity of this experience into something which becomes nothing more than a kind of *need,* and thus stuck in the economy of the traditional notion of desire as a force arising out of some perceived absence, aimed at some determinate object/aim, and concluding in the subject's eventual satisfaction (*EE* 30, 86; *CPP* 164; *TO* 64ff.; *TI* 114, 254). Ultimately then, the Platonic account of Eros fails to fully arrive at the kind of trans*ascendence* which he ascribes to metaphysical desire. As a result, Platonic Eros ultimately remains little more than a kind of nostalgia, and thus must be distinguished fundamentally from his metaphysical desire. Levinas even goes so far as to state that what he aims at in his account of metaphysical desire is a kind of "Love without Eros" (*BPW* 140).

This is of course rather curious, for Plato explicitly states, at least according to Diotima's account in the *Symposium,* that Eros is a movement toward the Good, the beautiful, or the divine, all of which are certainly associated with the above or the beyond. And the *Phaedrus,* for its part, is filled with images likening erotic transcendence to an ascent. There the soul of the desirous is compared to a winged horse; and, of course, "the natural function of the wing is to soar *upwards* and carry that which is heavy up to the place where dwells the race of the gods" (246d–e; italics mine). Levinas even seems to recognize this element with Plato's account of Eros, identifying therein something resembling his assertion that *height* must be attributed to the movement of this phenomenon. This he acknowledges citing Plato's claim in the *Republic* that "in my opinion that knowledge which is of being and of the unseen can make the soul look *upwards*" (*TI* 34–35; italics mine).

Levinas's problem with Plato's account of Eros then seems to lie not so much in the *way* in which the movement of desire is characterized, but in how *the end* of that movement is understood. The *ascent* lacking in Plato's account of Eros, as critiqued by Levinas, thus seems to stem not so much from the kind of movement it presents, but in the object, aim, or trajectory of that movement. Thus, though it may mount the subject on wings, those wings fail to carry the subject toward that which is truly transcendent, the metaphysical proper.

According to Levinas, the movement of Platonic Eros is not one directed toward the otherwise, but toward a *return*. Recounting Aristophanes's myth in the *Symposium* "in which love reunites the two halves of one sole being," he identifies Platonic Eros as an "adventure as a return to the self" (*TI* 254; cf. *BPW* 139–40). Like need, then, Platonic Eros seems to resemble for Levinas the travels of Odysseus. The problem is then that for him Plato's Eros ultimately aims at a kind of homecoming, a return to and reappropriation of that which was lost or removed by time. This is why it is a movement which Plato defines as fundamentally guided by memory and recollection (*anamnesis*). Eros, it seems, operates alongside recollection as a means to repossessing that which has been lost to the subject. It is not aimed at any real exteriority, as metaphysical desire is, but at that which is held interiorly by memory (*TI* 51, 56–57; *EN* 149). On other words, Plato's Eros does not appear to be aimed at that which is truly other or outside the self, but ultimately at that which belongs to the self, indeed to the self proper.[11] As such Eros appears to be less a kind of metaphysical longing than a form of need or nostalgia. This is further demonstrated in the fact that, according to Levinas, Plato's account of erotic transcendence seems to position it as a movement which eventually ends, like consumption, in the satisfaction of the subject—in the *fusion* of the subject with the object of his affection such that the subject is made whole again, and is returned to his primordial rest (*EN* 113). In this way, the dynamics of Eros appear to be much more circuitous than they are linear. It is thus, for Levinas, representative of a kind of desire like need which fails to break free from the gravitational pull of the subject's being and which, therefore, endlessly orbits the self from whence it was launched.[12] This is not to say that Eros is somehow "bad" for Levinas, that it is a mendacious metaphysical desire, or some sort of moral danger. Rather it is simply to state that Eros does not demonstrate the same metaphysical trajectory and power as his longing. The two are for him divergent and should not then be read as different expressions of the same tendency.

But is this an accurate reading of the Platonic account of Eros? If so then Plato's account of Eros must, like any other need, hold out the possibility of some eventual satisfaction, if not in this life, then at least in the next. Its transcendence must move toward that which will ultimately fulfill it, even if that object is infinitely removed. And, moreover, in its movement toward this end, it must find itself slowly, but ever increasingly, becoming whole again, nearing its eventual return to fulfillment. This is in part why, after all, Levinas was so insistent upon the fact that metaphysical desire, in pursuing its end, by contrast, becomes ever increasingly desirous of its object. This phenomenon, he seems to maintain, testifies to the fact that its end does not complete it. It stands to reason then, that in Plato's account, where satisfaction is understood to be the ultimate aim of Eros, the subject's desire should not "deepen" as it proceeds but, in a sense, become "shallower" as its lack is filled. To weigh the validity of these claims we must turn to the Platonic texts themselves.

PLATO'S EROS REEXAMINED

We will not trifle here with the structures of Plato's thought in general with which the reader will be familiar (i.e., the divided line, the forms or the soul's movement through recollection toward them, and so on). Let us begin instead by first refamiliarizing ourselves with Diotima's mythologization of the biography of Eros. The *Symposium* is filled with such accounts of the origins of Eros. Beginning with Phaedrus's retelling of Hesiod's account of Eros as one of the oldest existing forces emerging from the depths of Chaos itself, and achieving its greatest literary accomplishment in Aristophanes's account of the troubles of mankind and the power of Eros as a mediator therein, these accounts, though differing in content, all revolve around a few central themes. As is usually the case in the Platonic dialogues, these themes find their locus and clearest expression in the words of Socrates. Thus, Diotima's version of the birth of Eros serves in many ways to concretize what Plato takes to be the most important elements offered.

We are led into this recounting of Diotima's wisdom by way of Socrates' inquisition of Agathon: "Now try and tell me about Love [Ἔρως]: is he a love of nothing or of something," he asks (*Symposium* 199e). To this question Agathon readily replies that Eros is most certainly directed toward something, which is to say that it strives after definite end and purpose, it has an aim. If this is the case, Socrates concludes from Agathon's assertion, then Eros must not currently possess that which it pursues. That is, if Eros is driven toward some end, then that end cannot be included within its very being, though indeed the drive for it may make it inexorably attached to that end. Eros it seems, in line with Levinas's suspicion that it is like need, must then derive from some definite *lack* within the subject. However, as Diotima will soon show, this is not necessarily the case. Though Eros may not be able to remove itself from its pursuit toward some object, this object does not necessarily correspond to some absence within the subject. In other words, the erotic object's exteriority to the subject may be more than a temporary displacement of that which properly belongs interior to the subject.

The object of erotic striving is for Plato, as we all know, beauty. This of course begs a question for Socrates concerning the nature of Eros itself: since it does not possess beauty within itself though it may be bound to it, must Eros then be understood as ugly? It is this question which leads Socrates to recount his tutelage under Diotima. We are told Diotima was a woman of many talents. A kind of midwife and folk doctor she was not only savvy in matters concerning Eros, but she was also familiar with diseases and how to cure them.[13] By Socrates' reckoning, it was her advice which forestalled the "advent of sickness," among the Athenians (*Symposium* 201d). And, it was from her that Socrates received his lessons in "love matters." According to Diotima, while it is true that Eros may not be properly spoken of as beautiful, he must not be immediately understood as ugly either. These sorts of binary categories do not seem to apply to something like Eros. Instead, she suggests, Eros appears to be some kind of "halfway," as it were, between these two seemingly opposed positions. Just as right opinion is deemed by Socrates in the *Meno* and other texts to be halfway between truth and ignorance, so too must Eros be considered halfway between the beautiful and the ugly (202a–b). The curious mixture that composes Eros is not, furthermore, the result of the fact that it *lacks* a portion of goodness or beauty. Eros is not the result of a temporary displacement of some fullness nor representative of some *absence*. Instead, the halfway that Eros inhabits expresses the very way in which Eros *is*. It is the being of Eros as such, and thus expresses a strange kind of *presence*.

Eros, it seems, *is* between, between ugly and beautiful, good and bad, and so on. This *between* must not be understood as a Hegelian middle ground, the resolution of two opposing forces. The mediation between ugly and beautiful, or good and bad, is not one of compromise. Nor is it some fixed position—some chartable or measurable mixture. It is rather a dynamic movement between two poles. Eros is, in a sense, the current that runs between these two extremes. It is between, then, as one in transition. By personalizing Eros as a daemon (δαιμόνιον), as a messenger between the mortal and the divine, Diotima accounts for Eros as anything but a placid and peaceful middle ground. There is no resolution in Eros. It is instead the very principle of movement, of movement away from the ugly, the base and temporal and toward the beautiful, the good and the divine. Eros is "in-between" *only* in this sense. This trait Diotima explains by way of Eros's curious parentage.

Eros, by her account, was born the child of Resource (Πόρος) and Poverty (Πενία). In his very essence then, Eros is the union of an inexhaustible *Lack* (Πενία) and *A Way* (Πόρος) out of that lack, a way across into abundance.[14] Combining in his being the linage of both parents, Eros is eternally in a state of transition between absence and presence, striving after fullness and yet ever denied its acquisition. Eros is thus at one time:

> ever poor, and far from tender or beautiful as most suppose him: rather is he hard and parched, shoeless and homeless; on the bare ground always he lies with no bedding, and takes his rest on doorsteps and waysides in the open air; true to his mother's nature, he ever dwells with want. But he takes after his father in scheming for all that is beautiful and good; for he is brave, impetuous and high-strung, a famous hunter, always weaving some stratagem; desirous and competent of wisdom, throughout life ensuing the truth; a master of jugglery, witchcraft, and artful speech. By birth neither immortal nor mortal, in the selfsame day he is flourishing and alive at the hour when his is abounding in resource; at another he is dying and then reviving again by force of his father's nature. (*Symposium* 203c–e)

As a daemon, Eros is not unidirectional. Unlike need Eros does not move exclusively from the absence of indigence to the presence of resource. Instead, its being is maintained in the passage between these two—it *is,* in a sense, the path uniting them. Eros thus unites in its being abundance and absence in such a way that it expresses a kind of superabundant absence and completely indigent abundance, if such a thought can be had.[15] Thus, in the words of Robert Lloyd Mitchell, "*Eros* is always needful, always seeking and devising a way out of need, always on the way—toward beauty, goodness, wisdom, deathlessness, but never in final possession of any of them."[16]

Though Eros appears to hunt fulfillment and completion, this pursuit appears to be denied any eventual homecoming or consummation. Nevertheless, thinks Levinas, the very fact that it pursues what it supposes to be its own gain, regardless of whether it ever achieves it or not, is enough to condemn it as a kind of need and distinguish it from his metaphysical desire. But, this of course implies that the ends that Eros seeks are not only deemed good and the source of some possible gain, but that their recovery would constitute a kind of return. After all, the ends of metaphysical desire are certainly deemed by Levinas to be good as well, and one cannot deny that any pursuit of them would also involve, therefore, at least a kind of latent self-interest. What distinguishes metaphysical desire then, as we have said, is not that its end is not good, but that its end is deemed entirely *otherwise*—if it is good then, it is not a good *for me* but one which others me. The approach to this good would not constitute a form of homecoming; but, as we have mentioned, a form of alienation. But, is the end pursued by Plato's Eros a kind of eternal home or resting place? Does the fact that a subject would be made whole or more complete were it to ever achieve the aim of its erotic transcendence necessitate that what it strives for is something familiar to it? Put another way, is the good pursued by Platonic Eros the good of or for he or she who seeks it? Clearly these are questions which must be answered if we are to understand in more detail the singularity and difference of Levinas's account of metaphysical desire.

AN EROTIC HOMECOMING?

While Levinas is right to identify Aristophanes's account of Eros as ending in a kind of erotic homecoming, we cannot take Aristophanes's position to be representative of the Platonic position as such. He even seems to recognize as much stating in at least one place that Socrates' recitation of the Diotima myth appears to be a kind of rejection by Plato of the Aristophanic account of Eros (see *TI* 63). After all, Diotima describes Eros as "homeless," and this attribute does not appear to be merely accidental. For Plato Eros appears to be more than merely temporarily homeless—momentarily displaced from the homely but nevertheless carrying the promise of home within it and sallying forth toward its retrieval. Homelessness seems to be essential to the nature of Eros for Plato. Indeed, it seems tied to the very way in which it *is*.

Since in its very essence Eros is the union of absence and presence—since, as a daemon, it is always in transition between the here below of mortal life and the absent life of the divine—it seems that it is not only homeless now, but is in fact by its very nature homeless. Eros does not belong fully to either realm. Not one of the Olympians he is denied access to the holy dwelling places, but neither fully human he cannot make his home here on earth. Thus when Diotima describes Eros as indigent "hard and parched, shoeless and homeless; on the bare ground always he lies with no bedding, and takes his rest on doorsteps and waysides in the open air," she is not describing any merely ephemeral state, but how Eros *is,* as such, denied a home (*Symposium* 203c).

This is an idea which is seconded in the *Phaedrus* during Socrates' famed analogy of the soul's transcendence through Eros to the flight of a winged beast. There, Socrates argues that as the soul is borne aloft toward the divine on the back of Eros, "the wings of the soul are nourished and grow" (*Phaedrus* 246e).

The path which the soul takes on this flight is determined by its specific character or nature, a character which was established primordially in heaven before the birth of the living being itself. Before the demarcation of mortal time, claims Socrates, the soul traversed the heavens in a holy throng led by the 12 great gods of the pantheon. In that primordial procession every human soul, immortal like the gods, followed in tow, each in the train of one of the gods. When the soul takes flight again through the inspiration of Eros it flies upward to join once again the path it once pursued. Thus, the followers of Zeus are carried upward as philosophers while devotees to Hera "seek a kingly nature." All of the gods participate in this movement, he asserts, except one, and this is essential. According to Plato, Hestia, the goddess of the home and the hearth whose being is tied to the essence of things and is more fixed than any of the other gods (*Cratylus* 401c–d), does not participate in this cosmic cycle. While the holy throng takes to the skies she "alone remains in the house of the gods" (*Phaedrus* 247a). So it would seem that according to Plato no soul can erotically transcend by way of the homely, for no soul's character was formed in the wake of Hestia's flight—no soul can erotically transcend without becoming alienated from the homely, without diverging from the paths familiar to it. For Plato, it seems, the erotic path to the transcendent good is not one which leads us home, but one which carries us elsewhere.

It does not seem then that, as Levinas seems to claim, the Platonic account of Eros ultimately aims at a kind of return or homecoming. Precisely the opposite, it seems erotic transcendence is for Plato anything but a homecoming, even though the movement realized through it is one which is determined by character and charted in a time immemorial before the very birth of the subject. Instead, it seems, the path of Eros appears to embark toward an essential and immortal homelessness.[17] Thus, though the erotic movement seems to hope and strive for some eventual fulfillment, not only is it denied eventual acquisition of this fulfillment, but its very trajectory is away from the familiar. The fulfillment sought and hoped for at the end of the erotic movement must not be the recuperation of something lost, but the introduction of something new.

Stanley Rosen also reads Plato's account of Eros in this way claiming that "each movement of desire is radically incomplete, other than itself."[18] Similarly, Drew Hyland describes Eros as a movement toward a wholeness which it has never before been.[19] Thus, though perhaps the path of the soul's erotic flight is preprescribed before the very birth of the subject, the movement upon this trajectory is not toward any redemption, return, or reconciliation with some lost good. Any good attained through it is achieved as a kind of progression, not as the result of a regression. Any wholeness promised at the end of Eros is thus not the recovery of a past presence. Instead it must stand for the promise of a new perfection, the map to which has been inscribed upon our very being since time immemorial. The fact that erotic flight may be accompanied and aided by recollection thus does not necessitate its being understood as a kind of nostalgia as Levinas would have it.

Longing, the Good, and the Other

Seen in this way, Plato's account of Eros begins to resemble remarkably Levinas's claims concerning metaphysical desire, as noted by Adriaan Peperzak who sees in this account of Plato's something resembling the first lines of *Totality and Infinity*, "'The true life is absent.' But we are in the world" (*TI* 33). For Peperzak, this longing for an eventual homecoming and union with a "true life" so much a part of Levinas account of metaphysical desire is drawn directly from Plato's account of Eros.[20] Of course not everyone agrees with this reading of Plato's relation to Levinas insisting that while Levinas's account offers us a nuanced reformulation of Plato's Eros which ultimately diverges from it.[21] Either way, it is read, it cannot be denied that, at least concerning their respective accounts of the *ends* of desire, Levinas and Plato have much more in common than at least Levinas would have had us believe. Whether or not he recognized this similarity, or relied upon Plato's comments on the homelessness of Eros to develop his account of metaphysical desire remains unclear. In either case, it is undeniable that Plato's concept of Eros and Levinas's descriptions of metaphysical desire overlap on this point. Still, despite this similarity, it is not enough to fully reconcile their respective accounts. For despite the sundry similarities, Levinas still maintains the difference of his metaphysical desire from Eros in terms of their respective discernible *aims*.

According to Levinas, though the subject may indeed be drawn by the Good in metaphysical desire as it is in Eros, this momentum is interrupted in the former in such a way that the Good cannot be counted properly as its end as such, as it is in Plato's account of Eros.[22] This trajectory is not interrupted by the being of the subject itself, however, says Levinas. Remember that the distinguishing features of metaphysical desire do not result from the finitude of the subject. The transcendence of metaphysical desire is not merely a "failed immanence" (*BPW* 158). Instead, he claims, the appeal of the Good felt in metaphysical desire is broken up by *the goodness of the Good itself*. The Good, it seems, deflects the pull of its attraction onto a determinate other. Though one may feel drawn *by* the Good, he maintains, one is not drawn *toward* the Good directly.[23] Instead, this attraction is diverted onto another such that one's route to the Good is forever directed on what Michael Purcell calls a "detour."[24] This detour functions for Levinas such that the Good never becomes the *object* proper of metaphysical desire. Instead, this power is absorbed into the realm of the ethical, the realm of social interaction.[25] It is the concrete and determinate other, my neighbor, the beggar, who takes on the mantle of the Good. Hence, "metaphysics is enacted where the social relation is enacted—in our relations with men" (*TI* 78).[26] Metaphysical desire, it thus seems, does not propel us toward some celestial throng, but instead affects us with the compunction of responsibility for the other, the neighbor. Indeed, the Good *cannot be thought* outside of a relationship with the Other (*BPW* 29). Thus, though it is true that one is related to the Good in and through metaphysical desire, this interaction is, as Levinas terms it, a "relation without relation" (*TI* 80).

As the inheritor of the Good's autodeflection, the Other, as the Good itself, can never be reduced to the status of an object by the subject (*TI* 75, 211). The Other "does not enter entirely into the opening of being where I stand" and cannot be reduced to an object within the horizon of my interests (*BPW* 9). The Other is never "wholly in my site" or my field of grasp (*TI* 39). The Other is not something at-hand for us. This is not to say however that the Other stands entirely outside of my field. If he did then the subject could not even feel the pull that the Good exercises as the Other. What Levinas aims to say is that the Other cannot be conceptualized by the powers of consciousness—that the Other emerges from the "hither side of consciousness" (*BPW* 83). In forwarding this assertion, it is Levinas's intention to radically restructure the powers of consciousness and thereby remove the authority of the self-obsessed subject of desire.

According to Levinas, the subject's powers are manifest, in part, through its ability to objectify the world, and in so doing, lay claim to it through conceptualization. This power is grounded in the subject's mastery over all that is presented to it visually (*TO* 97).[27] By Levinas's read, the subject establishes and maintains its dominance over the world by illuminating all that which appears to it therein and attempting to control those appearances by reducing them to objects of possible knowledge (*TI* 44). "Vision" functions to "measure my power over the object" (*BPW* 9).

This results in the subject's misapprehension of the origin of appearances. Mediated through the power of vision, one encounters that which appears as something which can be possessed, as something which *belongs* to the structures of subjectivity, appearing as it does in the subject's field of vision as if illuminated by the eyes which are raised to it. The appearance of the Other on the scene, however, changes all of this. The Other, bearing the power of the Good, appears as a kind of super bright phenomenon which outshines all the intelligible powers of the subject. Thus once a subject is brought into relation with another the origin of visibility is reversed. A subject's power to perceive is revealed therein not to have originated in itself, but in the Other. The appearance of the Other reveals that it is not I who measure the world but he who "measure[s] me with a gaze incomparable to the gaze by which I discover him" (*TI* 86).

Emerging in the trace of the self-withdrawal of the Good, the Other exceeds the bounds of one's comprehension. Like the Good, the Other cannot be illuminated as an object of possible categorization. The Other's appearance thus reveals that illumination itself cannot be accounted for solely via the powers of the subject, but must be recognized to have emerged from elsewhere; namely, the Other. The subject can see not because of his or her own powers, but because the Other's appearance illuminates the scene.[28] The Other is, in a sense, the light in which things appear. As such, the Other appears in its *own* light. In light of the Other's appearance the world is revealed not to be ordered and structured around the subject's needs, but primordially oriented toward the otherwise—and available for use *for the sake of* the Other.

Levinas names the illuminative power of the Other the *face* (*TI* 51). As the bearer of the light of the Good, the face "*signifies* otherwise" than my powers (*BPW* 10). It signifies precisely the limit of those powers. "The face is present," claims Levinas, "in its refusal to be contained. In this sense it cannot be comprehended, that is, encompassed" (*TI* 194). Yet, this face still expresses itself in that which is present. But, in expressing itself "the face resists possession, resists my powers. In its epiphany, in expression, the sensible, still graspable, turns into total resistance to the grasp" (197). It is this face, this *refusal* of my powers in the world, that absorbs the power of the Good.

The interruption and deflection of its attractive powers is not merely an accidental trait of the Good, but is rather the very thing which identifies it as Good for Levinas: "the fact that in its goodness the Good declines the desire it arouses while inclining it toward responsibility for the neighbor, preserves *difference* in the non-indifference of the Good, which chooses me before I welcome it" (*OB* 123). It is because the Good has chosen me *before* I can choose it, that I can even identify and respond to the solicitation of the Good felt in metaphysical desire. The Good, it seems, places something within us which precedes the very formation of our identity. To use Levinas's language, it leaves a *trace* within us. Thus, though the Good is maintained by Levinas as absolutely other, falling entirely outside the subject's cognitive framework, it can still be recognized, as it were, and its pull can be felt. This trace left by the Good *before* my time only comes alive and becomes visible through the interruption of the subject's power and cognitive faculties affected through metaphysical desire.[29]

But if this is the case, then the movement initiated toward the Other in metaphysical desire cannot be wholly alienating. After all, it is only because the Good precedes me that I can exist as a being with an interior life at all: "Inwardness is the fact that in being the beginning is preceded" (*CPP* 133). For Levinas, the Good's claim over the subject is the very condition for its existence. Thus, the interruption of its being initiated by the Good in metaphysical desire does not appear to mark the onset of any irrevocable alienation. Instead, it seems to initiate a kind of ethical distancing within the subject from its ontological self in order for it to arise to another form of self, what Levinas terms elsewhere the subject's "true self."[30] In other words, the illumination provided by the appearance of the Other reveals an aperture in being through which the Good solicits one outward toward something greater.

Indeed, claims Levinas, the responsibility for the other that I am called to by the Good and which is mediated through my metaphysical desire *does not,* in the final analysis, alienate me. Instead, it brings me across the limits of my existence into a "beyond being," that I could not have attained on my own. In a sense, it inspires within me the birth of a new selfhood, not hemmed in by the confines of my own being, but elevated into the realm of responsibility (see *OB* 114).[31] As a result, "no one is enslaved to the Good." Instead, through the responsibility for another the deflection of the Good's attraction occasions and solicits, one is in fact *liberated* into the curious condition of "finding oneself while losing oneself" (11). It is precisely upon this notion of being freed by our devotion to the Good as manifest in another that we must concentrate.

By Levinas's read, though the power of the Good binds us to the Other in an ethical relationship, this restriction must be understood as a kind of emancipation (*TI* 88). The other's appearance on the scene does not leave the subject unchanged, but instead draws it up short and disconcerts it by revealing not only the limits of its powers, but the way in which it is confined by those limits (75). In doing so, the Other reveals to the subject the rut of its own existence and provides for it another way of living, a way out of the servitude to itself it is forced into by its very being.[32] The Other reveals that instead of succumbing to the whims of one's own being, one is free to devote oneself to the Other. Through the Other one is freed from the demands of *need*—free to follow the Other to whom he or she is solicited by his or her metaphysical/ethical desire. In this way metaphysical desire can be read as awakening a subject from the slumber of ontological actuality into the true life of ethical potentiality. Thus the trans*ascendence* initiated in metaphysical desire is not only an elevation out of oneself *to the Other,* it is also an elevation out of oneself *to another level of selfhood,* a level which was hitherto unavailable to the subject, and yet a level which was primordially placed within the subject by the Good. So "it is only in approaching the Other that I attend to myself" and "am brought to my final reality," my "final essence" (178–79). In the words of Adrian Peperzak, "the other's emergence answers the deepest desire motivating me," which leads him to conclude that "exteriority and otherness do not destroy all elements of anamnesis, but they respond to what we already are before we know it. Desire is oriented before we can discover it. In trying to say what and how we desire, we thus try to reach back to that which precedes our consciousness."[33]

But there is something that we must stress here. For Levinas, the recognition of this trace placed within us and apparent as a metaphysical longing—this potentiality that we are solicited to but were previously unaware of—occurs only *after* we have been broken open by the Good. It occurs only *after* metaphysical desire has revealed to us the limits of our being, calling into question our naïve enjoyment of the world and our powers therein. Its temporal relation thus expresses what he calls the "posteriority of the anterior" (*TI* 54; cf. *BPW* 81–82).[34] Essentially, what his concept expresses is that though one may have been marked by the Good *before* one's arousal to the Good through responsibility and metaphysical desire, this marking cannot be conceived as a part of the subject's biography, as a part of who he or she *is*. It pertains to a *before* which is only introduced *after,* posterior to, the interruption of the continuity of one's existence by the Good through the appearance of the other. It does not then belong to the order of the subject's being, but to another order *beyond* that being.

By inverting time in this way, Levinas is able to account for the way in which metaphysical desire, though striving after a Good which will lift the subject into its "final essence" nevertheless constitutes an interruption of the powers of the subject. By this account the very roots of a subject's identity fall outside of the subject's being and time in the world. It thus presents the subject with the curious possibility of having been established on a foundation which is only introduced posterior to its solicitation by the Other.

Though terribly curious, the account of the way in which metaphysical desire works nevertheless begins to resemble again what we have just shown to be found in Plato's account of Eros. In both cases the subject is called away from its self toward a beyond which carries the weight of the Good, not to reclaim some identity that had previously been lost, but to arrive at a higher and entirely novel, but nevertheless more complete, expression of its potential, a potential inscribed upon its being in a time before its own. Does this then, finally, reconcile these two accounts? Not yet, claims Levinas. For, there is still another crucial difference between his notion of metaphysical desire and Plato's description of Eros: namely the origins from whence each spring.

LEVINAS AND PLATO ON THE ORIGINS OF DESIRE

As we saw at the beginning of this chapter, desire, and its correlates—satisfaction and enjoyment—have traditionally been interpreted as functioning within an economy established in some concrete *privation* or *lack*. This is not the case, as we saw, with what Levinas chronicles in his descriptions of metaphysical desire. Metaphysical desire seems to arise not from some *absence* but instead from some determinate *presence,* indeed abundance, albeit an abundance which operates otherwise than our own being, namely the trace of the Good and the appearance of the Other.

Levinas names this *presence* within the subject the *idea of the infinite*. Drawing from the work of Descartes, he describes the idea of the infinite as "exceptional" and distinct from all other ideas "in that its *ideatum* surpasses its *idea*" (*TI* 49; *CPP* 54). It is thus an intuition *within* the subject that cannot be conceptualized *by* the subject—contained by the powers of ratiocination. Levinas writes, "In thinking infinity the I from the first *thinks more than it thinks*. Infinity does not enter into the *idea* of infinity, is not grasped; this idea is not a concept" (*CPP* 54). As such the idea of infinity is the expression of a *presence* within the subject of something that *exceeds the bounds of subjectivity itself*—a presence which, despite our attempts to master, grasp or comprehend, will perpetually evade our powers, remaining "radically, absolutely other" (54). Thus the determinate other, on whom the power of the Good collapses and toward whom metaphysical desire is directed, as the subject proper of this thought and desire, also "*infinitely* overflows the bounds of knowledge" (*BPW* 12). Since by its very nature the idea of the infinity defies any finite attempt by the subject to wrap its mind around it, and yet nevertheless resides within the finite subject, it expresses a kind of openness within subjectivity—a breach within the totality of interiority that exposes the subject to exteriority and the beyond. As such the idea of the infinite expresses wonderfully the curious relationship metaphysical desire establishes between the subject and the transcendent proper: though it emerges in and through a finite subject, its infinite insatiability enunciates the presence of something within the subject which is superior to it.[35] As such, both metaphysical desire and the idea of the infinite serve as proof for Levinas of the subject's openness to the metaphysical—evidence of the fact that the subject's interiority is not complete or whole unto itself, but instead has always already been breached by the Good. In the idea of the infinite and metaphysical desire the Good lays claim to the subject and *possesses* it (*TI* 50).[36]

Possession is an apt analogy for detailing the way in which the Good operates within the life of the subject, for it is something which comes over someone and takes a hold of them driving him or her out of his or her customary paths. It is the passivity implied in this kind of possession that is the salient point for Levinas. Since "the finite thought of man could never derive the Infinite from itself," it expresses something *within us* which could not have been produced *by us,* which could not have originated with us. Thus, "the idea of the Infinite, *Infinity in me,* can only be a passivity of thought" (*CPP* 160).[37] It must, therefore, be understood as having "been put into us" (54). The gaze of the other through which the infinite and the Good is mediated "slip[s] into me, *unbeknownst to me*" and without my assent, but, as quoted before, without enslaving me (145). The infinite can thusly be understood as a kind of foreign agent which has infected the subject, its host, debilitating its powers to fully contain itself within itself.[38]

It is this notion of an infinite put in us which seems to distinguish for Levinas his own thinking from Plato's. Indeed, he claims that "this placed 'in me' is a scandal in the Socratic world" (*GDT* 217). Levinas's problem with Plato's notion of Eros is not that therein no phenomenon corresponds to his notion of an idea of the infinite. Indeed, he claims that "we find that this presence in thought of an idea whose *ideatum* overflows the capacity of thought is given expression not only in Aristotle's theory of the agent intellect, but also, very often in Plato" (*TI* 49; cf. *CPP* 47, 54, 57; *BPW* 51; *TI* 63, 103). After all, one of the most infamous aspects of Platonic thought is his praise in the *Phaedrus* for the sundry positive effects of being "possessed," by the power of the Good in Eros, especially as it becomes manifest as a kind of mania. Rather the problem seems to be that in this account Plato still allows the subject to retain some power by which to surmount the passivity implied by the idea of the infinite. For, in Plato, Eros and the idea of infinity is still directed by the subject's power to recollect. As such, thinks Levinas, Plato misses the radical passivity of human life implied in longing and therefore prevents the independence and radical alterity of the Other such that every other, encountered by Plato's Eros, ultimately gets reduced to the structures of subjectivity. Thus, though the other may be recognized as a phenomenon by Plato, this recognition lacks the power to initiate a breach in the interiority and powers of the subject.

By contrast, Levinas's own concept of the idea of the infinite is of something which "is not a reminiscence. It is experience in the sole radical sense of the term: a relationship with the exterior, with the other, without this exteriority being able to be integrated into the same," by anything as paltry as memory (*CPP* 54). It signals the presence within the subject of an "exteriority that is not reducible, as with Plato, to the interiority of memory" (*TI* 51). Ultimately, Levinas seems to claim that in Plato, though the seemingly infinite insatiability of the phenomenon is recognized, because Eros still functions in conjunction with a subject's memory and thus strives to attain satisfaction by going back, Eros ultimately remains nothing more than a kind of *nostalgia*. It does not break radically enough with the realm of being and pursue the otherwise, as he proposes metaphysical desire does. Thus it remains trapped within the economy of the traditional rendering of desire as need.

But there is a difficulty here: for if, as Levinas claims, we must grant the radical exteriority of the idea of infinity due to it being, by definition, beyond the capacity of the subject's powers to either contain or produce; and, if he has already identified within Platonic thought the presence of some rudimentary version of precisely this idea, then how can he now claim that for Plato the idea of infinity is made manageable by the powers of recollection. Must not it, like his own idea of the infinite, be, by definition, the result of a radical exteriority? And if so, regardless of how Plato himself understands it, would not it testify to the fact that what Levinas identifies as a metaphysical desire may in fact be, in the end, something akin to what Plato names Eros? Why, then, Levinas's insistence that these two phenomena are so distinct? Why this claim that ultimately Plato's teaching is "to receive nothing of the Other but what is in me, as though from all eternity I was in possession of what comes to me from the outside—to receive nothing, or to be free" (*TI* 43)? Given what we have seen so far to be the remarkable similarity between Plato and Levinas's rendering of the phenomenon, despite the latter's insistence on their differences, it is perhaps worth investigating these claims more closely, specifically concerning any possible appearance of possession and passivity in Plato's account of Eros.

According to Socrates, one is *possessed* by erotic madness when one "sees the beauty of earth, remembering the true beauty, feels his wings growing and longs to stretch them for an upward flight, but cannot do so, and like a bird, gazes upwards and neglects the things below" (*Phaedrus* 249d). Notice the way that time moves here. Socrates claims that it is only *after* seeing the "beauty on earth" that one remembers "true beauty." One cannot remember true beauty until temporal beauty has awakened it. So it seems as if temporal beauty solicits within the subject the memory of something of which it was previously unaware in much the same way that it is only after the illumination provided by the appearance of the determinate other that one can recognize that his or her subjectivity has always already been breached by the Other.

Furthermore, according to Socrates, erotic possession can enter someone unawares—it can slip in, unbeknownst to the subject, from without. Near the end of the first major part of the *Phaedrus* Socrates introduces a curious anecdote about the power of the gaze and the role it plays in the subject's participation in the transcendence of erotic madness. According to Socrates, when one is overwhelmed with erotic desire through the perception of a beautiful other, such as a young boy, the power of his or her *mania* can at times overflow the bounds of the perceiver and enter into the soul of the perceived (*Phaedrus* 255c). In this way the perceived, though consciously unaware of the admiration he or she received, can feel him or herself drawn toward another not of his or her choosing. While Socrates initially relates this phenomenon on behalf of the lover who *affects,* he quickly expands it into an analysis of what happens within the beloved who *is affected*. The perceived and admired, he claims, enraptured by the gaze of the other, can him or herself become a lover and share equal part in the effects of erotic madness, though he or she "knows not with whom," and "does not understand his [or her] own condition and cannot explain it" (255d). In other words, not only does it seem that Eros reveals a kind of passivity within the subject, but also reveals the limits of what can be known by the subject, the limits of what a subject can understand. Furthermore, this is a passivity which, though perhaps driven toward heavenly beauty and rising upward toward the eternally Good, is mediated through the gaze of another and introduced from outside the subject. Socrates likens this aspect of erotic love to infection, a disease passed through the eyes.[39] This note on the possible passivity of the soul is far from *hapax legomenon* within the Platonic oeuvre, especially within the *Phaedrus*. Instead, this concluding observation serves only to punctuate and elucidate that which he earlier named as the aim of his endeavor: to understand "the truth about the soul divine and human by observing how it *acts* and *is acted upon*" (245c; italics mine). Notice the forthright recognition that the soul not only acts, but is passive, can be *acted upon*.

This notion of Eros, as an expression of a presence within the soul which is introduced from outside it and reveals its fundamental passivity, is also presented in the *Theaetetus*. There Socrates addresses young Theaetetus's inability to find "any satisfactory answer" regarding his questions concerning the nature of knowledge (*Theaetetus* 148e).⁴⁰ This dissatisfaction, claims Socrates, is not the result of any indigence—it does not derive its poignancy from any object of knowledge which Theaetetus lacks. Instead, says Socrates, it is the same kind of "suffering" one undergoes when in "the pains of labour" (148e).⁴¹ It is thus not the expression of some absence within Theaetetus, but of some presence, some abundance. Theaetetus, it seems, has been impregnated—he has been made pregnant by philosophical questioning—filled by its significance.⁴² Theaetetus's relation to the pain and suffering of his erotic striving for answers is thus not the result of his own agency, therefore, but something which, like pregnancy, is initiated by the introduction of something other.⁴³ Thus though it resides within him and when emerging appears to have sprung spontaneously from him, it is not something which in the final analysis could have spontaneously originated in him alone—after all, one cannot make oneself pregnant without at least the tacit help of another. Pregnancy always involves the introduction of the Other. Socrates' role as midwife then is to aid into the world that which has been placed within his interlocutors by this Other.

So it seems that the distinctions which Levinas sets up between his metaphysical desire and Plato's Eros once again collapse. But we should be reticent to fully reconcile these two accounts, given Levinas's strong language concerning Plato. Lets return once again then to the Levinasian oeuvre in attempt to exhaust any possible grounds of distinction between his perception of human longing and Plato's.

LEVINAS ON THE ENDS OF DESIRE

Remember that traditionally desire has been defined and understood as arising out of some determinate absence, pursuing some determinate object and culminating in the satisfaction of the desiring subject as its natural end. What seems to be unique about human longing, at least as accounted for by Levinas, is that it does not seem to arise out of any perceived lack, but in fact a kind of super abundant presence. Indeed, as we saw for Levinas, this longing is occasioned by the introduction of something new within the subject, namely the other. And, moreover, this Other never serves as the ultimate aim or object of this desire, making the desire interminable and infinite—never ultimately resolving in satisfaction, but instead growing ever more desirous with the passage of time. But, thus far we have failed to locate the real singularity of Levinas's accounts in the first of these two differences, finding correlates to them in Plato's account of Eros. So it would seem that at least at this point in our investigation we have yet to find sufficient grounds to understand and justify the way in which he seeks to distinguish his account of longing from that of Plato. What has become clear, however, is how much both of these accounts diverge significantly from the traditional conception of desire: giving rise to the question whether or not longing can still be thought of as a desire and if so, how might this change our understanding of the operation of desire? In order to approach an answer to these questions we must settle the question of how Levinas's account of metaphysical desire differs from Plato's account of Eros; and, since this difference cannot be found in their respective origins or aims, it must lie in their ultimate ends.

Levinas's account of the nature of enjoyment and pleasure is one of the most novel and intriguing elements of his thought. According to Levinas, enjoyment, like metaphysical desire, should not be understood as occasioned by some absence or lack, as, he contends, has traditionally been done; but instead should be seen as the natural outpouring of a kind of presence, namely the being of the subject itself—its presence in the world. It is not because a subject has first been displaced from some comfortable, complacent position in the world (i.e., finds itself in *need*), that it can later enjoy the *pleasure* of a return. A subject's pleasure, he contends, is not motivated by any initial loss and should not, therefore, be accounted for solely as an experience which accompanies one's release from an indigent or agitated state, as Freud famously argued. Instead, the subject's enjoyment of the world should be viewed as established upon its very being, the very way it *is* in the world; and not the way in which that being may have been interrupted. Pleasure, he contends, is not the result of the recovery of being from some absence or privation, but concupiscent with the being of the subject—with its life: "The bare fact of life is never bare.... Life's relation with the very conditions of its life becomes the nourishment and content of that life. Life is *love of life*" (*TI* 112). Thus, "happiness," he argues, "is made up not of an absence of needs, whose tyranny and imposed character one denounces, but of the satisfaction of all needs" (115). The subject is naturally a subject of pleasure. Its very way of being discloses the world to it as an object of pleasure (111).

The pleasure enjoyed by the subject serves to more fully establish its being in the world. According to Levinas, when one *enjoys* the world then, one relishes in the myriad delights offered therein and celebrates the ways in which those delights avail themselves for consumption by and integration into the subject. In this way, enjoyment is not a movement away from one's being, but the ultimate affirmation of it. Thus when a subject enjoys, it is not propelled toward that which is exterior and otherwise, as it is by longing, but is instead drawn further inward toward its own being. Levinas thus typifies the movement of enjoyment as "a withdrawal into oneself, an involution," what he calls a *coiling* inwards (*TI* 118).

Quotidian desires such as hunger or thirst seem to operate for Levinas within this trajectory of this involution. It is thus not they which establish the possibility of pleasure, but pleasure and enjoyment which establish the possibility for such desires. These needs, which arise within the field of the subject's enjoyment of its own being, do not function then to affirm anything truly outside the of the subject, anything truly other, as Levinas contends human longing does, but instead serve to reaffirm and reassert the natural supremacy of the subject. Given this relation between pleasure and the being of the subject, it would seem that any desire which operates within the framework of enjoyment would be restricted to the realm of the immediate, the realm of ontology, and denied any relation to the truly metaphysical, the Other. Such desires, then, would seem to ultimately differ in kind from longing, operating as they do on an entirely different level.

Perhaps it is here then, finally, that we find the point of divergence between Levinas account of longing and Plato's account of Eros. Though Plato's Eros, as we have seen, may actually arise out of an abundance, like the idea of the infinite, and though it may strive toward that which is situated on a height and is otherwise than it, such that its end is not ultimately a homecoming, nevertheless, it seems, its aim is ultimately not for that other *as* other, but rather solely as a means of achieving a higher pleasure. The other toward which it moves is thus not recognized and respected in and for its otherness, but remains cognized and treated as an object promising the possibility of fulfillment. In other words, Plato's Eros fails to push beyond the enjoyment it derives in the movement of its desire thus remaining within the orbit around the self-interests of the subject and its being. Thus while Eros may transcend, and even *ascend* in its movement, its ascension is not toward the otherwise, but merely toward some distant pleasure attainable only in the Olympian realms. For Levinas, it seems, though Eros may break with the traditional accounts of desire, and escape being named alongside need as a kind of nostalgia, it nevertheless fails to attain the difference demarcated in his own account of metaphysical desire, and our experience of human longing. He writes:

> Might the Platonic myth of love as offspring of abundance and poverty be interpreted as the indigence of wealth itself, as the desire not of what one has lost, but absolute Desire, produced in a being in possession of itself and consequently already absolutely 'on its own feet'? Has not Plato, rejecting the myth of the androgynous being presented by Aristophanes, caught sight of the non-nostalgic character of Desire and of philosophy, implying autochthonous existence and not exile—desire as erosion of the absoluteness of being by the presence of the Desirable, which is consequently a revealed presence, opening Desire in a being that in separation experiences itself as autonomous?
>
> But love as analyzed by Plato does not coincide with what we have called Desire. Immortality is not the objective of the first movement of Desire, but the other, the Stranger. It is absolutely non-egoist; its name is justice. (*TI* 63)

The alignment of Plato's conception of Eros with the egocentric enjoyment of abundance does not prohibit the experience of pain from its movement.

Indeed the *Phaedrus* spends considerable time exploring the curious mixture of pain and pleasure involved in erotic transcendence (see *Phaedrus* 251c–e), not to mention the sections of the *Philebus* dedicated to the attempt to understand the impure "nature" of pleasure (*Philebus* 46c–b; cf. *Theaetetus* 151a). In the *Phaedrus,* in fact, pain and suffering appear as essential and inescapable aspects of erotic transcendence. But the recognition and inclusion of a kind of inexorable pain in Eros is not enough to rupture it from its attachment to the soul's interest in its own pleasure. Any pain which accompanies this pursuit is not essential to it then, but merely an accidental accompaniment to its ultimate aim. After all, Levinas too addresses the necessity of encountering pain in one's pursuit of the pleasurable (see *TO* 68–69, 89; *TI* 144). The difference is that in Plato this pain, like the pain of an exercise regimen, derives its meaning on the basis of a subject's more primary aim at the prospect of a more complete expression of itself—that is, of more pleasure—redefining this pain as part of the larger movement of the pleasurable. Thus though Plato's account of erotic transcendence may include a level of pain—indeed, by his account, great pain and hardship—the hardcore of its movement is still directed toward the pleasure it awaits through this pain. This has led Adriaan Peperzak to note that despite the number of similarities between Levinas and Plato's respective positions, "the Platonic Eros still has too many features of need to be a model for a description of the desire *without lack* that opens up the most radical dimension," of metaphysical desire.[44]

Thus, for Levinas, ultimately Plato's account of the soul's march up the divided line via Eros, though perhaps trans*ascendent,* nevertheless remains entirely a journey forged within the realms of the subject's being and self interest—and not one which ever arrives at the metaphysical heights introduced by the Other and intuited in longing. So it is that in Plato's Eros any otherness encountered ultimately becomes reduced to the status of a possible object of pleasure by the transcending subject. The Good thus appears for Plato not on its own, independent of the subject, but as that which promises ultimate fulfillment for the subject. So it would seem that erotic transcendence remains forever hampered by the interests of the subject—bound within the realm of interiority.

METAPHYSICAL DESIRE AND DESIRE PROPER

From what we have seen there is no doubt that what Levinas details in metaphysical desire is a radical departure from the traditional account of desire as occasioned out of some lack, proceeding toward some determinate object and striving through it to attain satisfaction. It is so radical in fact that it merits the reconsideration of the traditional rendering of desire as such, as we have already noted. From what we have seen, the phenomenon detailed as metaphysical desire in Levinas's thought cannot merely be slotted within the order of the traditional understanding of desire; it is more than merely another, rather peculiar, species of desire, and yet it remains, nonetheless, at least to our thought, a kind of desire. But how are we to conceive this relation? Does the nature of longing require that we rethink the nature of desire as a whole? Or, can they coexist as separate though similar phenomenon? To approach these questions we must endeavor to understand the relation between metaphysical desire and other desires more fully.

One of the curious things one first notices about Levinas's account of desire is his inconsistent capitalization of the letter *d*. At times he speaks of Desire, capitalized, while a few lines later, seemingly, in reference to the same movement, he speaks merely of desire, small *d*. One is immediately reminded of the somewhat obtuse distinction between the Other and the other elsewhere in Levinas's work. But here, as there, though inconsistently used, this distinction seems to serve a purpose. Desire, capital *d,* for Levinas, is always used to connote metaphysical desire, whereas desire, lowercase *d,* is more often than not the expression of a more quotidian desire. This seems to suggest that determinate desires relate to metaphysical Desire as truncated or abbreviated expressions of the same movement. It seems that these desires are, in a sense, the expression of a kind of failed or incomplete metaphysical Desire. Metaphysical desire thus does not seem to differ in kind from desire, but in degree. Their difference is not like the one between black and white, but is instead like the one between reality and shadow. As such, metaphysical desire, Desire proper, cannot be cut entirely free from desire, as Peter Pan can cut himself free from his shadow. It is fundamentally tied to other such determinate desires, and yet it remains fundamentally distinct, for both seem driven by the same fundamental pursuit of the other, but only in metaphysical desire does this pursuit remain pure and expresses itself as such.

The distinction he establishes between metaphysical Desire and desire is one which, he claims, "can not be reflected in formal logic, where desire is always forced into the terms of need" (*TI* 104). It is one which can only be understood within the ethical register in terms of the Good and its emissary, the other. Driven by a metaphysical movement, determinate desires such as love seem to arise out of an abundance and seek that which is other, but only in metaphysical desire is this pursuit maintained and is this movement expressed in its fullest. Thus, whilst desires like love may be predicated upon the existence of the exterior and ultimately in pursuit of the other, they nevertheless *fail* to recognize the otherness of the other in its own right—though they may be launched from a ground that is not their own toward a height which is not a home, they somehow fail to break the atmosphere of being and thus fall into orbit around the ego of the desirer. So, while the transcendence of metaphysical desire is, as we saw, more than a failed immanence; perhaps the immanence of everyday desires is the expression of a kind of failed transcendence.

This relation can be seen in Levinas's efforts toward the end of *Totality and Infinity* to distinguish sexual desire (which, in line with tradition, he names Eros, or erotic desire[45]) from metaphysical desire.[46] Eros, more than any other desire, exhibits the legacy of its ground in metaphysical desire by pursuing the otherwise: "the loving intention goes unto the Other, unto the friend, the child, the brother, the beloved, the parents" (*TI* 254). Love thus exhibits in some inexorable way the transcendence of metaphysical desire; and yet it seeks to instantiate this transcendence precisely in that which is immanent, namely the beloved, through what Levinas characterizes as the caress (257–58).[47] As such "it brings into relief the ambiguity of an event situated at the limit of immanence and transcendence," and reveals the curious relation between desires and Desire (254).

Erotic love "remains a relation with the Other that turns into need, and this need still presupposes the total, transcendent exteriority of the other, of the beloved" (*TI* 254).[48] It is thus a desire, a need that still expresses its origin in the metaphysical. Thus though it occurs entirely within the framework of the subject's being, it manifests a break in the totality of that being by pursuing what Levinas calls the *not yet,* the possibility of a "future never future enough" (255). Like need then it seeks its end in satisfaction; but "the desire that animates it is reborn in its satisfaction, fed somehow by *what is not yet,*" by the possibility held out in metaphysical desire (258). Thus, though Eros is "rooted in [the] animality" of the subject's tie to his or her own being, it also reveals the "vertiginous depth of what *is not yet,* which *is not,* but with a nonexistence not even having with being the kinship that an idea or a project maintains" (259).

This ambiguity of the *Erotic* phenomenon is exhibited in its natural outcome: *fecundity.*[49] For, the product of the erotic relationship, a child, carries an ambiguous relation to the subject. "My child is a stranger (Isa. 49)," says Levinas, "but a stranger who is not only mine, for he *is* me. He is me a stranger to myself" (*TI* 267). The child is thus an expression of the same that breaks with the totality of the same—it is a continuation of the powers of the subject but in a way in which the subject is no longer in control, no longer has free reign over those powers. Richard Cohen sums up well the relation between fecundity and the erotic encounter writing that "Ultimately, in the love for the other's love, the lover wants, per the impossible to *be* the other, to be lover and beloved at once, to be same and the other."[50] It is this impossible union of oneself with the other that is witnessed in the birth of a child.

From this it should become clear that though Eros is not a metaphysical desire, a longing, but instead circulates within the realm of being and the interests of the subject (it is interested in *being* the other); it is not yet wholly otherwise than metaphysical desire, for it maintains the legacy of metaphysical desire—still somehow signals otherwise.[51] Erotic love transcends, like metaphysical desire, only it "does not transcend unequivocally—it is complacent, it is pleasure and dual egoism. But in this complacence it equally moves away from itself; it abides in a vertigo above a depth of Alterity that no signification clarifies any longer—a depth exhibited and profaned" (*TI* 266). So it is that though not entirely different from metaphysical desire, erotic love nevertheless remains fundamentally distinct from it.

This relation between more determinate desires, like erotic desire, and metaphysical desire, Desire proper, is also reflected in Levinas's *Existence and Existents*. There he suggests that while desire may aim for the merely satiable, "*unconsciously* desire presupposes more than its object and can go beyond the desirable" (*EE* 28). Determinate desires, it seems, intuit the trace of the beyond in their pursuit after attainable aims. Thus, though they remain within the realm of object, ends and pleasure, they, in a sense, know more than they know. Their failure is constituted in not pushing beyond the object-world, into the realm of the Other who allows for the appearance of those objects. As such, they fail to attain to their grounds.

By suggesting that there is something in the determinate ends in the world pursued by desires which signals the otherwise beyond them, I am in no way suggesting that some sort of natural theology can be made of Levinas's work. He openly sets himself against any such suggestion declaring that "there is no natural religion." There are no mystical claims suggested in the "autonomy of the sensible in the world" (*TI* 62). The subject encounters the world as if it has come from *nowhere*. We should not see the Other suggested by objects of possible satisfaction in the world as some sort of divinity resting behind all that appears; but rather as that otherness which establishes and allows one to enjoy the world. The Other allows for subjects autonomous enjoyment of itself and the world by relinquishing any claim it could have on the world prior to our arrival—this it does so that the subject can emerge as somehow separate and distinct.[52] As a result, though the subject encounters the world independently and enjoys it on its own, on the basis of its own being, ultimately "the I is not the support of enjoyment" (118). The support of enjoyment, though experienced *interiorly,* is the *exterior,* the world *outside* the subject; and, moreover, the Other who by withdrawing its claim upon the world allows the subject to take possession of it.[53] Thus, though the subject finds itself at-home in the world "the interiority of the home is made of extraterritoriality," and this extraterritoriality "is produced in...gentleness," a gentleness which "comes to the separated being from the Other" (150). Metaphysical desire seems to distinguish itself from other forms of desire in the fact that it, at least unconsciously, recognizes the primordiality of the Other in the world and remains tied, somehow, to that Other from whom the subject exists as separated and independent.[54] Other desires, on the other hand, seem to emerge alongside the natural forgetting which accompanies the subject's autonomous emergence on the scene. They do not carry within them the latent memory of the Other who may have come before, but instead bear solely the mark of the separated subject who emerges through the erasure of the Other. So it is that in enjoyment "the I is ignorant of the Other" (62).

This seems to be the case with need, which, as we have seen, is perhaps furthest in Levinas's mind from the likes of metaphysical desire than any other human desire. By his read, "human need already rests on Desire" (*TI* 117). Though it differs from Desire, it nevertheless rests on the trajectory set in the fundamental human drive for the other expressed in such a Desire. For this reason, Levinas is willing to suggest that the kind of pleasure one can attain through the fulfillment of needs is not irreconcilable with Desire for "this Desire is a desire in a being already happy" (62–63). Nostalgia too then, though different from Desire as such, nevertheless reflects in some incontrovertible way metaphysical Desire—it bears a trace of its immemorial origins in the Other. This is demonstrated, for instance, in his earliest work, *On Escape,* where he explores how the need for escape and the accompanying nostalgia for a land or beauty wherein one can make such an escape hints at a movement toward the beyond only realized in metaphysical desires (see *OE* 54–55).

Given this relation between metaphysical desires proper and desire as typically experienced it becomes clearer why it was such a difficult task to determine the precise nature of Levinas's problem with Platonic Eros. Both, it seems, differ from the traditional notion of desire compared to which Eros appears to be very close to metaphysical desire, indeed motivated by the same drive for otherness. But, ultimately it nevertheless fails to attain the heights suggested by its origins, or pursue the otherwise proper though it is propelled toward it. It thus remains a reflection of metaphysical desire, but a reflection cast "through a glass dimly," as it were.[55]

Plato's Account of Desire Reconsidered

If we have read Levinas correctly in understanding determinate desire such as Eros to be motivated by the same basic movement as metaphysical desire, then we should pause perhaps to question whether or not a similar structure exists previously undetected in the work of Plato. Is there a phenomenon, akin to metaphysical desire, which appears in Plato under which Eros can be subsumed and understood anew? To answer this requires a brief foray into the Greek.

As is well known, the *Phaedrus* contains two different Socratic discourses on the nature of Eros, the second of which is intended as a kind of penance for the sin committed in the first (*Phaedrus* 242c). From this we may safely assume that the latter speech is offered by Socrates with a bit more humility and sincerity than his first one, which he judges the result of a man overcome with ambitions. While this may or may not be the case, depending on the hermeneutic with which one approaches the Platonic texts, there can be little doubt that a profound difference does exist between the two accounts given by Socrates, and that it is the latter one which he, at least, recognizes as the more sincere of the two. In any case, by exploring the friction between these two accounts, the sin and its accompanying penance, the structure of Eros and its relation to other desires becomes clearer.

Socrates' "sin against Deity," essentially amounts to his having borne false witness against Eros and consequently denigrating its status. But, it is the nature of *how* exactly he bore false witness that is of such consequence to us. Socrates began his first speech by defining Eros as a kind of "desire" (*Phaedrus* 237d). But one should be cautious here as this is no neutral assertion. For, the "desire" which Socrates binds to Eros here has a very specific and determinate meaning.

The word he uses here to identify Eros as a kind of desire is ἐπιθυμία (*epithumia*), which is perhaps better translated as "lust," as "the desire for pleasure or enjoyment."[56] The consequences of this association will become immediately apparent. Firstly, says Socrates, "we must observe that in each one of us there are two leading principles...one is the innate desire for pleasure [ἐπιθυμία ἡδονῶν], the other an acquired opinion which strives for the best [ἐπίκτητος δόχα, ἐφιεμένη του ἀρίστου]" (*Phaedrus* 237d–e). And, he goes on, it is the first of these two which, overpowering the former, guides us and takes the name Eros (238c). Thus Eros is reduced to nothing more than the "innate desire [ἐπιθυμία] for pleasure," hence our discovery that it is ultimately on the basis of pleasure and enjoyment that Plato's Eros and Levinas's longing differ. From this we see that what appears at first, and in translation, to be a seemingly benign identification is actually wrought with significance. This definition of Eros as a kind of lust pursuing pleasure is maintained throughout the rest of the first speech ultimately leading Socrates to condemn erotic desire as base and immoderate.

This is, of course, not the first time that ἐπιθυμία appears within the Platonic oeuvre. The *Symposium,* which is considered by those interested in dating the Platonic texts to have been composed earlier than the *Phaedrus,* also contains the word ἐπιθυμία. There it is used by Aristophanes to identify the sexual hunger of erotic movement (*Symposium* 191b). In fact almost every time that Eros is addressed by Socrates as something to be avoided it is referred to as a kind of ἐπιθυμία (*Republic* 437c). But, ἐπιθυμία and Eros, though often related to one another, cannot be absolutely identified. That is, Eros need not be the expression of a kind of ἐπιθυμία, as we will see; it can be the expression of other desirous aims as well. Nevertheless, the equivocation of these two terms dominates the reading of the Platonic texts.

According to Drew Hyland, much of the confusion within Platonic studies on the nature of desire in fact emerges from the obfuscation of the difference between Eros and ἐπιθυμία resulting in a conceptual collapse within the vast majority of secondary literature between what, in the final analysis, are two fundamentally different terms.[57] According to him, "'Ἐπιθυμία we know to be the lowest faculty of the soul, the brute desire to possess what one lacks. Ἔρως also desires, but unlike ἐπιθυμία, which only desires, Ἔρως both desires and loves. The difference between Ἔρως and ἐπιθυμία, then must lie in this 'and loves.'"[58] This confusion is understandable of course since, as we have seen, Socrates himself at times identifies one with the other. Nevertheless, Hyland is right to draw our attention to it for, as we will see, it is an identification which Socrates himself seems to want to make at times introducing at least one other term by which Eros can be oriented. In fact, the nature of Socrates' "sin against" Eros seems to be wrapped up in this identification of it with ἐπιθυμία. His error was thus not committed in his condemnation of Eros, but in his false identification of its nature. After all, if Eros truly is nothing more than a kind of ἐπιθυμία one cannot help but reject it if they are to maintain a Socratic perspective on the world. The sin of his first presentation of the nature of Eros thus consisted not in his *condemnation* of its impurity, but in the *misalignment* of it to ἐπιθυμία which precipitated this condemnation. His redemption must then proceed through a realignment of the nature of Eros to another kind of desire.

Socrates begins his second account of Eros by invoking the name of "Stesichorus, son of Euphemus [Man of pious Speech] of Himera [Ἱμεραίου, Town of Desire]" (*Phaedrus* 244a). Under this guise Socrates immediately renounces his previous teachings and begins to praise Eros as a kind of madness (μανίας) by which one is inspired by the divine and propelled toward it. Eros is still identified as a kind of desire here, only it not associated with ἐπιθυμία anymore, but with ἵμερος (*himeros*). His "pious speech" thus begins with the rebaptism of Eros as a sojourner from Ἱμεραίον.

This identification of Eros with ἵμερος remains consistent throughout this second presentation of its nature. It is thus Eros as a kind of ἵμερος which Socrates discusses when detailing how it is that that the soul is driven upward toward the Good, an experience alternatively tortuous and nourishing (*Phaedrus* 251c–e). And, it is again under the form of ἵμερος that Eros is discussed as holding the soul away from the homely and yet overflowing it with the abundance of the divine (255c). This latter reference is particularly telling for two reasons. Firstly, it is on the basis of this reference to the overflowing abundance manifest in ἵμερος that Socrates argues for the passivity of the subject in relation to erotic transcendence, the way in which the subject can be infected, as with disease, by erotic desire. Secondly, by associating ἵμερος with divinity, Socrates has in a sense made it the perfected expression of Eros, what becomes of Eros when it is purified of a subject's desire for pleasure. Remember, in the *Symposium,* Eros was described not as a god, but as a messenger, a daemon (δαιμόνιον) uncannily caught between the divine and the mortal. When ordered among the mortal, Eros seems to present itself under the form of ἐπιθυμία, but when it approaches its divine nature Eros thus seems to be a kind of ἵμερος. Ἵμερος thus emerges in the Platonic texts as a kind of perfected Eros, purified of the mortal craving for pleasure, ἐπιθυμία.

This reading seems to be supported by the *Cratylus*.[59] There the mixed nature of Eros is alluded to through an etymological reading of the word *Hero*. Hero (*ΗΕΡΟΣ*), claims Socrates, is derived from Eros (*ΕΡΟΣ*) because a hero is one who is born out of a love which binds the gods to the mortals (*Cratylus* 398c–d). Later in the *Cratylus*, Socrates asserts that in addition to this Eros ('ἔρως) "is so called because it flows [ἐσρεῖ] in from without, and this flowing is not inherent in him who has it, but is introduced through the eyes" (420b–c). Again we see Eros figured as an element introduced to the subject from outside of it—as an experience not inherent to the subject, but preceding from "the eyes" of another.

The *Cratylus* also defines ἐπιθυμία and ἵμερος. The former, Socrates claims there, "has its name from the raging [θύσις] and boiling of the soul" (*Cratylus* 419e). It thus appears again as a kind of lust or compulsive desire emergent from a disruption, imbalance, or privation within the soul. Ἵμερος, on the other hand, was the name "given to the stream [ροῦς] which most draws the soul; for because it flows with a rush [ἱέμενος] and with a desire for things and thus draws the soul on through the impulse of its flowing" (419e–420a). Thus whereas ἐπιθυμία seems to emerge from an imbalance or privation within the soul, ἵμερος seems to follow a course which has the urgency of an abundance, a rush which sweeps up and carries the soul with it. Socrates adds to this list in the *Cratylus* one more form of desire, namely πόθος (*pothos*) which he describes as the same desire as ἵμερος only differing in that it "pertains not to that which is present, but to that which is elsewhere ['ἀλλοθίου] or absent" (420a). It is thus another form of ἵμερος which is motivated not by a presence, an overflowing abundance, as in the *Phaedrus,* but by an absence, by the lack of that toward which it moves.

So it seems that Eros can appear ordered under at least two different forms. It can either present itself bound to the mortal and earthly under the form of ἐπιθυμία, or it can manifest as tied to the divine as a form of ἵμερος, and therein it can either be ordered according to ἵμερος proper and occasioned by abundance, or as the derivative form πόθος wherein it arises from out of a lack and absence. In either case it is clear that Eros should not be understood as an independent term, but one which must be modified by other forms to have any real determinative power in language. That is, it seems to be something which derives its meaning from the superstructures to which it is attached, either ἵμερος or ἐπιθυμία.

Given this discovery, to return to the Levinasian taxonomy briefly, is it possible to understand Eros as a kind of desire which can be ordered under the form of Desire? If this is the case, then ἵμερος seems to correspond to this Desire. For, as we have seen, Eros when ordered under the form of ἵμερος resembles metaphysical desire in every way, even overcoming the difference which ultimately separated Eros as ἐπιθυμία from metaphysical desire, namely the pursuit of pleasure (i.e., the interests of the subject). And, Eros, when modified as a kind of πόθος appears to be what we identified as nostalgia at the beginning of this chapter; for though it resembles the longing of metaphysical desire and ἵμερος, it is occasioned by the loss or absence of some beloved object.

Conclusions

By reexamining the nature of longing through an investigation of Levinas's descriptions of metaphysical desire and Plato's determination of a kind of erotic ἵμερος we have seen that longing is in fact a very distinct phenomenon—one which differs radically from the traditional understanding of it as a kind of desire, as traditionally defined. By breaking with the traditional account, longing thus calls for a reexamination of the order of desire itself. Its singularity as a phenomenon calls for the dismantling of the traditional structures supporting our understanding of how desires function. In fact it turns them on their head, revealing how determinate desires can more easily be understood when subordinated to a more fundamental longing than longing can be when understood as simply a different kind of desire. Understood thusly, determinate desires would be understood as immanent expressions of a primordially transcendent movement. In this way they would express an incomplete or failed longing, a longing which attempts to satisfy itself with objects (and thus constantly recurs, finding itself always only temporarily satisfied, like Hemingway's hunger).[60] This is even then the case with nostalgia, with which we began this chapter. As a species determination of human longing, nostalgia seems to bear the trace of its origin and carries within it the mark of insatiability. But it nevertheless makes that trace immanent, locating its origin within the history of the subject instead of in that which falls elsewhere and otherwise. Determinate desires like nostalgia thus express a subject's failure to recognize that his or her true self or final essence, the ultimate aim of his or her longing, lies elsewhere; and, that no determinate satisfaction will fill the yawning hunger inside of him or her for something else or quiet the haunting suspicion that there is something more to be had behind all concrete, graspable objects—something which signifies otherwise than the immediately possessable or consumable.

Two

Longing and Striving for the Beyond

Levinas and Heidegger in Dialogue

Levinas's Heideggerian Roots

The influence of Martin Heidegger on the thought of Emmanuel Levinas cannot be overestimated. As Philippe Nemo put it in an interview with Levinas, though he may have gone to "Fribourg to follow Husserl's teachings, [he] discovered there a philosopher he did not know beforehand, but who would have a capital importance in the elaboration of [his] thought: Martin Heidegger" (*EI* 37). The influence of Heidegger can be felt in almost all of Levinas's major works and ideas, from his account of the nature of the subject's interaction with the world to his insistence on the superiority of the Other and the transcendence of the Good, both emergent as direct refutations of elements within Heidegger's thought. It should not be surprising then that one of the places this influence is most apparent is in Levinas's conception of the nature of human longing.

It is, however, a bit counterintuitive to see Heidegger's work positioned as a positive influence on Levinas thought. One is much more accustomed to seeing Levinas and Heidegger contrasted or presented as bitter opponents within the history of philosophy. After all, Levinas himself openly contrasts his work to Heidegger's.[1] Heidegger is unquestionably one of the most obvious targets of Levinas's harangue against the history of Western philosophy. One finds repeated attempts throughout the Levinasian oeuvre to decry the Heideggerian universe. *Totality and Infinity*, for example, is littered with examples of Levinas's contestation of the Heideggerian system (see *TI* 89, 109, 113, 138, 242). And, it is commonly held that one of Levinas's main interests is to establish a system of thought that fundamentally undermines the Heideggerian project of reconceiving Being—Levinas's evocation of the Platonic *beyond being* serving as a kind of condemnation of the limits of Heidegger's thought.[2]

So it would seem that Heidegger's work should only be viewed as a negative influence on Levinas, one to which Levinas defined himself in contrast, in much the same way he sought to contrast his thought from that of Plato's. Indeed, Levinas explicitly compares Heidegger and Plato on more than one occasion describing the history of philosophy against which he strives as one continuous chain of violence leading directly "from Plato to Heidegger" (*TI* 294; cf. *BPW* 5). Levinas even links the two when discussing the singularity and difference of his account of metaphysical desire from all previous accounts (see *BPW* 51). But on closer investigation we discover, that at least in terms of his conception of human longing, Levinas is profoundly indebted to Heidegger both for providing a framework upon which to build his understanding of metaphysical desire, and for providing a system with which Levinas can disagree in the attempt to enunciate more fully his own understanding of the phenomenon. It is also interesting to note that both Levinas and Heidegger sought to inform their respective understandings of the nature of human longing in dialogue with the Platonic texts. They did not, however, approach these texts in the same way. Whereas Levinas's interaction with Plato is mostly negative—as we saw, his attempt being to demarcate metaphysical desire from the traditional rendering of desire exemplified for him in Plato's Eros—Heidegger's employment of the Platonic texts, on the other hand, is almost entirely positive. Heidegger, for the most part, approaches Plato as a source from which to draw and not as a foe to be defeated. In order to understand this difference fuller, and trace the Heideggerian influence on Levinas's understanding of human longing, all in the attempt to understand our own experience of the phenomenon, we must turn our attention then to Heidegger's treatment of Plato's Eros and its surrounding concepts.

Heidegger's Treatment of Plato and Eros

Though Heidegger's approach to the Platonic texts is largely positive compared to Levinas's, his relation to them is not entirely unambiguous nor all together straightforward. To the contrary, like Levinas, Heidegger had great qualms with the Platonic project. This is due to the fact that according to Heidegger, Plato's thought is situated at a turn in the philosophic history of the West. It demarcates for him a change in the nature of its metaphysical thinking, a change which bears grave consequences on the way in which we think today. Specifically, Plato's work represents for Heidegger the precise moment in Western thought when the ontological difference between the idea of Being as a whole and the nature of apparent beings is obscured, an obfuscation which, he claims, has resulted in a kind of prevalent nihilism in the twentieth century (see *GA* 6: 173 / 171). Still, thinks Heidegger, the resultant history of this change must be distinguished from the thinker upon whom it was founded. Thus while Heidegger wants to reject almost entirely what he calls the "Platonism" of

Western thinking, he still holds out hope for Plato as such (153 / 151).[3] Situated as it is on the watershed of Western thought, Plato's work seems to hold for Heidegger not only insight into the ways in which Western thought has come to err, but also a window into its primordial origin. For Heidegger, this origin, though perhaps forgotten now, nevertheless holds sway and influence over the trajectory of Western thought. But he claims, in order to see through Plato's work into that lost prehistory, requires an overcoming of the Platonism in Plato (190–91 / 188); a task Heidegger elsewhere names the attempt to say the "unsaid" therein (*GA* 9: 203 / 155). It is this task, when posited more generally, that Heidegger thinks is what "the whole effort of philosophizing is about"—namely, approaching that which is unsayable at the heart of philosophy (*GA* 34: 19 / 13).

Philosophy for Heidegger consists in the attempt to enunciate that which lies unspoken at the heart of existence and to illuminate whatever lies hidden therein (*GA* 34: 82 / 61). It is with this goal in mind that Heidegger turns himself to the Platonic texts in hopes of uncovering the primordial insights they contain. Nowhere is this more apparent than in his 1931–32 winter semester lecture course on *The Essence of Truth: On Plato's Cave Allegory and Theaetetus* (*GA* 34). Though there, as elsewhere, Heidegger's main interest is in exploring the Platonic conception of truth as ἀλήθεια (*aletheia*) and how it reveals the "*transition* from truth as unhiddenness to truth as correctness," a transition he links to the confusion of Being with beings—he nevertheless also touches upon a number of other important themes, not least among them Plato's treatment of Eros (17 / 12).

It is interesting to note before examining this text, however, that though Heidegger mentions the notion of Eros a number of times throughout his extensive collected works (*GA* 6: 198 / 194; *GA* 19: 315 / 219; *GA* 53: 141 / 113), he very rarely treats it exhaustively or devotes to it anything more than a passing reference. This is even the case with his most exhaustive treatment of it here in the 1931–32 lecture courses where it is addressed as a means of understanding the intimate and inexorable connection between human beings and Being as such. Thus though Heidegger mentions the notion of Eros, desire, and love relatively often, he does not seem to be terribly interested in it as a phenomenon worthy of independent study—at least not as much as he is in other similar phenomena such as boredom or anxiety. Thus, though he counts the erotic phenomenon among those other essential emotive attunements (*Grundstimmungen*) explored so thoroughly throughout his oeuvre (see *GA* 34: 238 / 170),[4] his treatment of it there is generally woefully inadequate. Recognition of this fact has lead Heidegger scholar Ben Vedder to remark that "at first sight, th[e] notion [of desire] would appear to be completely absent" in Heidegger's thought, an observation which should strike those familiar with the goals of the Heideggerian project as somewhat unusual.[5] After all, it is Heidegger's expressed interest, at least in the early works, to investigate the nature of Being by way of Dasein and its comportment in the world. Certainly erotic desire and longing are amongst the most fundamental ways in which human Dasein experiences itself in the world. One would think then that the concept of desire would figure prominently in Heidegger's analyses. But, when called upon to exemplify or explore Dasein's emotive connect with Being, Heidegger much more often turns to boredom or anxiety for illumination, leaving his few comments on the concept of desire generally undeveloped. The one exception to this tendency is found in this 1931–32 lecture course. Fortunately, what is found there is profoundly informative, not only regarding his understanding of the nature and role of desire, but for our experience of human longing as such and our emergent understanding of Levinas's metaphysical desire.

HEIDEGGER ON THE EROTIC PHENOMENON

Heidegger begins his 1931–32 investigation into the nature of Platonic Eros with a word of warning. Though the word Eros has been grafted onto contemporary culture to express a kind of love, "we should not," Heidegger cautions, "understand the Platonic and Greek 'έρως in terms of what is nowadays called the 'erotic,' but nor should we think that the Greek 'έρως would be suitable for bigoted old aunties" (*GA* 34: 216 / 155). Eros, he seems to claim, though perhaps not as strictly limited to the realm of what we today conceive of as the erotic or the sexual, should, at the same time, not be conceived of as neutered and placid. Though it may not pertain to the sexual, it is not a benign or impotent phenomenon. It is instead, as we shall see, one of the most profound and significant phenomena of human existence for Heidegger—one which inscribes upon human existence a terrifying and uncanny trace of Being.

In order to approach the phenomenon of erotic desire outside of our bigotry concerning it and our traditional understandings of the realm of the erotic, Heidegger begins by redefining Eros. Eros, he claims, must be understood first and foremost as "not only the most authentic striving [*eigentlichste Streben*] by which the Dasein of man is carried, but, as this latter it is simultaneously authentic having [*eigentliche Haben*]" (*GA* 34: 216 / 155). Note that by designating Eros as exclusively that striving (*Streben*) and having (*Haben*) which is determinatively authentic (*eigentliche*), Heidegger already reveals something about the nature of human Eros: namely, that it can appear in different modes depending upon its relation to itself—its authenticity. Heidegger's notion of authenticity, however, though perhaps one of the most well known and certainly one of the most discussed elements of his early thought, is nevertheless perhaps also one of the most difficult concepts to penetrate. This is due in part, at least within the English world, to issues surrounding the translation of his texts. For in order to understand the way in which Heidegger employs the concept of authenticity properly one must be able to hear it in the original German as *Eigentlichkeit*.

The root of *Eigentlichkeit, eigen,* is an adjective which in its everyday use ascribes possession to an object or person as in the word *Eigentum,* which designates a piece of *property*. The word *eigen* can thus be rendered into English by the adjective *own*. Note that *eigen* does not designate the active English verb *to own*. It does not refer to *ownership,* to the activity of overseeing or maintaining a particular object or property.[6] Instead *eigen* designates that which is *one's own,* it modifies and describes an object or action by identifying it with a particular person. It thus expresses that which *belongs* to someone, that which somehow *naturally fits* or characterizes someone. As such *eigen* can equally be rendered into English with the words *peculiar, particular,* or *singular,* as it relates that which sets something or someone apart from its others.[7] When it is thus nominalized as *Eigentlichkeit* it can be understood to express a property or quality such as *ownness* or *singularity*. It is for this reason that Heidegger's translators have traditionally rendered *Eigentlichkeit* as *authenticity* in reference to the Greek root *auto* (αὐτο), meaning *one's own self*. It could thus also be Latinized as *proper,* referencing the root *proprius,* meaning one's own or personal, to express that which belongs *naturally* to someone or something; as in the phrase "it is *proper* that a fish should swim." Inauthenticity (*Uneigentlichkeit*), as the negation or turning away of that which is proper to one's being, thus expresses a kind of betrayal of one's true nature, it occurs when one has abandoned what is natural to his or her inmost character and chosen a path which is foreign or otherwise to his or her nature—one which diverts from the trajectory demarcated by his or her being. When one comports oneself inauthentically, one does not sever oneself wholly from the path of one's nature. This is of course impossible. One is always bound to be whoever he or she is—this is, of course, what it means *to be:* wherever you go, there you are. Inauthenticity, as a divergence from being, is thus not an escape from being, but an improper, artificial, or dissimulated expression of that being. Thus, whereas to be authentic is to be in line with one's true self, exhibiting straightforwardly the being one has always already been given over to, to be inauthentic is *cover over* one's being, to act otherwise than one's own being—it is, in a word, to be false.

This relation between, on the one hand, authentic comportment and truth and, on the other hand, inauthentic comportment and the false or untrue is further illuminated in *Being and Time*. There Heidegger defines truth as the "uncoveredness" (*Entdecktheit*) of a particular being. It is thus the active revelation and appearance of an object solicited through the care of Dasein.[8] Truth thus occurs, he claims there, when "entities get snatched out of their hiddenness," out of their coveredness (*GA* 2: 222 / 265). As such, the activity of truth inherently references the nature of Dasein, its being-in-the-world—Dasein's disclosedness (*Erschlossenheit*) (220 / 263). Being-true, as a form of Being-uncovered (*Entdeckt-sein*) is a possibility, thinks Heidegger, which is grounded on Dasein's being—the way in which Dasein *is* in-the-world. When Dasein comports itself to entities authentically they are revealed/uncovered and appear truly without distortion or dissimulation. When, however, Dasein turns away from its being-uncovering and comports itself inauthentically, entities remain covered over and hidden showing themselves improperly and falsely. This same relation bears on the way in which Dasein comports itself to itself. Authenticity is a mode in which Dasein is toward itself in such a way that its own being is uncovered and revealed in its true form.

According to Heidegger, the temptation to act inauthentically, to cover over the trajectory of one's own being, is part and parcel with the way in which Dasein finds itself "thrown" (*werfen*) into the world. That is, the possibility of acting inauthentically does not denote an active turning away from the call of one's own being, it is instead the refusal to actively tear oneself away from the distractions of the world into which one finds oneself thrown and to instead "fall" (*fallen*) in the trajectory of that "thrownness" (*Geworfenheit*). Thus, claims Heidegger, "Being-in-the-world is in itself tempting [*versucherisch*]" (*GA* 2: 177 / 221). Still, inauthenticity does not express for Heidegger the natural nor primordial expression of Dasein. Though Dasein is thrown into the world such that inauthenticity is always a temptation, it is not, in a sense, *natural* for it to be inauthentic. Inauthenticity is always a derivation from and negation of its primordial calling. It is always the result of heeding the temptation offered in the world instead of listening to the primordial call issued by one's own being. Thus, whilst authenticity expresses for Heidegger an attainment to the true expression of one's being, inauthenticity is always somehow privative, a derivative modification of that being, even though the temptation to be inauthentic is inexorably a part of the way in which Dasein is *in-the-world*.

This temptation to derivate from the path to which one is called by one's own being is, especially presented in the collective being of others, in the collective being of other Dasein, which Heidegger infamously terms the "they" (*das Man*). By Heidegger's read, *falling* into the temptation of being-in-the-world, "this downward plunge into and within the groundlessness of the inauthentic Being of the 'they,' has a kind of motion which constantly tears the understanding away from the projecting of authentic possibilities" (*GA* 2: 178 / 223). One way in which inauthenticity appears for Heidegger is thus as a mode of being wherein one rejects the call of one's own being by immersing oneself within the collective nature of others and taking on that nature in lieu of one's own. In this case inauthenticity appears as the refusal to actively distinguish the singularity of one's own existence from the *hoi polloi* and to treat oneself as one of them, to take on the mantle of others instead of attending to the call of one's own being. Inauthenticity can thus result from allowing the clamor of the masses to drown out the persistent demand of being. To be truly or authentically, one must reject the temptation offered in the they, and this is only done by uncovering and revealing one's ownmost being—by attending to the voice within which beckons.

One can perhaps already hear the possible Levinasian rejoinders to such a concept. For, as we saw in the last chapter, one attends to one's true self not by rejecting that which comes from the outside or appears in the form of another, but by abandoning the path which is natural to one's own being in order to accept and receive as a host that which is otherwise and comes from beyond one's own being—in order to heed the ethical call which comes from another. It is thus, Levinas claims, only once one rejects the ontological insistence of one's own being and assents to the ethical primacy of the other that one can truly arise to his or her "final reality" or "essence." In this sense, he reverses the order of the "true" or the "natural" referenced in Heidegger's notion of authenticity. By Levinas's account, that which is true or natural to a self should not be situated within the order of being but, as we have seen, beyond or exterior to it. For Levinas, authenticity must run otherwise than being. Authenticity for him would thus require rejecting that which is natural to one's way of being in order to embrace that which is foreign or otherwise to that being. Heidegger's alignment of the true with that which is interior to a phenomenon's being seems to establish him firmly within what we have seen Levinas identify as the Odyssian mode of thinking which favors return over estrangement and prioritizes sameness over the otherwise, a criticism which has been repeated throughout the secondary literature on the differences between Levinas and Heidegger.[9] Of course, as we shall see, Levinas's thought cannot be figured as a complete rejection nor reversal of Heidegger's insights, after all, even Levinas's rejoinders to the Heideggerian system can still be figured as functioning, at least to some extent, within the logic of the Heideggerian system, as other scholars have demonstrated.[10]

Indeed, even here Levinas seems to make distinctions within his own thinking, akin to Heidegger's distinctions between the authentic and the inauthentic. This is especially true in his conception of desire. Remember, after all, that this foray into Heidegger's conception of the authentic and the inauthentic was intended to illuminate his designation of Eros as a particularly *authentic* mode of striving and having. So while for Heidegger authenticity refers primarily to Dasein's mode of comportment in relation to itself, it only becomes of interest to us as a concept in as much as it designates a particular expression of Dasein's erotic striving—in as much as it can distinguish certain kinds of erotic transcendence from others and thereby grant deeper phenomenological insight into the nature of longing as investigated by Levinas. By suggesting that Eros proper is a particularly authentic mode of striving and having, Heidegger implies not only that there can be equally inauthentic modes of striving and having—modes which would express a kind of inauthentic Eros, but also the fact that what designates Eros proper from its modified inauthentic form is how it relates to its ownmost nature. Authentic Eros would thus be for him a having and striving which remains true to its trajectory and calling while inauthentic Eros would express a striving and having which diverts from its natural course. Strangely, this insight seems to be repeated in some of Levinas's claims concerning the nature of desire.

As we saw toward the end of the last chapter Levinas demarcates the difference between metaphysical desire and other forms of desire in part by capitalizing the first letter of those desires which pursue the otherwise. From this we inferred that for Levinas, other desires, those desires bound by the limits of ontological interest, represent a kind of fallen, or lesser order, metaphysical Desire. So it seemed that metaphysical desire expressed for Levinas the true form of Desire, while other desires, such as Eros, by diverting from the trajectory of that Desire and subsuming themselves into the realm of being, resulted in an incomplete demonstration of the natural trajectory of Desire proper—that is, such desire failed to testify to the priority of the otherwise and the foreign. By falling short of the call of Desire to pursue the absent and the otherwise, determinate desires like Eros thus expressed for him a kind of betrayal of the true trajectory of Desire as such. Could it be that such desires could thus be termed, employing the Heideggerian language, inauthentic? If so, could metaphysical desire, on the other hand, as that human longing which tirelessly pursues the otherwise and testifies to its elevation and infinity, be called somehow authentic? Clearly, we take the terms beyond their intended meaning at this point, but it nevertheless seems that Levinas's thought on the nature of human longing, at least covertly, employs what could be called the "logic of authenticity" in Heidegger. If this is indeed the case then we must rethink our intuitions concerning his possible exceptions to Heidegger's so called "ethics of authenticity." Indeed we must claim that while Levinas may stand in opposition to some of the ways that Heidegger employs this logic of authenticity—in as much as it is applied to the structures of subjectivity, for example—he nevertheless relies upon that same logic in ordering his account of desire. Thus, Levinas's thought seems to differ from Heidegger's not so much in the logical structure employed therein, but in the content with which each informs that structure. For, whereas for Levinas Desire's authenticity is maintained in its commitment to the otherwise than being—its commitment to the metaphysical proper (that which exceeds and transcends as such)—for Heidegger a desire's authenticity is maintained through its commitment to the primordial trajectory and call of Being. Thus, while an authentic desire for Levinas is necessarily metaphysical, moving away from and beyond being by attending to the call of the otherwise, an authentic desire for Heidegger is deeply and truly ontological, liberating and disclosing the true nature of Being.

So it is that we begin to approach the Heideggerian legacy in Levinas's analysis of the nature of human longing. But, the plot thickens the more we examine this possible connection. For, as we will see shortly, Heidegger is none too clear on the ultimate aim and ends of erotic striving, not because he fails to investigate the matter fully, but because, by his read, those aims and ends seem to fall beyond the limits of representation, a fact which will significantly affect our reading of the differences between his analysis of desire and Levinas's. But in order to approach these possible differences more fully we must first investigate further Heidegger's claims concerning the nature of the erotic phenomenon.

THE INTERNAL INHERENCE OF HAVING AND STRIVING IN THE EROTIC PHENOMENON

Heidegger's claim that Eros proper is only a determinately authentic striving (*eigentliche Streben*) and having (*eigentliche Haben*) suggests that, Eros is the original and primordial expression of striving and having as such. This also implies, of course, that there are other derivative/inauthentic expressions of that phenomenon which must be defined as *inauthentic* expressions of having and striving. To determine what these possible phenomena are, and in doing so more sharply define our understanding of the nature of the authentic expression of Eros, we must begin by understanding what Heidegger means by striving and having.

According to Heidegger, when considered in terms of their participation in the erotic phenomenon, having and striving should not be taken as two distinct phenomena independent of one another. Instead, they must be conceived of as inexorably coconstitutive. This is revealed in the very way in which we understand and talk about human striving. For, he says, "we [only] strive for what we *do not yet have*" (*GA* 34: 211 / 152). This fact is not merely ancillary but pertains to the very essence of striving. Indeed, says Heidegger, "in its *essential nature,* striving is such that we strive only for what we do *not yet* have" (204 / 147; first italics mine). Striving is thus *essentially* tied to the way in which it *has*—or, to be more precise, the way in which it *does not have*. In any case, having seems to pertain essentially to the nature of striving for Heidegger. And, likewise he goes on, "striving is not just itself a kind of having, but even necessarily belongs to the essence of authentic having" (214 / 153). Authentic having is thus in essence a form of striving.

Defined in terms of its having, Heidegger claims that striving must be understood in relation to that which it does not yet have. That is, striving, thinks Heidegger, must be conceived in terms of its aim and the way in which it relates to that aim. The aim of authentic striving is more than a merely passive end however, claims Heidegger. It is, instead, that which motivates and occasions the striving as such. The object of striving, he claims, "pulls and draws us towards it...it holds us to itself" (*GA* 34: 210 / 152). The object of striving exerts a force upon the striver such that his striving should not be thought of as an active project or conscious engagement. Human beings are not the origin of their own striving—they are caught up in it, engaged by it. As such, striving seems to express for Heidegger a kind of passivity within human existence.[11] Humans are not the author of all of their experiences, but are subject to the whim of something else—something which, though seemingly other, nevertheless exerts a force upon them and defines the way in which they are.

Heidegger's emphasis of the passivity of man in relation to the aim of his striving is so great that in the 18th appendix to the text, taken from Heidegger's own notes on the lecture course, the word "striving" is entirely left behind. Heidegger seems to have thought that the word "striving" implied too much subjective activity within human existence. He thus replaces it entirely with the reflexive term pull (*Zug*) or ground-pull (*Grund-zug*) (*GA* 34: 350 / 234). Erotic striving, he seems to suggest, is some sort of pull that we are subject to—in Eros we are *pulled* or *drawn* by some force which does not originate in us, but which exercises a power over and through us as an iron filling is drawn by a magnet. Thus though the force experienced in erotic striving seems to be other than us, it is not our subjective being which is at work in erotic striving, it nevertheless corresponds to something within us, it resonates at the frequency of our inmost being.

By establishing the origin of the momentum present within erotic striving on something other than human agency, Heidegger is able to abandon all questions of the activity of some supposed subject in Eros. Eros is not for him the result of some latent interest within the human subject, but is instead the effect of the presence of some *presence* or force which draws human existence toward it. As such, erotic striving evidences for him the fact that the human Dasein is in its ownmost nature not a closed totality. It does not express for him a kind of inside from which some determinate outside can be distinguished. Eros, as the effect of a pull upon human existence of some other force which defines the very way in which it is and expresses its being, testifies to the fact that the traditional conception of the subject is flawed, that human beings are not entities wholly unto themselves, capable of shutting themselves entirely off from any outside world. Instead, Eros as an expression of the *authentic* having and striving of human existence, and yet nevertheless motivated by and directed toward something other than that existence, demonstrates that its true nature inheres to something beyond it—something which cannot be localized within any particular entity or being such as a subject.[12] The experience and nature of Eros thus testifies to the fact, for Heidegger, that humans are not ultimately the source for, nor in charge of, their ownmost being—no Dasein is truly the decider of his or her own nature. Erotic striving, as that "by which the Dasein of man *is carried,*" announces the fact that human Dasein is swayed and influenced by something other than its own being, though this something other always already corresponds to its nature (*GA* 34: 216 / 155; italics mine).

Authentic striving is nothing more than this being drawn, this "*being carried,*" this *pull* experienced within human existence toward something beyond the limits of its own being. It is for Heidegger the way in which this feeling of being summoned beyond oneself is expressed in language. Since this pull is already being felt in striving, its aim or object must be conceived as somehow already "*there* in the striving and [as] absent precisely in non-striving. Only *in* the striving for it do we have it 'there'" (*GA* 34: 211 / 152). The object or aim of striving presents itself in and through the striving itself. Thus, though striving pertains to that which one does *not yet* have for Heidegger, it should not be seen as arising out of some absence—it is not privatively motivated. It is instead the testament to some presence within human existence—something that is *had* within and holds before itself.[13] Heidegger even identifies that which is held before human existence in erotic striving as some kind of "excess" (*Mehrbestand*)—some kind of strange surplus present within it (190 / 138).

Though this excess is always already present and held before human beings in their erotic striving, human existence nevertheless appears incapable of concretely grasping or having fully that toward which it is drawn in its striving. It can never fully appropriate nor make its own that which it has through its striving. In this sense, though tethered to the nature of human existence, the aim of erotic transcendence is forever held away at a distance and perceived as that which one does not have. Thus though striving may testify to a kind of presence within human existence, this presence can appear to be somehow absent—can be felt as a kind of absence.[14]

Clearly this is an uncanny understanding of the nature of having, which Heidegger himself seems to confess: "The whereto of the striving, the object of striving as such, is had *in* the striving; it is had *as* the object of striving—and yet still as something striven *for;* and thus *not*-had. A curious phenomenon this: had and yet not had! The striving relationship is intrinsically a having-before-oneself, a having that is at the same time a not-having" (*GA* 34: 211–12 / 152). Still, it is clear why, on the basis of this argument, Heidegger linked the nature of striving to the nature of having so inherently. To comprehend more fully Heidegger's claims concerning the nature of erotic striving, it is thus necessary to turn our attention to the nature of authentic having. Indeed, "the problem of determining the essence of striving is not so much a question of what striving is, as of what *having* is, where having is understood as human *comportment*" (212 / 152).

Heidegger's claim that the "problem" in "determining the essence of striving" by way of having is no accident. It is a difficult task partly because of the seemingly paradoxical nature of the way in which one has in erotic striving, but also partly because of the way in which having has been traditionally understood. When one thinks of how he or she can *have* something one naturally understands this having in terms of possession (*Besitzen*). But possession (*Besitzen*) is only *one* way of having (*Habens*) (*GA* 34: 212 / 153). To elucidate what he means by possession Heidegger examines the way in which human beings comport themselves to things in "*one* way of possession (the most familiar to us)," which he claims is "having disposal over things" (212 / 153).

This kind of possession "is marked precisely by immediacy of disposition and arbitrariness of employment, thus by a kind of *freedom* in having" (*GA* 34: 212–13 / 153). It thus testifies to the power and the spontaneous freedom of the possessor. One who possesses in this way, claims Heidegger, "is not subject to any other claim. He can employ what he possesses in any arbitrary way depending on his desire and needs" (213 / 153). This having of an unrivaled ownership over one's possessions thus seemingly promotes the freedom of the subject who possesses. That is, it seems to testify to his mastery and independence from that over which one exercises dominion. But, it actually does just the opposite, for it confuses the difference between one who owns and that which one owns. That is, when one defines his or her essential human freedom in relation to that which he or she possess, one has made the grave error of identifying too closely with mere objects—with that which is merely at hand for use. As such, one risks losing oneself amidst that which he or she possesses. Thus, the kind of "freedom" to which ownership testifies reveals itself to be a kind of slavery; for therein, he argues, "the autonomy of the self gives way to the contingency and arbitrariness of needs and desires to be immediately satisfied [*der unmittelbar zu befriedigenden Bedürfnisse und Reize*]" (213 / 153). As such, possession appears to be an inauthentic mode of having "because its apparent freedom of disposition fundamentally amounts to servitude under the arbitrary and contingent rule of needs [*Wahllosigkeit und Zufälligkeit der Bedürfnisse*]" (213 / 153; translation amended).

Note the way that Heidegger links possession, as an inauthentic mode of having, to need, which one can only conclude is the corollary inauthentic mode of striving.[15] Indeed, claims Heidegger, "striving can be an inauthentic comportment in just the same way that possessing can be this" (*GA* 34: 214 / 154). Thus whereas "inauthentic possessing proved to be an unrestricted claim upon arbitrary needs [*andrängenden Bedürfnisse*]," inauthentic striving is "a mere chasing after what is striven for" (214 / 154). When this occurs, the movement of striving becomes "fixed in *one* direction," such that the striving consumes "itself in its striving and mere self-abandonment" (214 / 154).

This mode of striving resembles remarkably what Heidegger names a kind of *craving* (*Gier*) in *Being and Time* (*GA* 2: 346–47 / 397). There, craving is addressed in passing to reveal the etymological, and it seems, existential root of inauthentic curiosity (*Neugier*). Curiosity is a kind of "craving for the new" in such a way that it never satisfies itself with the actual. As a result, it "is characterized by a specific way of *not tarrying* alongside what is closest," of constantly becoming distracted and "never dwelling anywhere" (172–73 / 216–17). This uprootedness seems to characterize the movement of inauthentic striving, or need. As the desire to possess and consume in search of satisfaction, inauthentic striving remains perpetually on the hunt — perpetually in search for some new object to possess or delight in. It appears to be a kind of insatiable hunger than cannot rest nor tarry with itself. It is, it seems, a kind of *greed*. When this form of inauthentic striving is paired with its correlate, inauthentic having under the form of possession, we witness the inauthentic expression of the erotic — what happens to the erotic when it is diverted from its ownmost course and natural trajectory: namely a desire which attempts to satisfy itself in object possession.

Authentic striving, on the other hand, which along with authentic having is constitutive of authentic Eros, Eros as such, "does not strive to possess the object, but strives for it to *remain* as striven for, as held in the striving, in order that the striver finds himself *from* that for which he strives" (*GA* 34: 215 / 154). Since possession is not the aim of this kind of striving, claims Heidegger, that which is striven for in authentic Eros "always remains *untaken* as something striven for" (216 / 155). The kind of having which is maintained in such a striving then is, according to Heidegger, one that "still somehow stands in the light of *in*-completion," not only unsatisfied; but, it seems, unsatisfiable (212 / 153). Clearly at this point we begin to perceive some similarities between Levinas's account of longing and Heidegger's analysis of Eros.

AUTHENTIC EROS AND PRIMORDIAL LONGING

Operating in relation to the object of its striving in this way, Heidegger's conception of Eros, as authentic striving and having, appears, like Levinas's account of metaphysical desire, to be a kind of reversal of the traditional understanding of desire. For, as we have seen, whereas determinate desires are usually posited as a striving which emerges out of some absence and moves toward some determinate object in order to possess and consume that object for the sake of the striver's satisfaction, authentic Eros, like metaphysical desire, is occasioned by the *presence* of some force already in its striving which draws it onward toward that which precisely cannot be *taken* as some object of possible satisfaction. As such, authentic Eros appears to be a kind of drive which remains essentially *incomplete*. This latter movement, as the authentic and original expression of the nature of Eros, is thus the true expression of erotic transcendence. Other more determinate expressions of this erotic movement which attempt to satisfy erotic striving by possessing or grasping some concrete aim or object, as the inauthentic derivation of the ownmost trajectory of erotic transcendence, thus appear as derivative manifestations of true erotic transcendence. The inauthentic expression of the erotic present in greed for instance, is thus the result of the perversion of the original primordial call of the erotic. Nevertheless derivative desires of this sort, as expressions of Eros, however inauthentic, must be conceived as occasioned not by some determinate absence, but by the presence of some force which motivates their drive toward whichever object upon which they become fixated. The status of any particular erotic transcendence as authentic or inauthentic is thus determined by Heidegger in how that transcendence is related to the beyond toward which it is pulled. When the aim of Eros is taken as some sort of object which is made the goal of some eventual possession this transcendence deviates from its original trajectory and becomes inauthentic. When, on the other hand, it is allowed to relate to the force which motivates it in such a way that no eventual satisfaction is aspired for and in such a way that respects the indeterminacy of its end, Eros seems to remain authentic.[16]

Michael E. Zimmerman distinguishes between these two expressions of erotic striving as "ontical craving" and "ontological desire" respectively.[17] Thus whereas the former is a kind of "desire for what is pleasurable and useful, for what increases our chances for survival, for what will make us more powerful," ontological desire or authentic Eros, on the other hand, maintains itself above what Zimmerman identifies as the merely animalistic and grounds the possibility of being human by holding itself in proper relation to its object.[18] Ben Vedder, for his part, also sees in Heidegger's analysis a difference between authentic desires, which recognize and respect the absolute difference between striver and what is striven for, and inauthentic desires which toil to take possession and actualize the presence of its aim.[19] Vedder suggests, in part, that this difference has to do with how the striver comports himself to a primordial absence within him, either by, authentically allowing it to be, or inauthentically attempting to fill it with presence. Though we have to diverge from Vedder's analysis that authentic desire consists in an absence, given the fact that according to Heidegger it demonstrates a kind of over abundant presence, his analysis of the goals of inauthentic striving certainly stand.

In contrast to its inauthentic form, Heidegger dubs this authentic relation to the object of erotic striving as the "most primordial longing [*ursprünglichsten Sehnsucht*]" (*GA* 34: 239 / 171; translation amended). Though relatively unexplored in his treatment of Plato, Heidegger turns his attention to the nature of this longing more completely in his 1936 lecture course on *Schelling's Treatise on the Essence of Human Freedom* (*GA* 42), which we shall examine more thoroughly.[20] There he begins by invoking the strange alterity present in this kind of striving: "Who has ever completely dismissed the possibility with adequate reasons that what we call 'longing' and live within might ultimately be something other than we ourselves? Is there not contained in longing something which we have *no* reason to limit to man, something which rather gives us occasion to understand it as that in which we humans are freed *beyond* ourselves [*über uns weg*]?" (216–17 / 124). This notion of being "freed *beyond* ourselves" through erotic longing is not exclusive to Heidegger's treatment of the Schelling treatise.[21] Indeed, in his reading of the *Theaetetus,* Heidegger claims that the way in which man is in his striving evidences the fact that "man as existing has always already stepped *out beyond* himself [*aus sich herausgetreten*]" (*GA* 34: 232 / 166; italics mine). According to Heidegger, one is distinguished as a human being precisely by "being out beyond oneself [*Über-sich-hinaus-sein*]" (236 / 169).

As such, it is only by attending to this *beyond,* thinks Heidegger, that one can attend to one's own inmost self. It is for this reason that longing is identified for him as an authentic phenomenon. For though, "every striving is indeed a striving toward (the object striven for)...this toward...is not necessarily an away-from-oneself" (*GA* 34: 215 / 154). To the contrary, by attending to the beyond to which one is called through longing one "strives for his own Dasein" (217 / 156). Moreover, "That the soul is as such [a] striving...means that man as existing has always already stepped out beyond himself....At the same time, striving...is the way the soul *is* in its own self" (232 / 166). So it seems that one only truly encounters and finds oneself in relation to this beyond. Thus, although longing is a moving "outside-of-oneself [*Außersichsein*]," it is simultaneously the "true coming-to-oneself [*eigentliches Zu-sich-kommen*]" (*GA* 42: 220 / 126; translation amended). Longing, it seems, by calling human existence away toward the beyond, beckons it home to its ownmost being. Clearly, as we will see in more detail later on, this is going to significantly affect our analysis of the differences between Levinas's account and Heidegger's.

Heidegger elaborates on this notion of finding that which is truly one's own by pursuing that which is beyond or foreign in his 1942 lecture course on *Hölderlin's Hymn "The Ister"* (*GA* 53). There is some question, however, concerning whether or not Heidegger's lectures on *Der Ister* can be taken to address the general state of human existence or whether it is intended to speak instead to a rather particular form of human existence, namely German existence. Written in 1942 during the height of National Socialism in Germany and the Second World War, many have read Heidegger's lectures on Hölderlin as the attempt at a kind of prophetic call to the German people in the hopes of revealing and inviting them to embrace their ownmost essence.[22] His explorations of the nature of the foreign journey needed to come into one ownmost being would not then be an analysis of the general state of human existence as such, but German existence (which for him needs to pass not through just any foreign, but the specifically Greek foreign in order to come home), and not, for instance, American existence. And, indeed, there are many passages in the text which suggest this (67–68 / 54). Nevertheless, it is my contention that Heidegger's claims concerning the German people in his lectures on *Der Ister* can be extended to the nature of human existence as such for two reasons. Firstly, because what he says there fits well with what is said in his other texts concerning the fundamental ex-centrism of the nature of human existence—its always already being out of and beyond itself. And, secondly, because the text itself often suggests that the journey beyond required by being has to do with the specific nature of *human* beings in general (*der Mench*) (107–08 / 87). Therefore, it is my contention that his references to a specifically German way of being human is a refinement of what he sees as the general condition of human existence as such, perhaps even because, for Heidegger at that time, the

German people were for him the *most* human of human beings (i.e., had the most potential to be authentically human).

Read in this way, Heidegger's *Der Ister* lectures serve profoundly to enlighten the way in which human longing, as one of the fundamental attunements of human Dasein, must carry human existence through that which is beyond itself in order to pursue its ownmost nature. There, it is only by passing through the foreign that one can come into what he calls the homely; and it is this "becoming-homely of human beings [*Das Heimischwerden des Menschens*]" (*GA* 53: 52 / 43). This "becoming homely," through the foreign "comprises [the] full essence of being human [*volle Wesen des Menschseins in sich*]" (52 / 43). Note Heidegger's language here however. It is not the *arriving* home which "comprises [the] full essence of being human," for Heidegger, it is the "*becoming*-homely."[23] The essence of human existence is thus not contained in the homely itself, but in the *passage* toward the homely, a passage which is pursued through the foreign. The foreign—the beyond toward which one is called in longing—is thus more than a merely temporary displacement. It is more than a merely momentary eccentrism from that which is truly one's own. It is instead concupiscent with the very *way* in which human Dasein *is* in-the-world—the very way in which human beings *are,* as such. Heidegger writes, "Coming to be at home *is*...a passage through the foreign [*Das Heimischwerden ist so ein Durchgang durch das Fremde*]" (60 / 49).[24] One's home, one's true/authentic self, is thus found, according to Heidegger, in the passage itself, and not merely in the end or goal of that passage. Thus, says Heidegger, "this *coming to be* at home in one's own self in itself entails that human beings are initially, and for a long time, and sometimes forever, not at home" (60 / 49).

The fact that one may be "forever" not at home does not entail for Heidegger that one has fallen into inauthenticity or somehow betrayed his or her true essence. To the contrary, this being not at home, however projected, *is* the true essence of human existence, thinks Heidegger.[25] It is for this reason that he nominates with Sophocles human nature as the "the most uncanny [*das Unheimlichste*]" (*GA* 53: 84 / 69). By his read, "the uncanniest of the uncanny is the human being [*Das Unheilichste des Unheimlichen ist der Mensch*]" (83 / 68). And moreover, "becoming-human is provenance from the unhomely [*Menschwerden ist Herkunft aus dem Unheimischen*]; the homely [*Heimische*] always remains related to the unhomely (*Unheimische*) in such a way that the latter is present in the former" (84 / 69). The foreign is thus for Heidegger "something that makes [human beings] into what they are and who they can be" (127 / 103).

The fact that one is drawn out *beyond oneself* into the foreign by longing is not thus the sign of an eternal estrangement, but the summons to a true expression of the essence of human existence—it is a beckoning home. It is for this reason perhaps that in the 1929–30 winter semester lectures entitled *The Fundamental Concepts of Metaphysics: World, Finitude, Solitude* (*GA* 29/30) Heidegger identifies a kind of *homesickness* (*Heimweh*) at the root of all philosophizing—a homesickness which he identifies as a kind of *restlessness* (*Getriebenheit*) that inheres to the very way in which the human Dasein is (*GA* 29/30: 8 / 5). In this way longing functions to reveal the nature of our being—the fact that we are bound by *finitude* (8 / 6). As such, homesickness is not for him, as it is for Levinas, a kind of nostalgia. It is not the expression of a desire to *return* to something that is our own—something that we have somehow lost. It is instead a determinate manifestation of the drive within humanity to stretch out *beyond* itself and find a home. It is therefore not an orientation toward the past, but an orientation toward some future, as we saw stated in Heidegger's elaboration on Hölderlin's *Ister*, only in and through an authentic encounter with the foreign. Homesickness thus appears to be for Heidegger something akin to Levinas's Eros, an ambiguous phenomenon which, in its future orientation toward a *not yet,* reveals its dependence upon a more primordial drive toward the beyond.

In keeping with this definition of longing as that drive to push *beyond,* Heidegger identifies within the nature of longing at least four different phenomenologically manifest attributes. Firstly, he associates longing with a kind of *stirring (Regung)* within human existence. Longing, it seems, awakens something within us. It *stirs* the waters of our existence, as it were—it unsettles us in such a way as to beckon us further, onward toward the beyond. Longing is thus a kind of propulsion or call to move out beyond the familiar and into the foreign and therein to seek one's true self. "Longing [*Sehnsucht*]" is precisely this "*stirring* [*Regung*], stretching away from itself and expanding" (*GA 42:* 218 / 125). Regarded thusly, longing appears to be a kind of inspiration—through it one feels inspired, breathed into from without and *beyond.* But, at the same time, it is this breath, this inspiration, which grants life and singularity. After all, Heidegger has identified the striving inherent in longing with the very essence of what it means to be human.

Secondly, claims Heidegger, though in longing one feels oneself summoned by the beyond, the whereto of that beyond remains forever *indeterminate.* Thus longing, as this drive toward the indefinite, itself appears as a kind of indeterminate phenomenon. "Longing is a will in which what is striving wills itself in the *indeterminate*" (*GA* 42: 218 / 125; italics mine). As such, it "never admits of a stable formation because it always wants to remain longing." Heidegger thus names longing "a will without understanding" (218 / 125). Though the experience of longing is certainly profound and unquestionably poignant, there is something about it which resists cognitive determination or categorization—something about it which resists the powers of ratiocination. According to Heidegger: "As a striving without understanding, it has nothing which has been understood and is to be brought to stand and stability, nothing which it could call something definite, unified. It is '*nameless*' [*namenlos*]; it does not know any name; it is unable to name what it is striving for. It is lacking the *possibility of the word* [*die Möglichkeit des Wortes*]" (218 / 125; italics mine, translation amended). Alongside the *stirring* inherent in longing and its fundamental *indeterminacy,* this *namelessness* constitutes the third aspect of longing's phenomenological appearance for Heidegger. Because longing is driven toward the indeterminate, and as such falls outside the powers of human conceptualization, there is something about it which denies the power of language. Words fail to describe the experience of being caught up in the indeterminate stirring of a deep longing. This in part entails the difficulty of the investigation under way. There is a sense in which one's experience of longing falls beyond the bounds of articulation. In longing one feels somehow struck dumb—unable to explain or describe what it is they are feeling or what it is they strive after.[26]

Though longing is essentially nameless, indeed perhaps because it is nameless, longing "always seeks precisely the word," according to Heidegger (*GA* 42: 222 / 127).[27] Thus though one may feel dumbfounded by the experience of longing, it is precisely this experience which drives one onward and forward encouraging articulation and inspiring new forms of communication by which to approximate that experience.

Finally, and fourthly, Heidegger identifies the experience of longing as somehow limitless and "eternal [*ewige*]" (*GA* 42: 221 / 127; italics mine). Indeed, he repeatedly refers to longing as "eternal [*ewigen*]" or "everlasting [*immer während*]" (218 / 125). Longing, it seems, is not contained by the finitude of the one who longs. Instead it signals the fact that there is a trace of something eternal and infinite within human existence and finitude.

HEIDEGGER AND LEVINAS REEXAMINED

Clearly there are a number of points of comparison between Heidegger's elaboration on the nature of authentic Eros and human longing and Levinas's description of metaphysical desire. Both, it seems, identify this drive within man with a kind of passivity. Longing, it seems, is motivated and occasioned not by that which is contained within man, but by that which resides outside of and *beyond* him. Both then recognize longing as the movement toward this beyond—a movement in which man encounters his own most essence, his true or final reality. Both contrast the movement of longing with that of need or craving, which they associate with other determinate desires like greed. But, neither fully separates these other desires from longing either. Instead both seem to suggest that these kinds of desire can result from an inauthentic expression of the trajectory toward the beyond expressed in longing. Furthermore, both describe this longing, and with it other forms of desire, as occasioned not by some *absence* within the subject, but by the *presence* of something else, though as we have seen some scholars disagree on this reading, at least with regard to Heidegger.[28] Finally, both assert the claim that there is something about the nature of longing which pertains to the infinite and the eternal.

Still, Heidegger and Levinas's respective treatments of human longing cannot be so quickly reconciled. Quite the contrary, some essential differences must be recognized between their respective accounts. Thus, though they may agree on the phenomenological structure of human longing, and though their respective treatments of it may inform one another's, there still exist some fundamentally irreconcilable differences between them. The heart of these differences lies, as we will see, in how each thinker treats the trajectory of human longing and how this treatment affects their analysis of the ultimate end and function of human longing.

Remember that for Levinas metaphysical desire is precisely *metaphysical* because it is categorized by its trajectory toward that which is *away*. It is on the grounds of the fact that it moved *away* from the interests of the subject's being that Levinas imbued metaphysical desire with such power; namely, the power to liberate us from the demand placed upon us by our needs and self-interest, and to reestablish our identity upon the grounds provided us by the Other. Metaphysical desire was thus posited by him as that desire which draws us away and beyond the gravitational pull of our own being and into the realm of the Good which, along with Plato, Levinas identified as "beyond being" (see *CPP* 175; *BPW* 21, 122–25; *OB* 12). In metaphysical desire, according to Levinas, one is thus called to a liberation not only *beyond one's own being,* but *beyond being* as such. It is only by being elevated into the height of this beyond being, he claims, that one is presented with the possibility of the ethical, a possibility which is not contained within the realm of being. And, as we saw, it was in the presentation of this possibility, that man is summoned to his true freedom and final reality.

Levinas nominates the realm of being which imprisons man within his determinate desires and needs with the impersonal term of the verb infinitive for being: "*there is* [*il y a*]" (*EE* 52). According to Levinas, "the *there is,* in as much as it resists a personal form, is 'being in general'" (52). While the realm *beyond being* is associated by Levinas with ethics, with concern for another who *regards* me, the reign of being as such is marked by a profound *indifference*.[29] Levinas's insistence on the indifference of being in the anonymous form of a *there is* should not be taken as a cue that one should oneself be indifferent to it. The *il y a* is not a neutral force for Levinas. On the contrary, he claims, that there is a very present threat contained within it. The *il y a* of being is, in fact, a kind of evil (*le mal*) according to Levinas (4–5). It is not evil because it is malicious, or because it is a bad thing, nor is it the expression of some kind of lack (i.e., the absence of some good). The evil of the *il y a* is not a defect; to the contrary, the evil of the *il y a* is grounded in the fact that it is a fullness so complete that no real determinations, such as that between good and bad, can be made within it (4). It express for him, a fullness of being so complete that no particular beings can exist within it, no beings which can elect or reject any moral good. Thus, he claims, "being is evil not because it is finite but because it is without limits" (*TO* 51). It expresses, employing the language of Hegel, a kind of "bad infinite" (*AT* 59; *OB* 142)—an infinite which does not elevate nor motivate transascendence, but an infinite which in its ceaseless monotony and homogeneity crushes all determinate existence and levels all difference.[30] The utter lack of determinacy and limits within the realm of being determined as the *il y a* prohibits the emergence of any sort of ethics or concern for the other because it delimits the possibility of a free action, and therefore a free choice for the good or the otherwise. Because being in general, the *il y a,* is completely free of all determinations, it is also utterly devoid of meaning according. He thus names it a kind of absurdity (*TO* 50). The totality of being thus expresses for him a horror (*EE* 55) which he compares to the curse of sleeplessness, to insomnia (see *EE* 61–64; *TO* 48). It is the ceaseless, monotonous, anonymous background hum of being which invades all attempts to close oneself off to sleep, rest, and interiority.[31]

Metaphysical desire, as a propulsion within the human being toward that which is beyond this being, thus signals the fact that one need not be dominated by the totalizing anonymity of being—need not participate in the realm of being in general as it is manifest in the *il y a*. It is the sign of a rupture within the continuity of being, the separation of a particular being from the totality of being in general. As such it signifies the possibility of the radical freedom present in the ethical relationship with another, another who stands outside the field of my being and signals otherwise. In ethics and metaphysical desire a singular being is liberated, affirmed and upheld from the morass of the *il y a.* Thus though one must *be* one's own being for as long as one *is,* in the ethical encounter one is given a way of eluding the absolute totality of that being—one is offered the possibility of committing one's being to the otherwise and thereby opening a space within being wherein one can truly be, as we saw in part in the last chapter.[32] It is thus essential to Levinas's argument that human longing be directed toward this otherwise, toward this beyond being.

In sharp contrast, Heidegger establishes the trajectory of human longing as definitively toward being, establishing a clear and seemingly insurmountable difference between his analysis and Levinas's. According to Heidegger, "Being is that towards which the soul strives, not just from time to time and to any purpose, but essentially" (*GA* 34: 203 / 147). The link between being and the longing of the human soul is so essential that, according to Heidegger, "the soul *is* this striving for being, in Platonic terms, the word 'soul' simply *means* striving for being" (203 / 147).[33] Longing, authentic Eros, is thus the authentic striving and having of being (218 / 156). That which is presented before human existence in striving, that which one *has,* "is grounded in a striving for being" (231 / 165). Thus, Heidegger says of the way Eros is presented in the *Phaedrus* that "the love Socrates speaks of, both the natural and the purified, is nothing else than the urge toward Being itself" (*GA* 19: 315 / 219). According to Heidegger, "in such authentic striving, man *holds himself* as an existing being in the midst of beings; man *has* the beings, and in these beings has himself, in the way he as man *can* have anything at all" (*GA* 34: 216 / 155). The *beyond* toward which one is summoned and in which one finds oneself is thus not a *beyond* that is otherwise than being, as Levinas would have it, but a *beyond* that expresses the fullness of being. Thus, claims Heidegger, "for all its unhomeliness, the unhomely remains within the sphere of being" (*GA* 53: 135 / 108). No matter how far away from the homely one may venture through longing, one never ruptures his or her position within being.

Clearly this difference in the trajectory and aim of longing fundamentally distinguishes and separates Levinas's analysis of the nature and aim of human longing from Heidegger. If the source of the final difference in their analysis of longing is their respective accounts of that toward which it is drawn, the Good beyond being in Levinas's case and Being itself for Heidegger, then our study demands that we attempt to understand the precise way in which these two forces function. This requires then that we endeavor to understand the precise way in which Heidegger characterizes the Being toward which he claims longing strives in contrast to Levinas's conception of the Good beyond being. Only once we've understood this difference will we finally come to understand the apparent difference between their respective phenomenological accounts of longing.

Heidegger's Being as "Beyond Being"?

As is well known, Heidegger posits much of his work as the attempt to reestablish what he calls the ontological difference between Being as such and the determinate beings which present themselves.[34] The problem, thinks Heidegger, is that this difference has more often than not been obfuscated over the course of Western philosophy resulting in confusion between the nature of Being as a whole and beings in particular. Indeed, Being has traditionally been understood as merely the highest expression of the same kind of being that beings exhibit. As such it has been taken to be a kind of absolute or complete presence. This confusion of the difference between Being and beings results in what Heidegger calls "onto-theology" (see "The Onto-Theo-Logical Constitution of Metaphysics" in *Identity and Difference*, *GA* 11). This confusion has had dire consequences for the West and has resulted in what he terms throughout his work a general "forgetting of Being" (*GA* 2: 2 / 21). In order to combat this confusion, Heidegger's recovery of Being, especially in his later works, appears as the attempt to distinguish beings, which indeed are fully present, from Being, which enables and empowers that presence and yet remains strangely absent, indeed manifests, as it were, as *nothing*.

According to Heidegger, whilst beings, as determinate entities are manifestly present- and ready-to-hand for Dasein, Being itself is that which is precisely not present as such, but rather that which presences (*anwesen*) the present, that which allows-to-presence (*anwesenlasen*), as is made clear in his 1969 lecture on "Time and Being" (*GA* 14). There, by playing upon one of the infinitive forms of the word "being" in German (*es gibt*), Heidegger defines beings as that which is *given* and Being as the *giving* of those gifts/beings. "Being," he claims, "belongs to this giving," it accompanies the manifestation of that which is given (6 / 6). This Being, he argues, "is not expelled from giving. Being, presencing, is transmuted. As allowing-to-presence, it belongs to unconcealing; as the gift of unconcealing it is retained in the giving" (6 / 6). Though it is "transmuted" and accompanies that which it gives, that which manifests through it, Being is nevertheless not present, argues Heidegger, in the same way as that which it presents. To the contrary, Being as such "withdraws [*entzieht*] in favor of the gift which It gives" (8 / 8). Being is in a sense that which opens up to allow room for beings to emerge. By opening/withdrawing in this way, Being does not appear as such, but only alongside the appearing of beings as the clearing in which they emerge.

To further elaborate the ontological difference between beings and Being, and thereby further define the nature of the latter, Heidegger also characterizes Being as a kind of "sending" (*Schicken*). Being, as "a giving which gives only its gift, but in the giving holds itself back [*zurückhält*] and withdraws [*entzieht*], such a giving we call sending [*Schicken*]" (*GA* 14: 8 / 8). Being is the sending of beings. As such a sending, Being is not present at the reception of the gift which it sends in the same way that the gift itself is, it is not immediately manifest to humans in whose perception the gift, beings/entities, is received. When one receives a package it is not the sending that concerns nor captures one's attention, it is the package itself. Nevertheless, it is only because the package has been *sent,* has been *given,* that it can be received at all. In the manifestation of that which is sent, the sending itself *withdraws*. So it is, claims Heidegger, that Being hides itself and withdrawals in its presentation of beings, that which is presented. Indeed, its very presentation seems to occur through its withdrawal such that Being itself becomes identified as a kind of presencing withdrawal.

Recognition of the strange nature of Being gives rise to his claim that "Being *is* not" (*GA* 14: 6 / 6). Being "*is* not" present in the same way that beings/entities are. This is not to say that Being is a kind of negation, as Heidegger goes to great lengths to show in his essay "What Is Metaphysics" (*GA* 9: 105–08 / 84–85). Being is not the negation of beings. Instead it is, in a way, its own kind of positive force, as it were, its own kind of showing. Struggling to give language to Being understood in this way, Heidegger at times takes to calling the Being beyond beings the nothing (106 / 94). Elsewhere he balks at this nomination as in his lecture course, the *Introduction to Metaphysics,* where he insists that "the [B]eing after which we inquire is almost like nothing, and yet we have always rejected the contention that [Being] in its entirety *is not*" (*GA* 40: 27 / 35).[35] Here Being appears to be "almost like nothing" precisely because of the way it withdraws from presence such that beings themselves may manifest, may take centre stage.[36] In either case, what Heidegger is trying to show is his contention that the Being toward which longing strives is not a determinate presence, nor is it the negation of such a presence. Instead it lies somehow beyond presentation and negation, beyond all logical formulation, what Heidegger calls in "On the Essence of Truth" a kind mystery (*GA* 9: 162 / 148).[37] What longing strives after, then, is the eternal withdrawal which allows determinate presences to manifest.

In order to emphasize the way that Being withdraws in favor of beings, and in this regard can be taken as that which "*is* not" present, in his last works Heidegger was taken to crossing out the word Being such that it read ~~Being~~. According to him "the crossing out of this word initially has only a preventive role, namely, that of preventing the almost ineradicable habit of representing '[B]eing' as something standing somewhere on its own that then on occasion first come face-to-face with human beings" (*GA* 9: 411 / 310). This crossing out of the word Being is thus intended to distinguish it even further from the mode of presencing exhibited by beings. Being, as ~~Being~~, is situated beyond beings, but beyond nonbeing as a negation as well.

Understood as it is, Heidegger compares the Being pursued by longing with Plato's conception of the Good as a kind of "highest idea, which can become visible *over* all ideas" and which empowers the manifestation of those ideas (*GA* 34: 99 / 72). This, of course, should immediately strike us as an unusual comparison given Levinas's explicit interest in the relation between metaphysical desire and Plato's conception of a Good beyond being. But, as we shall see, despite the fact that both return to Plato's conception of the Good in order to account for the ends of longing, the way in which they conceive of this end differs subtly, but significantly, as Noreen O' Connor has expertly demonstrated.[38] Still, this strange confluence bears further investigation.

According to Heidegger, like the Good which Plato famously characterizes as the light of the sun which illuminates all manner of things here below in his cave allegory (*Republic* 514a–521b), Being must be understood as the light, the visibility, by which determinate entities become visible and can be perceived at all. As such, he argues, like the Platonic Good, Being must be conceived of as "*out beyond* being (which is already most beingful) and primordial unhiddenness (unhiddenness as such)" (*GA* 34: 99 / 72). This claim should, of course, already strike those readers more familiar with Levinas as unusual, for it is precisely such a conception of a good beyond being that, according to Levinas, Heidegger cannot acknowledge and has no room for in his philosophy (*GDT* 126–27: "*the beyond being.* Now that is what, for Heidegger, would be scarcely defensible"). And yet, here it is, employed by Heidegger to illuminate a core concept within his thinking, the nature and meaning of Being. Still, we must insist their understanding of this concept ultimately diverges, as we shall see—and that the nature of this divergence fundamentally affects our analysis of their respective accounts of the nature of human longing.

According to Heidegger, "Plato calls that which empowers ἀγαθόν. We translate: the good" (*GA* 34: 106 / 77). This good is not merely another being, claims Heidegger, "τό ἀγαθόν cannot be a being [*nicht ein Sein sein kann*], therefore also cannot be unhiddenness, but is *beyond* [ἐπέκεινα], out beyond both being and unhiddenness" (108 / 78). "The good, the ἀγαθόν, is therefore," claims Heidegger, "the enablement of being as such and of unhiddenness as such. Or better, what Plato calls the good is that which empowers being and unhiddenness to their own essence, i.e. what is prior to everything else, that upon which everything else *depends*...*Empowerment* of being; not an existing 'good' (a 'value'), but what is *prior to* and *for* all being and every truth" (109 / 79). Heidegger situates the Good *beyond* because it is that upon which beings *depend,* that which is *prior to* and *for* their emergence. The *being* beyond which this idea is situated then is the Being of *beings*. The Good *beyond being* is thus that which empowers the emergence of beings—it is Being as such. "The expression 'the idea of the good'—which is all too misleading for modern thinking—is the name for that distinctive idea which, as the idea of ideas, is what enables everything else," it is Being (*GA* 9: 228 / 175). The good, like Being, "grants the appearing of the visible form in which whatever is present has its stability in that which it is" (229 / 176). Thus according to Heidegger, "when we ask about the *essence* of being and unhiddenness, our questioning goes *out beyond* these, so that we encounter something with the character of *empowerment* and nothing else. Empowerment is the *limit* of philosophy (i.e. of metaphysics)," it is the domain of Being (*GA* 34: 106 / 77).[39]

Note Heidegger's claim that the domain of Being, the domain concerning the empowerment of beings, that domain which is situated *beyond being* is the province of metaphysics. While Heidegger is generally opposed to the concept of metaphysics, since "metaphysics, insofar as it always represents only beings as being, does not recall Being itself" (*GA* 9: 366 / 278), in his text on Plato he seems to state that the domain of metaphysics engaged in properly would concern itself with the question of Being, the question of this beyond which withdraws in favor of that which appears, and the distinction of this Being from the manifestation of determinate beings. Indeed, Heidegger's whole problem with metaphysics and onto-theology, as we have seen, is that it has forgotten what is most essential to it, namely the nature of Being as such as withdrawal. Authentic metaphysics then, if such a thing can be posited, as the science which pursues that which is *beyond* (meta) *beings* (physics) would attend to the nature of Being proper, that which stands beyond all determinate presence and empowers it by withdrawing from it. Hence Heidegger's claim that "the recovery of metaphysics is [the] recovery of the oblivion of [B]eing"—its recovery begins with remembering that Being has been forgotten (416 / 314). Indeed, Heidegger's only interest in "overcoming metaphysics," as it is today is in order "to recall the truth of Being itself"—namely, that it is such that it *can be forgotten*—that it withdraws in such a way that it risks oblivion (367 / 279). Metaphysics must be overcome because it has forgotten the nature of Being—it has failed to retain the fact that Being erases itself—gives itself over to forgetting. Properly engaged in, however, Heidegger seems to suggest that metaphysics would attend to the nature of Being and the way in which it withdraws from presence. Done properly, metaphysical thinking would hold on to the self-erasure of Being and recognize the way in which Being is situated truly beyond being.

HEIDEGGER AND LEVINAS ON THE GOOD BEYOND BEING

Defined as belonging to the realm of the metaphysical proper, tied to Plato's conception of the idea of a Good *beyond being*, and understood as that which withdraws almost to the point of absence, almost to the point of being confused with the nothing, such that individual beings may differentiate themselves, Heidegger's conception of Being begins to resemble somewhat Levinas's notion of the transcendent proper which, as we have seen, is situated for him on a height and expressed in the idea of the infinite. But, we must resist such comparisons. After all, so much of Levinas's oeuvre is dedicated to decrying Heidegger's phenomenological ontology. And yet, when examined in light of their respective accounts of the transcendental movement of longing, their work reveals many more points of convergence than is typically portrayed both by Levinas and within the secondary literature on the subject. And, indeed, there are diverse opinions within the secondary literature on how to interpret the relation between Levinas and Heidegger's work.[40] For our part it is apparent that, at least in terms of how they account for the phenomenon of human longing, many more similarities seem to exist than we would have suspected. Not only do both account for the nature and movement of longing as a passive movement initiated within the human by some excess situated beyond it which remains forever out of reach, both furthermore appeal to Plato's conception of the Good *beyond being* to inform the nature of that beyond. Still, beyond all possible comparisons between their respective analysis of human longing, at least two essential and fundamentally irreconcilable differences remain between Levinas and Heidegger in their analysis of this beyond: 1) the ontological status of this beyond, 2) the way in which they inform the *value* of the Good identified with this beyond and thereby the transcendence enabled by it.[41]

With regard to the first, remember that for Heidegger though the beyond being expresses itself as a withdrawal it nevertheless appears, he claims, as a kind of positive power which, as we have seen, he at times calls the nothing. Because this withdrawal manifests through being, as that which empowers being, Levinas insists that, Heidegger's Being, though perhaps beyond the realm of determinate entities, is by no means free from the sway of the ontological in the same way that his conception of the Good is. It is not then, for him, truly beyond in any meaningful sense of the word—or truly otherwise than being, though it may appear differently. Instead, it is for Levinas something akin to the reverse or other side of the coin of determinate existence. Thus though it may fall beyond the realm of phenomenality, it remains inherently a part of it. For Levinas then, Heidegger's Being qua nothing, despite its appearance as a withdrawal from being, still retains a kind of ontological force. Levinas famously characterizes this force, as we have seen, as the *il y a* of Being which remains horrifyingly present in the nothing (*EE* 4–5).[42] So it seems that despite their mutual affirmation that the ultimate aim of human longing lies beyond being, Heidegger and Levinas's respective accounts of this beyond could not be more diametrically opposed. Ultimately what this comes down to is that while for Heidegger the beyond may appear as a kind of withdrawal toward the nothing, for Levinas the beyond toward which longing moves must be beyond even that. The good beyond being does not appear at all, thinks Levinas—it is entirely severed from the sway of the ontological. It thus does not function to empower beings, but to unsettle and decenter them from their own natures. The Good beyond being, then, is not only otherwise than being, it is otherwise than being's obverse, the nothing, as well (56). So, whereas for Heidegger the beyond appears as the nothing, for Levinas it must be figured as Alterity, or what he calls elsewhere illeity, the third option beyond beings and Being figured as nothingness.[43]

Just as importantly, Heidegger seems trenchantly reluctant to ascribe any moral value to the notion of the beyond being. The Good situated by Plato beyond being, and identified by Heidegger as Being proper, expresses a kind of suitability—something's ability to be put to use. Thus, "it does not have any kind of *moral* meaning: ethics has corrupted the fundamental meaning of this word" (*GA* 34: 106 / 77). Against the ethical corruption of the meaning of the Good, Heidegger defines the good as "the sound, the enduring, as distinct from the harmless meaning suitable for aunties: a good man, i.e. respectable, but without insight and power" (107 / 77).[44] This notion of the "moral good," he claims, "falls outside Greek thought, even though Plato's interpretation of the ἀγαθόν as idea offers the occasion for thinking of 'the good' 'morally' and ultimately for reckoning it to be a 'value,'" (*GA* 9: 227 / 174). Instead, claims Heidegger, the good should be understood as something which empowers a thing's utility, an argument which has given rise to the assessment, most notably by Stanley Rosen, that Heidegger's conception of the good is ultimately purely utilitarian.[45]

Defined as the sound and the orderly, or what in "Plato's doctrine of Truth," he calls the "orderliness of an order [*Geordneten einer Ornung*]"[46] (*GA* 9: 227 / 174), Heidegger is interested in realigning the concept of the Good with its function as Being, as an empowering force. "In Greek thought," he claims "τό ἀγαθόν means that which is capable [*taugt*] of something and *enables tauglich macht*] another to be capable of something" (227 / 174; italics mine). The Good, understood as the Being which stands beyond all determinate beings, is that which *presences,* which *enables* presence. It is that which *allows-to-presence* (*anwesenlassen*). It thus expresses for Heidegger a kind of power—a power which, he seems to suggest, accords to Nietzsche's conceptions of a will to power (233 / 179). This power or force which empowers presence, the "*empowerment* [*Ermächtigung*] of being," is thus never for him "an existing 'good' (a 'value'), but what is *prior to* and *for* all being and every existing truth" (*GA* 34: 109 / 79). The power of the good for Heidegger is that it enables the transcendence of beings toward being. It is the ground and condition for their power in the world.

This is in sharp contrast to the account of the transcendent Good beyond being given by Levinas. As we saw in the last chapter, the very goodness of the Good for Levinas is established in the fact that it deflects its attraction, what Heidegger defined as its pull (*Zug*), onto the Other. The Good for Levinas is thus not that which shines on its own, but that which shines in and through the social and is encountered only through the ethical recognition of another, as we will see in more detail in the following chapter. Hence Levinas's claim that "metaphysics is enacted where the social relation is enacted—in our relations with men" (*TI* 78). For Levinas, the Good cannot be reduced to some sort of power for being. Indeed, its very status is defined, as we have seen, in the fact that it relinquishes its power to that which appears otherwise than our being. As a result, the Good expresses for him, more than an empowering force, a very definite value—its *metaphysical* status is thus maintained for him in the fact that the Good extends beyond the logic of being and power, and expresses itself in the realm of the *ethical*.[47] Derrida has characterized the difference between Levinas and Heidegger on this point well. According to him, Levinas's problems with

Heidegger's concept of the beyond is that ultimately it is only situated *beside* beings, as it were, instead of properly *above* them and so lacks the critical distance of *height* so fundamental to Levinas account of the beyond.[48] The transcendence which the withdrawal of the Good beyond being effects, for Levinas then, is not the subjects ontological transcendence into being, but its ethical transcendence beyond being—the subject's freedom to escape the gravitational pull of his or her own ego and being to attend to the demands of the Other.[49] So whereas, by Levinas's read, the subject is *elevated* through his or her metaphysical desire in a transascendent movement, for Heidegger the subject is at best empowered by its longing, transcending only laterally and not horizontally.

Another way to characterize this difference is to say that Levinas's problem with Heidegger's conception of the Good beyond being, therefore, is that therein the social realm is forgotten—that the human, the ethical, is sacrificed to the ontological and the ethical value of singular individuals becomes lost in the totality of Being. As Levinas puts it: "to affirm the priority of *Being* over *existents* is to already decide the essence of philosophy; it is to subordinate the relation with *someone,* who is existent, (the ethical relation) to a relation with the *Being of existents,* which, impersonal, permits the apprehension, the domination of existents (a relationship of knowing), subordinates justice to freedom" (*TI* 45). This is the central core of Levinas's characterization of Heidegger's conception of Being as the insipid totality of the *il y a,* for it is a conception that cannot account for social or ethical value grounded in human life.[50]

Clearly, in the end Heidegger and Levinas's positions cannot be reconciled. Indeed, ultimately, as we have shown, their respective accounts stand fundamentally opposed to one another. But, at least with regard to their respective accounts of the nature of human longing, we have discovered more points of overlap between their two systems than we would have suspected.

CONCLUSIONS

Though Heidegger's conception of the Being beyond being and Levinas's idea of the transcendent Good beyond being remain fundamentally and irreconcilably opposed in their characterization of the metaphysical *content* of this beyond, their respective portrayals of the *structure* of that human desire which aspires to the beyond appears surprisingly similar allowing us to employ Heidegger's phenomenological account of human longing to gain further purchase in our attempt to explain and understand Levinas's conception of metaphysical desire.

Remember that for Heidegger, authentic Eros, primordial longing, was defined as an authentic striving and having of Being. This striving and having was not, as we saw, a kind of possession nor a kind of hunger, lust, or craving. These sorts of movements, claimed Heidegger, expressed the inauthentic mode of such a striving and having—they expressed for him the result of having confused the ultimate aim of authentic Eros with the immediately available and reducing the function of longing to a personal project of attaining some kind of satisfaction. But it is not longing's province to pursue such subjectivistic projects, however. To the contrary, longing appears, by Heidegger's account, to function to disrupt such projects; forcing us ever beyond our bourgeois goals and desires toward some greater power which holds sway over us. It belongs properly to the nature of longing not to seek satisfaction, but be content in pursuit of the unattainable ever distant and indistinct end which refuses to be made an object of consumption by us; but, instead, functions to break down such conceptions of subject and object, inside and outside, presence and absence. And in this description we find not only a remarkable similarity between Levinas and Heidegger but ultimately as well the source of their contention. And so, while these two conceptions cannot be ultimately reconciled, metaphysical desire for Levinas ultimately having an ethical value mediated in the social which distinguishes it from Heidegger's longing which remains restricted to the ontological, the two accounts nevertheless seem to inform one another, and more importantly inform our experience of human longing, especially with regard to how longing can be perverted toward more immediate forms of having and be converted into greed. In its own right, both seem to insist that longing be understood as a movement which is not occasioned by some absence, but initiated through the introduction of some excess which explodes the limits of subjectivity pushing the desirer out beyond his or her immediate way of being in-the-world without the promise of fulfillment of satisfaction. So it is that we discover a Heideggerian seed buried deep within Levinas conception of metaphysical desire.

PART TWO
ETHICAL LONGING

Three

The Ethics of Longing
Levinas and Fichte in Dialogue

Ethics: The Metaphysical Optics

Metaphysical desire is, according to Levinas, inexorably bound to the appearance of the Other, whose arrival on the scene opens up the possibility of the ethical choice by calling into question the subject's complicity with its own being.[1] Metaphysical desire is thus for him primarily an *ethical* movement, a movement which contends with choices made in the social realm—a realm situated outside of and beyond the self. As shown in the last chapter, it is this critical difference which perhaps more than any other, distinguishes his analysis of human longing from Heidegger's.

For Levinas, it is only because of its inherent tie to the Other, the fact that it is operational within the sphere of the ethical, that human longing is specifically *metaphysical* and not part of the *ontological* feedback loop of hunger and satisfaction. Human longing remains metaphysical only in as much as it exhibits and motivates an ethical concern for the Other.

As soon as this concern is lost, no matter how distinct it may appear, it can ultimately be analyzed as a kind of need. Only by maintaining its aim toward the Other, can human longing truly escape the temptation of being and empower the subject's transascendence away from its self-interest toward a higher or truer commitment.

This connection between the metaphysical and ethical is made so thoroughly by Levinas that the actual difference between the metaphysical and the ethical all but disappears therein. This is, of course, in keeping, however, with his thought on the nature of the metaphysical. Remember, according to Levinas, the Good functions such that it diverts the rays of its attraction onto the Other making the metaphysical accessible only through ethical responsibility in the social realm.[2] As we will see in more detail in this chapter, there is a sense in which, for Levinas, the metaphysical has collapsed upon the realm of the ethical such that questions concerning the *good* and the *otherwise,* the *beyond being* pursued by metaphysical desire appear only within the realm of the ethical. In order to understand further the nature of the ethical demands expressed in human longing, and how these demands function to distinguish human longing as determinatively metaphysical and not merely ontological, let us return once again to Levinas's assessment of the tendencies and excesses of the history of Western thinking.

THE HISTORY OF IDEALISM

Levinas's criticism of the history of Western philosophy is that it appears to be little more that the documentation of subtle variations within a pervading underlying idealism.[3] Thus by his read, even the most divergent philosophical systems, from Plato to Aristotle, Descartes to Spinoza, Kant to Hegel, all share the same fundamental orientation to the world—they are all, for Levinas, at least latently idealistic. This idealism becomes especially apparent for Levinas in the work of the German Idealists in general and J. G. Fichte in particular.[4]

The *idealism* which Levinas identifies and condemns within the history of Western philosophy he defines essentially as "the *myth* of a legislative consciousness of things, where difference and identity are reconciled," a consciousness which "rests upon the totalitarianism or imperialism of the Same" (*BPW* 14; italics mine). It is the story of a knowing I, Descartes's *cogito,* which finds itself in *possession* of a world—an I which can, thereby, define the world in relation to itself, understand the world as ordered and disposed unto it for its sake. In this story, argues Levinas, "every object can be spoken of in terms of consciousness," such that the world itself appears as little more than another mode of consciousness presenting itself—little more than the subject's outer projection of an object through which it can further realize itself (*TO* 65–66). This perceived ability, this possession over the world, is what idealism deems the freedom of the subject. This freedom is, at least according to Levinas, the ultimate status or final essence of the subject as it is understood and posited within the idealist tradition. Therein, the subject is defined first and foremost in terms of its freedom—a freedom which, as we have seen, is grounded in the way in which the I has disposal over the world. Because the idealistic consciousness holds dominion over the world, it thus understands itself as free from that world—as one who sits in authority over the world unfettered by its happenings such that though the world's order and structure may depend on the subject, the subject does not reciprocally depend upon the world, at least not to the same degree. The idealistic consciousness is thus declared *independent* of the world—and envisioned as an autonomously free floating power.

It is this vision of independence, claims Levinas, which constitutes the idealistic conception of freedom (see *CPP* 49). So it is that the subject becomes for the idealist the retainer of a kind of negative freedom—it is free *from* the bounds of any restraint other than those internally imposed upon itself either passively, by its own nature and thus still a limitation which can be reduced to itself, or autonomously and actively, as appropriated through a reasoned choice. This conception of the autonomous freedom of the subject is exemplified, thinks Levinas, in Kant's famous call to *Sapere aude* (dare to know).

Despite its diverse manifestations, whether in Descartes, Kant, or the Existentialist, this line of thinking amounts, concludes Levinas, to a philosophical system that grants the ego an almost absolute power and primacy in the world. It is for this reason that he defines this idealism a kind of *egoism*—it is not essentially then for him a *philosophy* understood properly as "the love of wisdom," but an *ego-ology,* a study of the self (*BPW* 14).

Given what we saw in the first chapter to be Levinas's persistent opposition to what he terms the tyranny of the ego, it should come as no surprise that he is considerably troubled by the presence of this kind of idealism within the history of Western thinking. What is curious however, is his nomination of it as a kind of myth. After all, given Levinas's own account of the way in which the I finds itself in the world of enjoyment prior to the epiphany of the other, one would think that the idealistic/egoistic account of subjectivity, though perhaps far from concerning itself with his presentation of the ethical, would not yet have given way to the realm of the mythological. That is to say that though this account may be limited, it nevertheless appears to be in keeping with his own descriptions of the way in which the I *naturally* functions in the world before the appearance of the Other, if such a before can be conceived. The idealistic position identified and criticized by Levinas would thus appear to be at worst a truncated, though nonetheless accurate, expression of the natural state of human consciousness. Thus, any fault presumed by Levinas to have been made therein should not be attributed to any flaw in reasoning, any turn to the mythological over the rational, but instead to a mere lack of investigative depth—a failure to push beyond the immediately apparent. Why his claim then that this brand of idealism constitutes a *myth?*

Levinas assessment of the mythological status of the idealist conception of the I as a purely legislative consciousness seems to stem not so much from what such idealisms *say* concerning the nature of human consciousness, but from what they *fail to say,* what they leave *unsaid,* either by intention or accident. The question seems to be for Levinas then not whether idealism has *accurately* or *reasonably* described the natural condition of the I, but whether it has *fully* described the life of human consciousness. The hard core of idealism's mythic status thus lies, Levinas suggests, in where it leaves off in its account of the life of subjectivity.

According to Levinas, by assuming from the outset the autonomy of the I, by making the subject's freedom in the world fundamental and on that basis establishing its power in the world, idealism makes of the subject an entity that must have somehow spontaneously arisen from out of the exercise of its own freedom such that it is in no way dependent on the world, but is entirely independent. Thus, the idealistic subject explored within the history of Western philosophy must be fundamentally self-positing, and therefore unquestionably autonomous and inaccessible to any form of authentic alterity (*OB* 162–63). This account, claims Levinas, severely delimits the possible experience of a radical alterity and thereby truncates much of the richness of the life of human subjectivity. It falls upon Levinas, then, in seeking to diverge from these idealistic traditions, to identify some of the shadows of its account of the nature of subjectivity—that is, to name and describe some of the phenomena that fall outside of its scope; and, by exploring these phenomena provide an alternative account of the origins and nature of consciousness not as a self-contained autonomy, but as a being emergent from a ground which is not its own.

Levinas embarks on this task by exploring the curious phenomenon of shame or bad conscience, two experiences which, according to him, reveal chinks in the idealistic account of the I. This is due to the fact that, according to Levinas, the experience of shame implies a level of passive affectivity within the subject that fundamentally contradicts what he sees as idealism's insistence on the absolute autonomy of the subject. The experience of shame, he argues, implies the vulnerability of the subject — its profound and primordial passivity before the world which, by his read, marks the nature of the subject much more than any of its active powers do. In shame, one feels oneself affected by another in such a way that is inexplicable by means of the active autonomous powers of the subject, for in shame, "the active ego reverts to the passivity of a *self,* to the accusative form of the *oneself* [*se*] which does not derive from any nominative, from the accusation prior to any fault" (*CPP* 147).

Note Levinas's claim that the radical passivity revealed through shame is composed in part through the fact that it is experienced "prior to any fault." It is integral to Levinas's argument that the experience of shame precedes any failure on the part of the subject. The kind of shame that Levinas is detailing here is not therefore the sense of shame which comes over one when he or she is guilty of some failure, either through action or inaction. It is not akin to the kind of disappointment one feels after having fallen short of some goal or standard, whether self or socially imposed, nor is it akin to the sorrow one feels over having done someone some wrong. These kinds of shame refer to and arise from some prior held commitments by the subject, they thus refer back to some value or good that has been adopted by the subject. As such these sorts of shame circulate within the system of the subject's aims and interests, and thus its conscious projects and being. These types of shame can thus be accounted for within an idealistic framework and do nothing to break with the totality of the knowing I posited therein.

The kind of shame that is of interest to Levinas, then, is the kind of embarrassment one can feel before the Other as if *for no reason.* It is the experience of being judged or examined by the Other—the experience of feeling gazed at or measured by another simply for being. It is thus the shame one feels for one's own being—for the very way in which one *is,* and not simply for what one has or has not *done.* It is the shame which is not precipitated by any fault or failure in how one *should be,* but which arises through an assessment of one's very nature and presence in the world. Subject to this kind of shame, one feels oneself somehow repelled from the world in which he or she had assumed a home, displaced from the center of one's very existence; and, subsequently thrown back upon oneself only now as an object of inquisition by the Other. Indeed, it is this very power of the experience of shame to cast consciousness back upon itself as an object for another—this power to objectify the subject—which makes it of such vital importance for him. For when shamed in this way, one feels the need to account for oneself, one is forced to ask the questions: "What have *I* done? Why have *I* been accused, rejected, judged, etc?" In other words, one begins to see oneself from the perspective of the Other.

How, Levinas asks, could such an experience be accounted for from within the idealistic rendering of human subjectivity? Does not the autonomous freedom so insisted upon within the idealist account of the subject imply the subject's freedom from any external influence of this kind? Could the truly autonomous subject simply choose to not avail him or herself to the Other in this way and thus entirely avoid such experiences? Is this not what is afforded one who is in complete and active possession of one's own being? If the idealist account of the subject is correct there is no accounting for the kind of radical passivity documented by Levinas in his analysis of the nature of shame. But, shame is a very real phenomenon. One can, and often does, find oneself feeling accused prior to any trespass or fault. No one is more aware of this than teenagers, who are keenly aware of the gaze of their peers and their inadequacy to stand up under such penetrative assessment regardless of their blameworthiness. The reality of such experiences, reasons Levinas, breaks open any possible naive assertion of the total active and autonomous power of the self fundamentally calling into question the idealistic understanding of human subjectivity.

But the poignancy of the experience of shame does more for Levinas than merely reveal the hidden cracks idealistic account of the I. Precisely by revealing these cracks, Levinas insists, it exposes what lies quivering in frailty beneath it—namely, the true essence and nature of human consciousness. That is, a truly phenomenological account of experiences such as shame serves to reveal the true ground of the human ego, which, as we shall see, is for him the Other and the ethical relation to which we are summoned by that Other.

Because of the way that it is able to not only strip away the naïve understanding of the self maintained in idealism but, in doing so, reveal its essential nature, phenomena such as "conscience and desire are not," for Levinas, mere "modalities of consciousness—but its very conditions" (*TI* 101). More than mere attributes of the phenomenon of subjectivity, conscience and desire are, in a sense, ontologically, or perhaps metaphysically, fundamental—they mark the very way in which the identity of the I is—an identity which, as we have seen, is only fulfilled in the otherwise; thus an identity which is always already given over to the metaphysical. It is thus incumbent upon us to explore alongside our analysis of that desire we have called human longing the nature of human conscience and shame; the latter hopefully serving to reveal something further about of the former.

SHAME: AN INTRODUCTION

It is a difficult task however to thoroughly discuss Levinas's account of the role shame plays within the life of the subject and the subsequent effects and revelations it bears there upon. This difficulty has to do in part with the nature of the phenomenon itself. Estimated and understood by Levinas as an integral part of the complex life of subjectivity, his explorations of shame weave together any number of the elements he explores in his work at large, metaphysical desire only one amongst them. Shame thus appears in his work as a kind of superdense phenomenon which does not yield itself easily to the light of philosophical investigation. But, the task of exploring the role played by shame in Levinas's work is rendered even more difficult by the author himself who seems to subtly change his perspective on it over the course of his career, and thereby our interpretation of its subsequent consequences upon the life of the subject. Levinas never wavers however on his estimation of its profound importance in enlightening the nature of the subject. Thus, despite the difficulties involved in attempting to dissect his understanding of shame, precisely such a dissection seems unavoidable if we are to forge a more complete understanding of the ethical life of the subject, and thereby the metaphysical nature of human longing. In order to initiate this task then, we must first make some basic delineations concerning his account of shame—that is, we must attempt to isolate it as much as possible as a phenomenon—all the while being cautious not to artificially separate aspects of his analysis of shame from their determinate context.

Firstly, in order to establish a basis on which our investigation can be erected we must briefly remind ourselves of the Levinasian account of the natural state of the I, or the I's ontic experience of itself. Thereby we will see that the I as described by Levinas—which admittedly never *properly* exists, but is rather a logical abstraction and interpolation from the natural tendencies of the ego in the world—resembles rather closely his descriptions of the idealistic understanding of the I.[5] Having thus, albeit somewhat artificially, separated out something resembling a pure account of subjectivity, we can then attempt to describe how shame operates and interpret how such an operation effects our understanding of the ethical commitments of the subject. Then reasoning with Levinas that such an encounter has always already happened within the life of the subject, we will be able to see more clearly precisely how his account of the subject differs from those of his idealistic predecessors. In our examination, however, we must distinguish, if only for the sake of connivance, Levinas's early descriptions of shame and its revelations from his later ones, dealing with each respectively and in its turn.[6] As we shall see, the two, though clearly distinct, contain many of the same elements such that the former naturally appears to lead to the latter. The difference between them lies not so much in the way in which the phenomenon is described or the role it plays in the life of the subject—in both shame reveals something to the subject—but in how each accounts for the *content* of that revelation.

As mentioned in chapter 1, according to Levinas the I does not experience itself as *thrown* into the world, as one at odds with an absurdity that must be taken in hand and related to as an object of concern, as Heidegger understands one's experience of one's being-in-the-world (see *TI* 140, 164). Instead, the I's primary experience of the world is enjoyment—*to be* an I, he thinks, is *to enjoy* the world (120), enjoyment being the primary referent to being. The world offers itself to the I as an object of delight and consumption; and, as such, the I feels itself to be at home in the world—it experiences itself as in possession of the world (132). This is not to say, of course, that everything is enjoyable, in the way in which we typically understand it. After all, there are unpleasant experiences. But, thinks Levinas, these experiences, as experiences by the I in a world disposed to the I, still fall under the rubric of enjoyment, as part of the way in which the I experiences the world as disposed to it, even if painfully, as we will see in more detail shortly.

Just because the world is encountered primarily via enjoyment as an object for the I's experience does not mean that the world is not distinct from the I. Levinas insists that the I's possession and enjoyment of the world does not give it complete license to make of the world a complacent facsimile of the structures of subjectivity. On the contrary, he fundamentally defines the world as something other to the I. Thus "every moment of life (conscious and even unconscious, such as consciousness divines it)," is lived, he asserts, "in relation with another than that moment itself" (*TI* 122).

The world is first and foremost a non-I, for Levinas, a kind of *other*. But the *otherness* of the world is not yet the Other presented in the experience of shame or sought in metaphysical desire. It is not yet an otherness so other than it cannot be related to. It is instead merely the otherness of ontic difference—a kind of outside which, though *other* than the interiority of the subject, can still be taken in hand and mastered by the subject—it is thus merely relationally other. The otherness of the world is not enough then to rupture the subject from its natural/idealistic relation to the world as an object of enjoyment and its understanding of itself as free therein. The cohesion of the identity of the I can thus never be fundamentally undermined or radically challenged by any surprise it experiences in the world, any encounter with the world's otherness. One needs more than an object to dislodge him or her from the center of his or her being. This is the case in part, says Levinas, because though the I experiences itself as at home in the world, its identity is not maintained on the basis of this experience but instead on its ability to reconnoiter the world and requisition what it finds therein to its own end. So it is, he argues, that the seat of the

I's identity lies within its own spontaneous ability to integrate the otherness of the world into itself.

According to Levinas, "the I is not a being that always remains the same, but is the being whose existing consists in identifying itself, in recovering its identity throughout all that happens to it" (*TI* 36). The I, in a sense, sticks to itself throughout its diverse encounters with the otherness of the world. No matter how much it may, at times, feel overwhelmed by the otherness of the world, it still remains a singular I throughout these experiences, absorbing and integrating them back into its own narrative and history. The otherness of the world is simply not enough to break the I's identity with itself. It is in fact on the basis of this inexorable identity with itself that the I can and does enjoy the world. For if no otherness in the world is so other as to threaten its identity, then that otherness can be taken in hand as an object of possible use and enjoyment. It is thus on the basis of the cohesive power of the I that the world is perceived by the subject to be little more than a resource for its diversion and empowerment.

The otherness of the world can, at its worst, appear *unpleasant* to the I, as for instance when it appears in the form of a hurricane or other natural disaster. But, even in these experiences, neither the I's authority over the world nor its identity with itself in relation to that world is challenged—for even here that otherness, the hurricane, drought, flood, and so on, is still defined in relation to the subject's enjoyment, only now negatively as unpleasant or distasteful. Thus even experiences as fundamentally life altering as these are not enough to change the I's identification with itself—are not enough to dislodge the I from its natural place at the center of its own existence. For, even these experiences can immediately be reintegrated and absorbed into the I's seamless narrative, becoming nothing more than another episode of the I's adventure in the world.[7] The being of the I thus remains ultimately unaffected by the otherness of the world, according to Levinas—it remains integral to itself, uninterrupted and whole. Despite its myriad possible encounters with this otherness, the continuity of the I is maintained—it is always still bound to itself, in possession of its faculties.

This identification throughout change, this perpetual dominance of the *same* over a series of relative *differences* is accomplished, in part, through the act of representation/thought; for part of the I's enjoyment of the world is constituted in the fact that it is a thinking entity (*TI* 124). The I is maintained through thinking, thinking of oneself, representing oneself to oneself. According to Levinas: "To remain the same is to represent to oneself. The 'I think' is the pulsation of rational thought. The identity of the same unaltered and unalterable in its relations with the other is in fact the I of representation. The subject that thinks by representation is a subject that hearkens to its own thought" (126). By his read then, by representing itself as a subject the I makes of the world an object of either reflection or enjoyment. This, he goes on to argue, amounts to an expression of the power of the I. Through representation, the I exercises its power over the world, drawing all otherness into itself and making it a part of its story. As such, "the knowing I," is best understood as "the melting pot of such a transmutation. It is the Same par excellence" (*BPW* 11–12). It is on the basis of this power to transmute the world in its own image, to make of the world nothing more than a backdrop and prop in its own adventure, which Levinas identifies as the subject's *capricious* freedom, a freedom which he distinguishes from its true freedom. The I, in its natural/ontological state, is *free* to absorb the otherness of the world into itself, making it a part of its own understanding of itself. Indeed, "such is the definition of freedom: to maintain oneself against the other" (*TI* 46). Hence our suspicion that the idealistic account may in fact be in accord, if only limited, with Levinas's own analysis of the natural state of the I in the world. It is the experience of shame which reveals these limitations and pushes our understanding of the I beyond the natural into the metaphysical.

The experience of shame, according to Levinas, inverts the traditional way in which the subject experiences and understands itself in the world. Unlike enjoyment or representation, "shame does not have the structure of consciousness and clarity. It is oriented in the inverse direction; its subject is exterior to me" (*TI* 84). In shame, I am no longer the subject of my own experiences—therein, I find that I am no longer at the center of my own world, that the world is not entirely disposed unto me but that I and the world are in fact disposed unto another. So it is discovered that the I is not the illuminative principle in the world, but rather that which is illuminated by a light which shines, furthermore, from the Other.

This reference to illumination as a metaphor to denote the revelation borne in the experience of shame, a reference we also explained briefly in the first chapter, is an apt analogy for informing the way in which the experience of shame operates within the life of the subject. In shame the subject feels itself put under an interrogative spotlight. It feels itself examined, measured and challenged to give an account for itself—for its way of being in the world (*TI* 86). Shame is in some sense the experience of being put on trial, made the *object* of an investigation. It is precisely this power of shame to radically displace the subject from its own subjectivity—making of him or her an object of observation—that is of such vital interest to Levinas. For there is a strange duplicity to the experience of shame as Levinas describes it: for shame is not only an affect, but it is, as such, also the evidence that the subject has already somehow been affected. That is, shame, it seems, is not only a kind of passive experience of the subject (one *is shamed* by the other), it is also an illumination of the way in which the subject *is* fundamentally passive—it uncovers a passivity on the level of the subject's own most being. Thus, the experience of shame simultaneously reveals that one cannot define oneself as the sovereign possessor of one's own being, for one is not in absolute control of that being—one cannot control how one feels before another nor how one appears in the light of another's perception. Shame, as the affectivity of having been open and exposed, reveals the way in which the subject is fundamentally vulnerable and available to the other and not hermetically closed in on itself. It thus reveals a disconnect within the identity of the I such that the previously and naively assumed autonomy of enjoyment and thought is radically called into question opening up a possibility within the subject of an entirely new understanding of itself.

The experience of shame thus casts the I back upon itself in a new way—it is, in a sense, the initiation of a new self-consciousness, one forged not from its own vision of the world, but forged in the light of the gaze of the Other before whom one feels that he or she must account. The possibility of this new-consciousness which is opened up through the appearance of the other and mediated through shame is a possibility which was previously unavailable to the subject, a possibility which is not available to the powers of representation. In shame one no longer *measures* one's own self in terms of his or her encounter with the world, which is a measurement of one's power over the world; instead, one finds oneself *measured* by the Other. Shame is thus the expression of a radical reorientation of the subject's understanding of itself outside the scope of its own powers. It expresses the subject's reexamination of the ontological ease with which it had previously experienced itself in the world and the freedom with which it had conducted its affairs therein. Shame reveals to the subject that its "freedom does not have the last word," that it is "not alone" (*TI* 101). It is on these grounds that Levinas argues that shame is a revelatory experience for the I.

Up to this point all that we have seen concerning Levinas's account of shame is consistent throughout his career. Henceforth, however, we will have to begin making some divisions within our analysis to take into account the subtle shift in thinking Levinas made over the course of his career. For while the Levinasian oeuvre is relatively synoptic in its analysis of the way in which the experience of shame reveals the subject to itself in a new way, his analysis of the effects of this revelation, which is the real hard core of its importance as a phenomenon, differs slightly from his earlier to his later works.

Shame's First Revelation: Self-Consciousness

When shamed the subject's natural response is to flee, to cover itself, to find shelter from the exposing gaze of the Other, like Adam in the garden. But, according to Levinas's early analysis of the phenomenon, precisely what makes the experience of shame so poignant is the fact that it cannot be so easily eluded. Indeed, what is revealed to the subject is its fundamental incapacity to distance itself from that which is being examined, namely its own being. This is, for the early Levinas, the essential revelation contained within the experience of shame: the intolerable inescapability of being oneself. It is thus a revelation which reverses the grounding structures of enjoyment making identity with oneself not a blessing which allows one's mastery of the world, but a curse which reveals one's slavery to his or her own being.

What is so burdensome about the experience of shame is the fact that in it what one feels accused of is no mere action or fault from which one can be easily exonerated or exculpated. It is, instead, a shame for the very way in which one is inexorably bound to oneself. Shame thus functions as a revelation of the terrible weight of having to be one's self. According to Levinas, one does not feel ashamed in this way "in as much as [he or she] is liable to sin [*susceptible de péché*]" nor as a result of his or her finitude or limitations (*OE* 54–55). Thus, as has already been intimated, the phenomenon of shame can be experienced without having been occasioned by any fault—it need not arise as the result of some indiscretion (*BPW* 94). Whereas one can escape the more pedestrian shame of having somehow failed by seeking forgiveness or by attempting to rectify the wrong, the experience of shame before the Other shakes the subject to its core, for it is the result of an accusation of the very way in which one *is*—one cannot simply escape it then by merely plucking out the proverbial eye that offends. One must stand it—bear up under the exposing the gaze of the Other—for as long as one has being. By addressing the being of the subject, the experience of shame reveals to the subject the nature of its tie to its own being—it brings the subject to consciousness of the very way that it inescapably *is* its being. Before the experience of shame provides this sort of hermeneutical distance, the subject is content simply being its own being—but, forced to reckon with it as the object of accusation instead of merely as the ground of enjoyment, this being, reflected now in the eyes of the Other, reveals itself as a burden. This then is what is revealed through the experience of shame for the early Levinas: the weight of being, the burden of being irrevocably bound to one's own being.

Accused by the Other, the subject finds itself reduced to an object with which it cannot immediately identify. In shame the subject feels itself as it appears from the outside, a perspective with which it had never reckoned while experiencing itself interiorly via thought and enjoyment. Forced to confront itself from another perspective, the I falters in the face of its own being. It cannot stand the presentation of itself offered in the accusation of the other experienced in shame—it cannot identify the I it experienced itself as with the *you* it is shown to be for another. In this way the experience of shame disrupts the seamless internal narrative which had previously guided the I's understanding of itself. It does not recognize itself in the story told in the accusative gaze of the Other, for in the shame in which this accusation is felt the I feels itself being called to account for something which it never had any control over or choice in—control and choice (i.e., freedom) being the operative mode in which the I is idealistically and naively understood. And yet, regardless of this fact, the I cannot distance itself from the object of accusation—it cannot escape (*TO* 55). As a result, in the experience of shame "the oneself does not rest in peace under its identity. And yet its unrest is neither a splitting nor a process which levels difference" (*BPW* 85). It is this *unrest* coupled with the fact that one cannot *split* with oneself that is so disturbing about the experience of shame according to Levinas. "Shame's whole intensity," he claims, "everything it contains that stings us, consists precisely in our inability to identify with this being who is already foreign to us and whose motives for acting we can no longer comprehend" (*OE* 63).

In this way the experience of shame reveals to the subject that what it previously took to be its freedom in the world was actually the bars of its imprisonment (*BPW* 12).[8] By reducing the subject to a *you* with which it cannot readily identify nor escape, the Other's gaze cuts through to the very core of the subjectivity revealing a fissure therein between the ego (*moi*) it naturally *is* and the oneself (*soi*) it *has to be*—the self to which it finds itself chained in shame. According to Levinas, "what appears in shame is thus precisely the fact of being riveted to oneself, the radical impossibility of fleeing oneself to hid from oneself, the unalterably binding presence of the I to itself [*du moi à soi-même*]" (*OE* 64). Therein, one is no longer simply *free* to be oneself—one is revealed to have no other option—one *must* be oneself. So it is that the subject discovers that the "freedom of consciousness is not without conditions" (*EE* 84)—that "the price paid for the existent's position lies in the very fact that it cannot detach itself from itself. The existent is occupied with itself [*s'occuper de soi*]" (*TO* 55).

Clearly, for the early Levinas, this "relationship between the Ego and the Self is not an inoffensive reflection of the spirit upon itself" (*TO* 56–57). To the contrary, what shame reveals is that "freedom is not as light as grace but already a heaviness, the ego is irremissibly itself" (56). In sharp contrast to the account of identification given within Levinas's descriptions of idealism and experienced by the subject in the world of enjoyment (prior to, as it were, the experience of shame), the identity of the I is revealed here to be a source of weariness (*EE* 11) and suffering (*OE* 55). And the bitter gall of this weariness is established in the fact that no matter how one strives against one's own being, one can never hope to free oneself from its intolerable confines. Neither self-improvement nor the distractions provided by the world are enough to ease the heavy load of having to bear one's existence alone. Not even death assures such an escape, Levinas suggests.[9]

Levinas's later and more major works, *Totality and Infinity* most notable among them, though voicing a similar expression of the experience of shame, nevertheless hold out hope for the possible, eventual redemption of the subject's experience—not the promise of an eventual release from the bounds of being, but the possibility of a solace for that experience. It is in fact the aperture of this possibility, this possibility of finding some solace in the course of one's being, that makes up the kernel of the revelation contained within the experience of shame as detailed there.

As we have seen, the experience of shame calls the subject's naïve understanding of its freedom into question by revealing to him or her that his or her freedom does not have the last word, that he or she is not alone. But, whereas in the early works Levinas places the accent on the first half of this revelation, how the subject's presumed freedom to be is actually a kind of imprisonment, in the later works Levinas seems to emphasize the latter half of this revelation, that the I is not alone — that there is another way of being, another way of experiencing the world than the one it naively invested itself in. In other words, according to Levinas's later work, by revealing to the subject "a resistance to my powers that does not counter them as a greater force, but calls in question the naïve right of my power, my glorious spontaneity as a living being," shame somehow liberates the subject to a new understanding of itself wherein a new possibility appears: the ethical commitment of oneself to the Other (*TI* 84). This possibility appears in the form of *responsibility*.

According to Levinas, the one must make a *response* to the appeal of the Other solicited in the experience of shame. One cannot simply ignore the accusation he or she feels before the Other, nor can one choose to not respond. All attempts to shut oneself off to this accusation, to deny its occurrence, or even murder the accuser all reveal themselves to be forms of *response* to the Other. After the appearance of the Other on the scene, all actions and nonactions by the subject reveal themselves to be little more than different ways of responding to the appeal and accusation leveled in the face of the Other. Responsibility thus becomes the primary way in which we experience the Other. The arrival of the Other thus denotes a fundamental reversal in the orientation of the subject from self-interest to responsibility. The appearance of the Other thus solicits the subject beyond its own being into the realm of responsibility — henceforth any action the subject takes is no longer defined in relation to the its own being and interests, but is oriented in terms of the Other, as a kind of response to the Other's accusation. So it is, claims the later Levinas, that the real kernel of the revelation contained in the experience of shame is the subject's responsibility before another. In shame the subject finds that it cannot refuse the accusations of the face—that it must make a response. This unavoidable responsibility thus appears, claims Levinas, as a kind of moral exigency. He writes, "Morality begins when freedom, instead of being justified by itself, feels itself to be arbitrary and violent" (*BPW* 17). According to Levinas, it is in this feeling where the possibility of a hope for the subject resides. For, once the subject becomes aware of its spontaneous freedom as something arbitrary and violent, and is called into responsibility by the Other, it is invited into a choice wherein its true freedom can be realized. That is, it is invited to choose responsibly for the Other.

Shame, Responsibility, and Freedom

Given the way that in shame the Other's accusation cuts through to the very being of the subject, the *I* finds its responsibility to the Other somehow *prior,* more primordial, than its commitment to itself, claims Levinas (*BPW* 17). Because it is able to call into question and reverse the traditional understanding of the I's commitment to itself, to its own being, the roots of responsibility appear to lie deeper than the roots of identity—deeper even, than one's very being. The power of the Other's accusation to break open the totality and interiority of the subject's identification with itself does not lie in the fact that it counters it as a "greater force." The accusation of the Other does not overpower the ego and wrestle it into submission. Rather, its power is grounded in the fact that it *precedes* and *conditions* the very emergence of the ego—it appears as a nonallergic gentleness (*TI* 197) which "instead of offending my freedom...calls it to responsibility and founds it" (203). "It is," what Levinas calls, "Peace" (203). The gentleness of this interposition by the Other reveals to the subject that there is another force at work within its life, the power of which is even more profound than the power of its attachment to its own being.

Here Levinas seems to claim that through the call to responsibility experienced in shame the subject finds itself somehow irrevocably split from itself in a more pertinent way doubled over by its own identity. Indeed, according to Levinas, "the other splits the same of consciousness which is thus lived" (*EN* 86). So it is that according to Levinas the subject is somehow *traumatized* by the appearance of the other. But this trauma is not one which cripples the subject, as it is presented in the early works. Instead, it seems to be a trauma that frees the subject, that *severs* the subject from the pull of its own being, that cuts it radically free and invests it with the possibility of the ethical choice.

"The relationship with the Other (*Autrui*) puts me into question," according to Levinas, and in doing so "empties me of myself and empties me without end, showing me ever new resources," upon which I can draw for the sake of that Other (*BPW* 52). The Other, thus, does not free the self from its misery by reconciling it to itself, but instead by releasing it from the totality of its own being—by providing it with another way. In responsibility one discovers oneself beholden to the Other, captivated by the Other and thus no longer a captive of one's own being. Responsibility thus frees the subject from the prison of identity by revealing to the subject the possibility of its being enslaved to the Other—a servitude which counters the claims of being upon it. The hope held out for the subject in responsibility is thus not the freedom from any bondage at all. The Other does not offer the subject a freedom of absolute license. Instead, by calling the subject into responsibility, the Other places upon it a new set of shackles which by binding it to the Other frees it from the tyranny of being. It is on these grounds Levinas claims that the responsibility to the other goes *beyond being* (121). In this way, responsibility elevates the subject out of the spontaneous freedom established in the way in which the I is and into the true freedom, the ethical freedom, of commitment to the Other. Levinas names this occurrence the *investiture of freedom* (*TI* 85).

Prior to the epiphany contained in the appearance of the face which is mediated through the experience of shame the subject understood itself to be free. What shame reveals however is that this freedom was really a prison for the subject, for while it could do what it wanted, it could do no more—that is, while it could pursue its ontological interests, it could not act ethically. But responsibility, by calling this freedom into question, liberates the subject to the ethical choice, a choice which somehow cuts to the very core of the subject. Responsibility is thus not the sign of the demise of the subject's freedom, but rather its true awakening and fulfillment. Freedom is not rejected as such, it "is inhibited, not as countered by a resistance, but as arbitrary, guilty and timid; but in its guilt it rises to responsibility" (*TI* 203). The appearance of the Other in shame thus "promotes my freedom, by arousing my goodness" (200). The Other to whom the subject is bound in responsibility "founds and justifies," the subjects true freedom—his or her freedom to be good, to make an ethical choice (197). So it is that for Levinas the subject's understanding of itself and its freedom in the world is redefined and regrounded through the experience of shame. After the appearance of the Other experienced as shame, this freedom is reconceived as the ability to make oneself available for the service of the Other. This turn, as we have seen, frees the subject from the bondage of the self in order make it a hostage of the ethical command of the Other (see *CPP* 150, *EN* 59). Put another way, responsibility frees the subject from the bondage of ontological necessity by releasing it into the custodianship of the ethical freedom offered by the Other.

Corresponding to this transformation, the subject also understands itself in a new way. As we have seen the trauma of the accusation severs the I from its identity as an ontological subject, revealing its indebtedness to the Other. Thus, whereas before the epiphany of the face experienced in shame the I understood itself on the basis of its ability to maintain its cohesion across a series of differences, in shame the I discovers its identity refounded upon its unique position with regards to the Other. Henceforth, the identity of the I must be understood as established on its incumbent duty to respond to the Other's moral command. The identity of the I is thus experienced in the ethical as an election, as being chosen or called forth by the other to respond (*TI* 245). "To utter 'I,'" claims Levinas, "to affirm the irreducible singularity in which the apology is pursued, means to possess a privileged place with regard to responsibilities for which no one can replace me and from which no one can release me. To be unable to shirk: this is the I" (245).

The call to responsibility by the Other does not come through some abstracted theory or moral code. It is experienced in the singular and concrete, it is a call placed upon a specific person at a specific time. When I see the suffering of the Other it is only *I* who can respond. No individual, bureaucratic institution or charity can mediate the demand the Other has placed upon me nor diminish the responsibility that I have before its face. It is upon this impossibility to shirk the demand of the Other that Levinas grounds the identity of the I anew. He writes, "The uniqueness of the I is the fact that no one can answer for me" (*BPW* 55). It is in the uniqueness of the ethical situation placed upon me by the Other that I find my identity. "The I," according to Levinas, "is summoned forth and faulty in the consciousness it has of a neighbor, in its bad conscience" (*CPP* 199–200). Therein, the I realizes itself to be no longer primarily defined as *for-itself,* but as *for-the-other.* It is this way of being *for-the-other* that affirms and truly grounds the identity and singularity of the I. On the basis of this argumentation, Levinas's claim that "it is only in approaching the Other that I attend to myself," that "I seek my final reality," as cited in chapter 1, becomes more clear (*TI* 178–79).

SHAME AND LONGING

However the product of shame's revelation is analyzed, whether in continuity with Levinas's earlier reckonings as a kind of burden or in line with his later as the initiation of a possible redemption, the susceptibility of the subject to this kind of shame is revealing. Through it we catch a glimpse of the underpinnings of human subjectivity and therein find that the ground of the ego is not the ego itself, but the otherwise and the elsewhere. For, what the experience of shame reveals in both the early and the later Levinas is that there is a connection within consciousness to the otherwise that runs deeper and more primordially than its connection to being. As such, our study of the experience of shame reveals the way in which the ego rests upon and is conditioned by another which precedes its emergence, which is *prior* to its own being. By laying bare the structures of human consciousness in this way, our survey of Levinas's analysis of shame is informative to our study of the nature of human longing by revealing the source of the breach through which longing travels. For, as we have seen, metaphysical desire is in a sense that passage way, that *poros,* through which one remains connected to the otherwise, to the transcendent proper. What was unclear up until now was how human beings in their finitude could be tied to an infinite Other. This is precisely what is revealed by way of a phenomenology of shame, namely: the way in which human existence, at its root, is always already preceded by the Other—not a closed totality, but broken open, and thus vulnerable to the introduction of the infinite, as experienced in metaphysical desire.

Shame and desire thus seem to be intimately linked in consciousness as two phenomenon wherein the subject is availed to the Other—wherein the subject is seen to exceed the very conditions of its being moving beyond its finite existence and bleed toward the infinite (*TI* 101). It is Levinas's claim that the availability of the subject to the Other, to that which lies beyond its being and is superlative to it, serves as the ground of its very emergence. Our analysis of shame, as a correlate phenomenon to human longing, thus serves to further reveal its nature and function in human life as a chink in the finitude which grounds and establishes the subject's being introducing the power of the infinite in its very core.

But this chapter cannot end so easily, for it began with the intent of showing how profoundly Levinas's understanding of the life of consciousness and subjectivity differed from what he claimed to be the position of the idealism present in the history of Western philosophy. And, indeed, it has become clear how these two systems differ, at least in as much as Levinas has presented them. We should perhaps pause to ask here, however, whether Levinas's presentation of the idealistic position was really representative of idealism as such? Or, whether it was instead merely a kind of artificial foil against which to distinguish his own understanding of the subject and its relation to the metaphysical, the otherwise? Is there really nothing within the idealist tradition that can encompass the story of this kind of freedom inducing radical passivity of the other? Is there really no ethical account of the metaphysical such that it grounds our understanding of human life and thereby the movement of human longing? Is this perhaps why the idea of human longing has been so little explored over the course of Western philosophy? To answer these questions it is incumbent upon us to turn to literature representative of the idealistic claims themselves.

IDEALISM REEXAMINED: FICHTE ON SOLICITATION, FREEDOM, AND RECOGNITION

Both Hegel and Fichte appear equally within the Levinasian oeuvre as symbols of the highest expression of the idealistic order. But, much more has been written on Levinas's criticisms of Hegel leaving his comments on Fichte largely unexplored. Nevertheless, it is often Fichte in particular whom Levinas takes to task when addressing the traditional accounts of the life of consciousness, attaching to him all of the predicates used to describe idealism in general. So it is that Fichte is featured in Levinas's work as the idealist *par excellence,* as someone in whom the latent idealism hovering throughout the history of Western philosophy finally becomes fully articulate. It is thus against Fichte and toward Fichte that much of his criticisms against idealism are made. Even his claim that the history of Western philosophy could be described as a kind of egoism is, albeit unacknowledged, culled from the work of Fichte, who first applied this term in reference to his own work.[10]

More often than not, Levinas's attacks of Fichte are veiled or implied, but nevertheless obvious to those familiar with Fichte's thought and language.[11] But occasionally Levinas addresses Fichte directly treating his thought as the very avatar of the idealistic insistence on the absolute autonomy of the subject. "Reason," by this account, argues Levinas, "is an archeology... The intelligibility of the subject itself can consist only in this return to the origin, a movement which, as the *Wissenschaftslehre* taught, is the very being of the ego, the 'self-positing' of oneself" (*CPP* 131). Therein, "everything that is in consciousness would be posited by consciousness" (*OB* 101). Thus, Levinas goes on to argue that in the Fichtean system, as in all of the idealists tendencies of the West, it is impossible to account for any experience of radical alterity and passivity, or, therefore, the strange freedom of responsibility made available in shame or the inexorable drive toward the Other experienced as metaphysical Desire. The Fichtean subject would have to be without holes, as it were, turned completely inward on itself and inaccessible by the otherwise in any real sincere sense and thus inaccessible to any such profoundly passive experiences. Indeed, by Levinas's read, Fichte's account of the ego is so focused on interiority that it becomes reduced only to that which can be accounted for by reference to the spontaneously self-contained activity of a fully autonomous subject. This is so much the case in Fichte, Levinas goes on to say, that even an experience as seemingly obviously passive as suffering at the hands of another, as in torture for instance, becomes merely another expression of the ego's totality—simply another experience grounded upon the ego's activity. According to Levinas, "all suffering due to the action of the non-ego is," for Fichte, "first a position of this action of the non-ego by the ego" such that all experienced suffering by the ego is ultimately reducible to some activity by the ego itself (124). If something as obviously passive as the experience of suffering is still seen in the light of the being of the ego as a kind of latent activity, then clearly nothing as fundamentally transcendent as the experience of human longing or profound shame could have a place in such a system.

We must ask then, whether Levinas's descriptions of the Fichtean system and his analysis of the conclusions of such a system, including its oversights, is really a fair estimation of the claims made in the *Wissenschaftslehre?* For, as has become apparent over the course of this study, we should perhaps be at least a little dubious of Levinas's dealings with his opponents. This is not to call into question the sincerity nor the validity of his criticisms against idealism. Rather it is merely to suspect that perhaps the relation of Levinas's work to that of the idealists in general and Fichte in particular, is in the end, much more complicated than he would lead us to believe. If it turns out, after all, there are structures at work in Fichte's account of the human subject which could allow for such passive experiences, then given its proximity to Levinas's work, if only by contrast, it should inform our attempt to understand Levinas's concept of metaphysical desire and our own experience of human longing. This thus requires a thorough examination of Fichte's account of the nature of the subject, especially where it is addressed by Levinas.[12]

Chief among Levinas's concerns is Fichte's claim that the I is self-positing. After all, there is a sense in which Fichte's fundamental thesis could be summed up in the claim that the I is self-positing. Unfortunately, however, this is a concept which is none too transparent. Taken as such, Fichte's claim could easily be misunderstood as a claim to the self-originary power of the I, as Levinas takes it to be. That is, taken out of context it could appears as if for Fichte the self is fundamentally self-creating and truly, therefore, purely and exclusively active. This position, however, is not really representative of Fichte's system and is in fact a betrayal of its overall tendencies. Taken in its appropriate context, Fichte's claim that the I is self-positing is not an account of its ontic genealogy; but merely a logical expression of its ontological relation to itself. It is merely to claim the logical *identity* of the I with itself.

Central to Fichte's work is the claim that the I cannot, and certainly should not, be understood as some *substratum,* as some actual *thing* that exists in the traditional sense of the word. This would be, perhaps for Fichte, an example of that kind of thinking that he eschews under the heading of dogmatism at the beginning of the *Wissenschaftslehre* (see *SK* 8–9). Instead, he insists, "the character of rationality consists in the fact that that which acts and that which is acted upon are one and the same" (*FNR* 3). Thus, he goes on to say that "what exists *for* a rational being exists *in* the rational being; but there is nothing in the rational being except the result of its acting upon itself...the I is nothing other than an acting upon itself" (3).

The I is thus not some*thing*, but a *way* of acting, a *doing*, one could even say that it is a way of being, in as much as being is understood in line with Heidegger as a verb and not a noun or substantive. Fichte terms this action that is the I, the action by which it identifies itself, as "self-positing." His claim that the I is self-positing is thus exclusively for him a description of the way in which the I is itself and not an attempt to describe the origins of the I. It is instead merely a description of how the I appears, how it *is:* the I *is* that *activity* which is acting as itself upon itself, which is positing-itself. The I is nothing more than this activity.

Now, it does seem that by claiming that the I is "nothing other" than this "acting upon itself" Fichte has radically cut the identity of the I off from the world, rendered a pure activity in relation to itself and impenetrable by any form of authentic otherness, and thus never truly passive. Were this the case then certainly Levinas's rejection of Fichte's position in favor of his brand of ethics would certainly be valid and perhaps even justified. But again, we must understand Fichte's claims in context wherein these claims not only seem tempered, but given an entirely different hermeneutic such that what is actually claimed in them barely resembles what seems to be claimed in them. One must remember that here Fichte is merely establishing the logical grounds for his account of selfhood, and this in contrast to a tradition he sees of making the I a kind of substance.[13] The claim that the I is self-positing, is fundamentally an activity in reference to itself, is not intended then to convey the idea that the I is some sort of solipsistic totality, complete in itself. It is rather merely an attempt by Fichte to move away from an understanding of consciousness, intellect, and identity *qua* substance. For him, the definition of the intellect in terms of a fundamental passivity before the world would be tantamount to making the I an object *qua* thing—an object which can be treated and manipulated by the world. This is, after all, precisely what Levinas claims: that in the gaze of the Other presented in the face and felt through shame one feels oneself reduced to the status of an object—objectified such that one becomes displaced from his or her natural position as a subject.

What concerns Fichte, however, is that this conversion of the subject into an object, this transition from an understanding of the self as an activity to its appearance as an object, betrays a substantive conception of the self as some*thing,* some object that can be acted upon like any other determinate entity. This however, he wants to claim, is a betrayal of the nature of subjectivity since, for him, the subject must be understood as essentially a kind of activity, never revertible into a static object. By denying the primordial passivity of subjectivity, then, Fichte is not declaring the I to be outside the sway of influence of that which lies beyond it, it is merely to indicate that this influence can never be such that the self substantiates. The I does not, and can never have the nature of a mere thing. His claim that the intellect exists as a pure activity then is merely intended to make sure that one does not make of the I some sort of material that can be acted upon. The affirmation of the I's fundamental *activity* in relation to its self, its own being, is not therefore the tacit denial of its *affectivity* but merely the declaration that when it is affected it is affected as an active movement and not some kind of object. The I is affected *qua* activity, thinks Fichte. In other words, the I can most certainly become caught up in something akin to the *activity of receptivity,* or the *activity of passivity,* if you will; but, nevertheless, this kind of activity still occurs within the greater context of its fundamental relation to itself as a mode of being, its fundamental way of being itself—of being self-conscious, self-positing.[14] Thus though fundamentally and primordially a pure activity, the I is not necessarily exclusively a being-*moving,* as it were, but it can also become a being-*moved.* In fact, according to Fichte, though the I's activity is understood as logically prior, this priority is based on an even deeper genealogical anteriority which is established precisely in the action of being-moved, in affectivity and passivity. Indeed, when genealogically accounted for, the I must, in fact, be understood as proceeding from another who summons it to itself.

By Fichte's reckoning, it is only through the encounter with another that the I truly takes up its rightful position in relation to the self. While by its very nature the self is an active self-positing, this is all it would ever remain were it somehow isolated or abstracted from its interaction with life. Such the self, for Fichte, would barely exist, would remain nothing more than an outwardly directed undetermined, and thus unrealized, empty activity (*SK* 71). The activity which is the self is for Fichte merely the ground for this realization through another. Without the influence of the outside the self remains little more than a sheer possibility which has not yet entered into existence as such. The world is that which modifies and, in doing so, actualizes the being of the self. For Fichte, only through the world is the I finally able to realize its potentiality and, in doing so, realize and recognize itself. In relation to this occurrence the world serves in some sense as the mirror through which the I comes to itself, and thereby becomes actual as itself. Thus, though the I is fundamentally a centrifugal act of self-positing it "must also be an activity that *reverts into itself and determines itself,*" that is, it must be capable of experiencing itself and positing itself as an object of reflection (*FNR* 18). This *reversion* is made available through the exteriority of the world. Through such an encounter with exteriority the I is able to move from merely *being* itself (being an empty potentiality) into *having* itself—being self-conscious, and thereby actual.

The world assists the I into actuality, in part, by limiting it, by revealing to it its fundamental finitude. For, according to Fichte, "the rational being's activity in intuiting the world...is constrained and bound" (*FNR* 19). The I, in relation to the external world experiences itself to be "curbed or held in check [*aufgehalten*] and limited" (20). Thus, alongside the logically fundamental understanding of the I as self-positing, is Fichte's claim that the I is finite and limited: "As surely as I posit myself, I posit myself as restricted, in consequence of the intuition of my self-positing. In virtue of this intuition I am finite. This restrictedness of mine, since it conditions my own positing of myself, is primordial in character" (*SK* 60).

Through its interaction with the external world the I experiences itself *checked* by something external to it. This check (*Anstoß*)[15] Fichte describes as an *intrusion* (*SK* 157) of the external world into what was logically postulated as the isolated activity of the I; it *clashes* (187) therefore with the I's primitive mode of being—its juvenile and imperfect form. The arresting nature of exteriority, by clashing with the I's previously uninterrupted activity and challenging its previously unperturbed way of being itself, forces the I into an awareness of itself—in this way it raises it from the realm of feeble mere being into the maturity of actual *having* being, self-consciousness. Fichte writes, "The endlessly outreaching activity of the self, in which nothing can be distinguished, precisely because it reaches into infinity, is subjected to a check; and its activity, though by no means extinguished thereby, is reflected, driven inwards; it takes exactly the reverse direction" (203). Before the *intrusion* of the exterior, if such a before can be spoken of, the I dwells unaware of itself as a sheer drive outward—as a kind of infinite and undetermined possibility. By way of the check provided by the external world the I discovers itself to be fundamentally finite. The realization of this finitude cancels the infinite undetermined possibility of the I by actualizing one particular finite possibility, namely the possibility for the I to not only *be* itself, but to *have* itself, to be conscious of itself. It is thus in the check to the I's unrestrained infinite movement, a movement which must be directed externally if it is to find its limit in the external world, that the self is slapped awake—that the self is able to emerge as itself, that the I is able to appear as self-positing. Thus, T. P. Hohler's conclusion that according to Fichte "without the independence of something outside the I, the I could never become conscious of its own self."[16]

Given the way that the exteriority of the world encountered by the I awakens it to itself Fichte identifies the alterity of the world as a kind of *summons* (*eine Aufforderung*). The exteriority of the world, by checking the limits of the I's primordial movement and thereby providing for it a limit and determination, summons the I to itself and to an awareness and attentiveness to its own nature (*FNR* 31). Fichte alternatively names this summons a kind of *demand* (*Anforderung*) upon the self—it is a call that the self cannot refuse (33). In summoning the I to self-consciousness the world summons the I to existence, to actuality. It is thus only through the determination of the external world provided in the check and the summons that the I begins to become a real entity, begins to take on individuality and singularity, become fixed and established (*SK* 182). This is essential in understanding Fichte's account of the I as self-positing in relation to Levinas's criticisms.

The summons is not made by just any exteriority however, claims Fichte; but by a particular kind of exteriority, namely the exteriority of the non-I, the other-I, what Fichte terms the *Thou* (*SK* 72). This is the hard core of the experience of the otherness of the world which checks the unrestrained movement of self-propulsion which logically precedes the actual emergence of a determinate identity. Hence Gunter Zöeller's claim that "Fichte argues that the actualization of the individual I's potential for self-determination can only take place through dynamic interaction with other intelligent beings that provide the solicitation [*Aufforderung*] to independent action."[17] It is only through the experience of the summons as it is *specifically* voiced in the existence of the Thou that the I ever moves from potentiality into actuality and is able to emerge as a singular individuality (73–74).

Furthermore, the summons of the Thou upon the I is a "summons to *freedom* [*Afforderung zur Freiheit*]" (*FNR* 34). But bear in mind that this freedom is made available through a check of the primordial activity of the self that summons it into actuality. The freedom to which the subject is summoned by the Thou is thus not an unlimited license to do as one pleases, but is instead established and maintained through the simultaneous *recognition* (*Anerkennung*) of the Thou's reciprocal claim to freedom and a subsequent self-limitation which corresponds to the initial limitation placed upon us by the exterior world. According to Fichte, "*I must in all cases recognize the free being outside me as a free being, i.e. I must limit my freedom through the concept of the possibility of freedom*" (49). Thus the Thou, by constraining the self, not only reveals to the self its efficacy to act in the world, its freedom (36), but simultaneously calls it to limit that efficacy on his or her behalf, to recognize his or her claim to freedom (85). "No one," Fichte writes, "has a right to an action that makes freedom and personality of another impossible; but everyone has a right to all other free actions" (86–87). It is this recognition of the demands of the Thou coupled with self-limitation that Fichte terms the invitation to the relationship of natural right (49–52). Since it is this relationship with a Thou which first allows the self to emerge as a self, the restrictions of the ethical relationship cannot be seen as an external imposition placed upon the self through some instruction or intuition. These limitations must instead be understood as somehow written upon the very essence of what it means to be a self—requisite for its emergence into being proper. This ethical situation is inexorably bound to how it is that the I becomes itself by way of the summons (87).

Since the summons is the path to the I's true emergence as a singular individuality, since it is by way of this summons that an I becomes a determinate actual reality and not merely an infinite potentiality; and, since this summons demands that the I recognize the rights of others by concretely limiting the exercise of its capricious power through which the I realizes its real and true freedom; it thus seems that it is only through the summons and recognition of others that the I truly becomes human. Indeed, according to Fichte, "the summons to engage in free self-activity is what we call upbringing [*Erziehung*]. All individuals must be brought up to be human beings, otherwise they would not be human beings" (*FNR* 38). Humanity, it seems, is a trait which is bestowed by another and only obtained through the ethical relationship with that other.

Fichte's establishment of the I as a self-positing activity is, as has now become clear, not intended to grant the subject an absolute spontaneous self-originary power, as Levinas seems to claim. Instead, Fichte's account of the activity of the I's self-positing seems to be much more properly understood as a weak force. All he wants to claim is that the I must be understood not as an entity, but as a kind of movement—a movement, furthermore, which only has any real efficacy and actuality once its infinite sheer potentiality is ruptured by the otherwise which summons it to itself. For subjectivity to emerge as a real/strong force the external world must first solicit it. The I thus needs, in a sense, the Thou to be itself. Hence T. P. Hohler's estimation that "the I's need for a non-I (as Fichte has shown in the *Grundlage*) is really a need for another subject. The I is essentially inter-subjective."[18] As we shall see shortly, this need for the external world is reflected according to Fichte in an insatiable desire which runs ever present within the life of subjectivity which Fichte terms human longing (*Sehnsucht*), revealing the relevance of our study of Fichte to the investigation at hand.

STRANGE BEDFELLOWS: FICHTE AND LEVINAS ON THE ETHICAL AND LONGING

It should be clear from our brief survey of Fichte that though he does, indeed, define the ego as self-positing, it is not entirely self-contained. Quite to the contrary, for Fichte it seems that the ego's emergence into the world is entirely predicated and grounded in an ethical call that issues forth from another, a *summons* to existence and freedom. In this way the self-positing ego is established to be genealogically passive, its emergence dependent upon its encounter with determinate others in the world. Hence Robert R. Williams's conclusion that Fichte's "ego is not self-creating: it is dependent in respect to its existence."[19] This dependence, as we have seen, is mediated through a check of the ego's powers issued in the form of a Thou who demands our recognition of his right to be. Existence thus proceeds for the ego not out of an explosive demonstration of power, but precisely through the opposite, through the limitation of those powers, through the de*finition* of those powers. Only by encountering its limits, only by realizing itself to be finite is the ego able to emerge from the status of mere infinite possibility, to definite finite actuality. Only in this way is the ego able to achieve its true identity and realize its final freedom, namely the freedom to truly *be* itself, to rise out of the realm of the merely possible. So it seems that, for Fichte, the ontological identity of the ego is established in its ethical encounter with another. Thus, though the I is first experienced ontologically, its dependence upon another reveals a deeper indebtedness to the ethical.

This notion of the ego being summoned to itself and its true freedom by another who calls it into question, who reveals its limits and demands its recognition — this elevation of the priority of the ethical — seems to establish a crossing point between Fichte and Levinas's thought. Indeed, Williams, who explicitly compares Levinas's position to Fichte's in his *Recognition: Fichte and Hegel on the Other*,[20] has gone so far as to claim that Fichte's work should be figured as a kind of philosophical predecessor and ally to the Levinasian camp. For example, when discussing Fichte's conception of the ethical as the predecessor to the ontological, Williams, in a direct reference to Levinas's claim that ethics must be considered first philosophy, claims, "Fichte clearly thinks that the problem of the other is not a derivative question. Rather he identifies the problem of the other as a prior question for *first philosophy*."[21] F. Scott Scribner has explored this connection between Fichte and Levinas in terms of the presentation of otherness in the face. According to his read "Fichte himself sought to account for the inadequacies of a transcendental description of intersubjectivity through reference to a pre-representational, pre-intentional affection, whose source is identified in the symbol of the human body and often even in the infinity of the human face [*das Gesicht*], and the transparency of the ego," leading him to conclude that "Fichte is closer to Levinas than Levinas would prefer to admit."[22] Simon Lumsden not only seems to support this claim, but to take it even further. In his examination of the overlap between Fichte and Levinas, he gives the impression of wanting to present the two thinkers as doing little more than echoing one another's insights—a kind of Janus head of the ethical account of the subject.[23] Indeed, his text presupposes the similarity between Levinas and Fichte to be so strong that rather than enunciating the points of connection between them, he instead dwells only on what he sees as the relatively few points of difference that may stand between them. In this way he reads Levinas entirely against himself, seemingly making of Levinas nothing more than a post-Heideggerian Fichtean.

The fact that "Fichte is closer to Levinas than Levinas would prefer to admit," as suggested by Scribner, most certainly seems to be the case, though whether their respective systems can ultimately be reconciled in the way seemingly recommended by Lumsden is yet to be seen. After all, there is another crucial similarity between their two systems that has yet to be examined, one moreover which pertains essentially to the larger study at hand, namely how human longing bears an ethical significance. For, according to Fichte, the ethical encounter with another through which the ego becomes itself is mediated by an insatiable desire which, as we have already mentioned, he terms, in line with our study, longing (*Sehnsucht*).

According to Fichte, the ego must be conceived as simultaneously finite and infinite. This is reflected in part through what we have already seen: for the ego arises out of an indeterminate ground of infinite possibility only achieving actual existence through the limitations placed upon it by another through which it realizes its finitude. Still, though the I discovers itself to be limited through an encounter with the Thou, and in fact only becomes real thereby, some trace of its movement toward the infinite is retained in its finitude. Thus, argues Fichte, though the I, in its very being, is inexorably finite it still *strives* to exceed that limit, to move *beyond* the finite and into the infinite proper. It is in fact this natural tendency of the I to progress toward infinitude that constitutes and grounds its ethical encounter with the Thou, through which it receives the limits that define it and make it real. Were the subject naturally self-limiting, Fichte seems to suggest, if it did not naturally strive for the infinite, then it would never *clash* with the exteriority of the world in such a way that it would realize itself to be finite.[24] According to Lumsden, "The very concept of striving involves finitude; finitude functions as the limit to be overcome by the I's striving."[25] The subject's natural proclivity for the infinite in a sense serves as the horizon on which its actual existence and finitude emerge. Still the infinite seems to cast a shadow upon the subject such that it always bears the image of the *beyond* within it. So it is that as much as Fichte identifies the being of the subject with its finitude, he nevertheless maintains that the subject must equally be understood in terms of its drive toward the infinite (*SK* 231). The subject, it seems, is simultaneously and inexorably finite and an overcoming of finitude—a movement into the infinite.

But there is a problem claims Fichte, for the infinite nature of the subject can never be fully realized by it; for if it were, the subject would immediately cease to be a subject. Remember that the subject's existence only becomes real once limits are placed upon it, once it *realizes* itself as limited. So it is that this movement toward the infinite, the drive to supersede the boundaries of its own being, leaves a radical and indelible incompleteness within the subject. Since the subject is by its very existence held away from that which its existence strives for, the subject necessarily experiences itself as somehow fundamentally incomplete. Indeed, the project of subjectivity as such seems irrevocably incomplete. Thus, although the subject manifests what he calls a *compulsion* toward the infinite, it is maintained in its *inability* to attain such infinitude (*SK* 254). This is of course in keeping with the logic of the infinite as such, for the infinite is that which can never be completed, consumed, or attained as such—by definition it has no ends or limits. So it is that the subject's drive appears endless, limitless and therefore not only eternally unsatisfied, but eternally insatiable (256).

Due to its very nature, Fichte claims, the infinite cannot be attained nor grasped by the subject—it always evades any attempt made by the subject to master or understand it. As such it cannot be comprehended by the subject nor reflected in conscious thought, nor can that which the subject strives to achieve through it—its ideal nature, its ultimate perfection, completeness, and satisfaction. Both remain the forever unthought, and indeed, the unthinkable (*SK* 115, 164). The self thus feels itself "*driven towards something unknown*" and unknowable (261). "Nevertheless," Fichte claims, "the idea of infinity to be completed floats as a vision before us, and is rooted in our innermost nature" (238). Thus, though the infinite is entirely incomprehensible to the subject, it nevertheless remains an indelible part of the life of subjectivity, influencing the very way in which the subject is and bearing a profound influence on how the subject experiences itself. The subject experiences this presence of the infinite within it as a kind of feeling (*SL* 262–63). And this feeling is human longing (*Sehnsucht*). According to Fichte, "longing is thus the *original, wholly independent manifestation* of the striving that lies in the self" (*SK* 267). Longing thus appears to be the only authentic manifestation of the subject's drive for the infinite. As such, it must be intimately identified with the life of subjectivity; it must be viewed as a kind of essential attribute of the existence of the ego as such. Indeed, this link is so essential to the constitution of the ego that "anyone who wants to be released from desire wants to be released from consciousness" (*FTP* 295).

As the expression of the subject's drive toward the infinite, though longing may, and indeed *must*, persist throughout the life of the subject to some degree or another, it will never be able to rise into the realm of ratiocination. Longing, it seems, by its very connection to the infinite, places it just outside the scope of the representational powers of the subject. As such, longing itself appears, like the infinite, to be a kind of indefinite phenomenon such that though one may experience longing one can never really know the nature or direction of that longing (i.e., what it is that one is longing for—for how can one know or conceive of the infinite?). Thus, claims Fichte, though longing may attempt to latch onto its end as a specific object (i.e., one may think that he or she is longing for some*thing*), the subject can never realize this "object" "as a thing, nor even *represent* [it] through ideal activity" (i.e., one never really knows what it is that he or she is looking for) (*SK* 265). There is thus no proper, knowable object or end to human longing. The attempt to attach longing to an object thus represents a feeble attempt on behalf of the knowing I to somehow regain control or mastery over its own experiences—a project necessarily destined to fail. Thus though a subject may presume to posit some determinate end to its longing—some object of possible satisfaction—in actuality no such satisfaction or end can ever be achieved and the presumed object of desire, once seized, will prove to have been a vainglory and meaningless acquisition.

So it is that satisfaction seems contrary to the very nature of longing as the expression of the infinite. Indeed, claims Fichte, were some eventual satisfaction able to be achieved, for instance in the eternal hereafter or in the presence of God, such a longing would immediately cease to be itself, would immediately cease to be longing. Longing is thus not merely a protracted desire, one in which the possibility of satisfaction is held out though denied to the desirer, it works in an entirely different way. It has no eventual satisfaction nor end just as the infinite has no limits or boundaries. Thus despite the myriad attempts to bring such a longing to an end, despite the sundry objects or ends to which longing may be attached—a new car, bigger house, or better lover, no final satisfaction to longing will ever be found: "longing," says Fichte, "necessarily recurs" (*SK* 286). The subject, by its very nature, cannot achieve any such lasting satisfaction, can never be fully complete or total in itself. This is the great irony of the Fichtean project, though it attempts to compose a *complete* philosophical system, the system itself rests upon the assertion that what it explores is by nature fundamentally and eternally *incomplete*.

Because longing functions in this way, because it can never become bounded by any object of possible satisfaction, Fichte argues that it is best understood as "an activity *that has no object whatsoever,* but is nonetheless *irresistibly driven out towards one*" (*SK* 265). Because that toward which it strives cannot be conceived of as such, nor can it ever properly attain the status of an object, longing must be viewed as objectless; but in our experience, as filtered through the intellectual need for limits, longing appears to us as driven toward some object. Still, in its essential nature, longing proceeds toward no such determinate goal. It is instead, he argues, the movement of the subject "*out*" of itself, over and beyond the limits of its own being and finitude. "Longing aspires," he claims, "to realize something outside the self" (267). It is in this sense, as a movement toward the *beyond* of its own being, a kind of striving for alterity—for an alterity that lies *otherwise* than its own existence. Longing thus appears for Fichte to be a truly *metaphysical* desire as understood and defined by Levinas.

As the expression of the presence of an infinite drive within a finite existence, longing can be understood as emergent from two different origins and drives. Understood in regards to the subject's finitude, longing can be understood as occasioned by the infinite gap between how the subject is and how it strives to be in its ideal nature. In this sense, longing can be presented as the expression of a profound lack within the subject: namely, the absence which separates its actuality from its ideality.[26] Thus longing can be understood in some sense as "a *need,* a *discomfort,* a *void,* which seeks satisfaction, but does not say from whence.—The self feels a longing in itself, it feel itself in want" (*SK* 265). But, the phenomenon of longing can also be interpreted in terms of its connection to the infinite. As such, longing is the expression not of some absence, lack, or disconnect within the subject, but of a superabundant presence—of a positive force and drive within the heart of the subject. It is in fact on the basis of this initial drive toward the infinite, this positive movement within the subject, that any negativity in its relation to longing emerges and is interpreted. The absence which can be interpreted as occasioning longing is thus established on the fact that it primordially arises from a positive drive toward the infinite. In this sense it appears similar to the Platonic notion of Eros as the perfect union of both *Poros* and *Penia*.

This of course resembles remarkably Levinas's claims concerning the nature of metaphysical desire. Remember that, for Levinas, metaphysical desire was posited as a kind of insatiable drive over and beyond the limits of one's own being into an otherwise that, though eternally insatiable, nevertheless carried within it the promise of lifting the subject into his or her true essence. Moreover, this metaphysical desire, like Fichte's *Sehnsucht,* was determined to arise not from the absence of some determinate object, but from the expression of the abundance of something which exceeded the bounds of the subject's finitude, something akin, he claimed, to the idea of the infinite. It was thus argued by Levinas that metaphysical desire was in some sense the expression of the infinite. But perhaps most importantly for Levinas, metaphysical desire was shown to be an ethical desire. That is, it was argued to be a desire that participated within the realm of the Other, a realm which is laden for him with ethical value. In fact, as we discussed at the beginning of this chapter, the metaphysical toward which this desire aimed in its drive toward the beyond was contained in the ethical realm of the Other. In this sense, metaphysical desire becomes the way in which our ethical relation to another is mediated. It was for this reason, after all, that in this chapter we sought to better understand the nature of the ethical life of the subject.

Not only do Levinas and Fichte's respective accounts of the subject appear similar, but so too do their accounts of the way in which that subject relates to the beyond, the way in which that subject longs—and this not only in their descriptions of the content of longing, but also in the function of longing. For, in Fichte's work as well as the expression of that drive into the infinite which is checked in the ethical demand of a Thou, longing appears in some way essentially tied to realm of the ethical.

LEVINAS AND FICHTE RECONCILED?

Though there is certainly more of a connection between Fichte and Levinas's work than we would have perhaps assumed at first, there are still a number of crucial differences which keep them from being as easily reconciled as thinkers like Lumsden argue. Firstly, in regards to what we have just seen concerning the connection between metaphysical desire and the ethical, we must remember that longing is for Fichte the attempt to supersede the limitation placed upon it by its being, a being it becomes aware of through the Other. Longing thus appears in some sense as the desire to transgress the limitations placed upon the self by the Thou. In this sense, though indeed intimately tied to ethical, it is does not appear to work in conjunction with the ethical limitations placed upon the subject in the other's demand for recognition. Thus though Levinas would perhaps not identify Fichte's *Sehnsucht* with need, he would nonetheless contest to identifying it as something which mediates the ethical relationship within the subject. Though Fichte's longing attempts to exceed the bounds of the self, it is still tied to the being of the self. That is, longing for him, still seems to be the expression of the *interests* of the self, whereas metaphysical desire for Levinas seems to go against the interests in of the subject.

This also reveals the two thinkers' differing approaches to the infinite. As we saw, for Levinas the infinite which gives rise to metaphysical desire also proceeds from the otherwise. This, he claimed, is in fact almost tautological—at the very least in keeping with the very nature of the infinite. Since the infinite, by its very nature, could not have been a product of a finite creature (i.e., a finite being could have never come up with the idea of the infinite) the presence of a drive that expresses a kind of infinite within the finite is evidence for him of the fact that within the subject there are things that are not of its own making, that originate somewhere else and are not in keeping with its natural state—which, in fact, exceed the very limits of its nature. In contrast, Fichte seems to ground the underlying structure of the infinite within the nature of the subject itself. The fact that it contains an infinite drive within it is not therefore the legacy of some other, but of its own primordial nature. The legacy of the other is, in contrast, a limitation or restriction which is placed upon that infinite drive—the other, the Thou, is thus the one who binds the subject's inmost drive toward the infinite. Though it is only by way of these binds that the subject realizes its actual existence, such that the ego remains forever indebted to the exteriority of the world and grounded upon it, this exteriority is not, for Fichte, associated with the infinite but with finitude. Thus though Fichte's *Sehnsucht* and Levinas's metaphysical desire appear to function in similar ways, the root of their respective accounts could not be more different. For Levinas, metaphysical desire is the expression of a pull exerted upon the subject from outside it, whereas, for Fichte longing is the outworking of a drive within the subject to realize itself beyond the limits placed upon it by the determinate outside. In this regard, Heidegger seems to mediate the difference between Fichte and Levinas presenting an account of longing as emergent from a drive initiated beyond the subject's being but which, as Being, nevertheless speaks to its core as opposed to displacing it from this core.

Though perhaps the most significant difference to our current investigation, this is by no means the only difference which distinguishes Fichte's thought from Levinas's. Another major difference is their respective conception of intersubjectivity. For Fichte's I, though initially solicited by the other, and thus dependent upon the other, simultaneously solicits the other to its own freedom. Hence Fichte's insistence on the mutual reciprocity of the I and the Thou such that were there "no Thou, no I: no I, no Thou" (*SK* 172–73).[27] The I and the Thou *interdetermine* one another in Fichte's conception, even though it is the Thou which is first pronounced, as it were (155ff.). This reciprocity could never be condoned by Levinas. Remember that what is at stake for Levinas is a notion of transcendence and height which insists upon the I being *commanded* by the Other and holding no claims upon its own being before the Other's gaze (see *BPW* 12). By making the other merely another I just as dependent upon me as I am upon it, Fichte's system fundamentally betrays the directionality of the call of the Other as described by Levinas. So while the I for Fichte needs intersubjectivity to be itself, and, in a sense, the other precedes the I, if not logically, then at least ontologically, this other-I still stands on an even footing with subject. This means that in Fichte's view the relationship with the other remains merely horizontal and not vertical. Any transcendence initiated through this relationship would fail to attain the truly trans*ascendant* movement inherent to Levinas account of metaphysical desire. Thus while the concrete operations of the intersubjective exchange upon the I may be read in a similar way in both writers, as we have seen, ultimately their respective analyses of directionality of this exchange keeps Fichte's work from being on the same page as Levinas's. Indeed, Levinas specifically addresses the dangers of a reciprocal understanding of the I-Thou relationship in his treatment of Martin Buber (see *TI* 68–69).[28]

Fichte's insistence upon the reciprocity between the I and the Thou also establishes a difference from Levinas in the way in which he accounts for the grounds of the intersubjective relationship. Remember that, for Levinas, the Other fundamentally precedes the I and that all interactions with the Other occur on the basis of the Other's self-revelation (see *TI* 65–66). Thus the intersubjective relationship is not only offered by the Other to the I, it is established on the existence of the Other, and not on the existence of the I. The Other not only grounds and conditions the ethical relationship, but the very existence of the I. In contrast, for Fichte the I is always already a potentiality before the entrance of the Thou. Thus, though the Thou may summon it into actuality, this Thou is encountered on the basis of the fact that the I is first a possibility.

This claim that it is only on the basis of the I's prior existence that the non-I or the Thou is encountered is not, as we have seen, intended to suggest that the exteriority of the world is somehow produced by the I. The world, the non-I, and the Thou are truly exterior for Fichte. Thus, Gunter Zöller can confidently state that for Fichte, "our existing world is all ready...Life is not a producing but a finding."[29] The I *finds* itself in the world, it does not create it. But, it finds itself in the world, caught up and actualized in exteriority, only because it is first a possibility—and this possibility is grounded in its own way of being, its own self-positing. Thus though it is not self-originating it still contains the ground of its existence within itself. Fichte compares the nature of the I's encounter and dependence upon the world with the hearing of harmony (*SK* 18). Harmony, he claims, does not exist in the heard, but in the hearing: it is not some thing-in-itself, out there in the air as it were, but only exists in as much as there is an I who hears it. Hence the fact that what is harmonic can be experienced differently in different cultures. Thus though the sound may not be interior to me nor produced by me, my hearing of it is, as is my judgment that it is harmonious. Likewise, though the world does indeed exist exterior to me, my encounter with it is grounded on the fact that I am and the specific way in which I am in the world.

In this respect, the Fichtean claims conflict profoundly with the Levinasian account not because it denies the reality of the exterior, nor because it denies the subject's dependence upon such an exterior, but because it establishes the ground of this dependence within the subject itself rather than on the alterity of the Other. For Levinas, all interaction with the Other and the otherwise, including interaction with the merely locally other in the exteriority of the world, is grounded on the illumination offered by the Other in the epiphany of a face. This means that, by Levinas's analysis, any alterity encountered within the Fichtean system would ultimately be resolvable within the subject—would be, in the end, merely relatively other, defined in terms of the subject's relation to the self. In contrast, the Other that is at work in Levinas analysis, the Other who is the ground of all otherness as such, is, as we saw in chapter 1, the Other *par excellence,* the absolutely Other. By Levinas's read then, though Fichte's I may encounter some form of otherness, it will never be able to escape itself—its movement in the world and interaction with the otherwise therein remains in the form of an Odyssian narrative. Hence Scott Scribner's analysis that "while for Levinas our exposure to the infinite is constituted in and through our ethical relation to the other, for Fichte, ethics is a work of the self even in the moment of its utter dispossession. In other words, ethics for Fichte, remains a task centered on self formation, even if its end point is an abandonment of the self."[30]

Because the I emerges on its own ground, even though it is elevated into existence by the Other, the I for Fichte must ultimately be understood as *for-itself:* "the self exists for the self" (*SK* 99). Consciousness for Fichte is thus fundamentally "nothing else but the *being-with-itself* and *being-for-itself.*"[31] Clearly this is a claim with which Levinas would take great exception. For Levinas, though the I may understand itself in its naiveté as a *being-for-itself,* this *for-itself* becomes transformed through its encounter with the Other into a *for-the-other,* such that the only way it seeks itself is through the Other. And so it is to the nature of this absolutely Other that we must turn our attention if we are to move further in our understanding of the nature of metaphysical longing.

CONCLUSIONS

From these few examples it should be clear that though Fichte and Levinas do ultimately share much more than Levinas's work initially suggests, they can never truly be reconciled to one another. For, despite their interests in the same phenomenon and their comparable analyses of that phenomenon, they ultimately approach the human subject and its insatiable desire in two fundamentally different ways. Levinas reads it in the light provided for by the Other such that through metaphysical desire the subject can be carried out of itself, whereas for Fichte longing is not only the expression of the self, but an operation through which it becomes even more riveted to itself. It is this fact, which for Levinas is the ultimate weakness of the idealistic position: that it fails to offer an exit to the burdensomeness of existence (see *OE* 72–73). Fichte's *Sehnsucht* thus remains what Levinas terms in *On Escape* a mere *ex-cendence* and not yet a *transascendance,* like metaphysical desire (54). Hence his claim that "at the very moment when idealism imagines that it has surpassed being, it is invaded from all sides" (73). The arguments of people like Lumsden, though perceptive to sniff out the connection between Levinas and Fichte covered over by Levinas himself, seem to belie a failure to take the Levinasian turn toward the Otherwise seriously enough—a failure to see that what is of interest for Levinas is a passivity within the subject still more passive than the one argued for by Fichte, a passivity that goes still deeper as it were, as is suggested for example in *Otherwise than Being.*

It is on the basis of this primordial passivity that the ethical implications of metaphysical desire are grounded for Levinas and its metaphysical implications further revealed. Indeed, the origins of that deeper passivity force us to probe deeper the metaphysical implications of human longing. It is this revelation, the fact that human longing must rest upon a metaphysical ground still more afield than one's own being, first intimated in our investigation into the relation between Heidegger and Levinas's respective accounts of longing, that has now become clearer by pursing the difference between Levinas and Fichte's respective analyses of the relation between longing and ethics.

We began this chapter in the hopes of gaining insight into the strange relation between longing and an ethical relation to the Other which led us through an investigation into the nature of shame and the constitution of the human subject. Along the way we discovered that shame, according to Levinas, reveals the fact that the subject is not entirely the master of its own being, for in shame the subject's interpretation and experience of itself is countered and contested by another. This contestation, however, does not come from a force which overwhelms the subject, he claimed, but rather from a force which can reach deeper than the ontological roots of the subject. What shame revealed for us then is the fact that the existence of the subject ultimately rests upon a ground which is beyond and otherwise than its own being. This is what Fichte's claims concerning the subject failed to recognize. As such his account of the ethical and the function of *Sehnsucht* therein ultimately remained limited to the realm of the ontological. Thus even though he defined *Sehnsucht* as the subject's attempt to go beyond the limits of its own being, because that attempt was not grounded in a ground still deeper and otherwise than the being of the subject, it ultimately does nothing more than act as a kind of further expression of that being. Levinas's metaphysical desire differs then in the fact that it not only moves away from and beyond the limitations of the subject's being, but also arises from a movement within the subject which runs counter to its being. Longing thus becomes for Levinas the expression of a kind of metaphysical aquifer which runs silently beneath the subject's being, buoying and supporting its existence and constantly driving it toward an ethical encounter with the Other.

It is the presence of this deeper metaphysical ground from whence human subjectivity arises, and with it human longing, which is thus revealed through our investigation into the relation between ethics and longing. And it is to this ground that we must turn again to gain any further insight into the nature of metaphysical longing.

Part Three
Divine Longing

FOUR

The Metaphysics of Longing and Creature-Consciousness

Levinas and Schelling in Dialogue

THROUGH SHAME TO CREATION

In *Totality and Infinity* Levinas famously identifies ethics as a sort of "spiritual optics," as a means of observing within the phenomenally apparent that which lies out beyond appearance, beyond essence—in other words, as a means of catching sight of that which lies beyond the pale of the visible and pertains properly to the metaphysical (*TI* 78). It makes sense then why Levinas would insist on identifying longing, which, as we just saw, distinguishes itself from other forms of desire primarily in its ethical inherence to an Other, as a properly *metaphysical* desire. Longing, it seems, testifies to some metaphysical depth at work albeit concealed within existence. The passivity that longing reveals to belong at the heart of human subjectivity, the fact that the subject is ultimately dependent upon an Other for its being, implies that the existence of the I, and with it the existence which avails itself to that I, rests upon an invisible, metaphysical ground beyond the bounds of casual observation. In order to bring the meaning of this deeper, more primordial metaphysical ground into focus then, it is necessary to further probe the ethical implications of the experience of longing. One way to do this is to pick up where we left off in the last chapter, investigating further the nature and meaning of the experience of shame.

As we have seen, shame is for Levinas, to use the words of Rudi Visker, a kind of "affect without a context."[1] That is, one does not feel ashamed because of anything that he or she has done or failed to do. In shame one feels oneself accused *prior* to the transgression of any laws or moral statutes. Shame thus references not the actions of the subject, but its very being. Indeed, according to Levinas, shame is the experience of having one's commitment to his or her own being called into question. It is thus an experience which is occasioned through the discovery of the very way in which one *is*, the very way in which one appears to another whose perception is accessible or controllable by the subject—another who cannot be illuminated but instead illuminates the subject in a light entirely its own. The power of the illuminative gaze of the Other to affect such a radical break within the continuity of the subject's experience of itself signals the fact that the subject is not the unrivaled master of its own existence. The experience of shame thus signals a break in the continuity of the subject's being as such. In this sense, the experience of shame goes *beyond being*—references that which falls outside the bounds of the subject's being. The fact that the subject can nevertheless be affected by such a *beyond* reveals, the fact that the very being of the subject cannot be explained on its own terms—that there is a trace of this *beyond* ever in the depths of being. Thus in order to fully understand the nature of the subject one must reference that which falls outside the bounds of the subject, beyond its scope—one must reference that which *precedes* the birth of the subject, that upon which the subject's being appears to be somehow dependent. Indeed, according to Levinas, what the experience of shame offers is the possibility of considering oneself in light of that which comes before, in light of that which conditions and occasions one's being. That is, it gives the subject access to a history which is not its own—a history which predates its own inception and existence—but a history which, nevertheless, determines it. It is only because the subject has always already been preceded by another that it can even be its being; hence Levinas's claim that "inwardness is the fact that in being the beginning is preceded" (*CPP* 133). Because this past which conditions the emergence of the subject precedes the history of the subject, it is not available to the subject through either memory or nostalgia—it is not something which the subject can ever take hold of and claim as its own. It is thus not a past to which the subject has any access outside of the illumination provided by the other, an illumination which comes through the experience of shame.

What shame reveals to the subject then, according to Levinas, is its possibility of having been *created* by another—of having been completely passive beyond all recognition in its own emergence into existence. It is to this possibility which, by Levinas's read, Fichte's work can never reconcile itself; for what Fichte's work resists is precisely "the very impossibility of a past that would never have been present, that would be closed to memory and to history" (*CPP* 131). Yet it is precisely such an im*possibility* that must be embraced for the life of the subject to be understood in such a way that the experience of shame and metaphysical desire can be made sense of in their profundity: "the account of creation [is] all the same necessary for the life of man" (58). Indeed, Levinas asserts, the very passivity of the subject, the fact that it can be affected by the Other, is vulnerable to the accusations of another, "is the condition (or uncondition) by which being shows itself to be a creature" (147). To understand what Levinas means here and to further illuminate the deeper metaphysical implications of human longing we must first examine what Levinas means by *creation*.

According to Levinas, creation should not be understood as an account of the subject's *actual* past, but instead as a merely *logical* determination of the past based on one's orientation toward a future offered by the Other—that is based on one's responsibility to another. Creation expresses for Levinas then not an accomplished history, but a present and future possibility presented to the subject in its ethical relation to the Other. It is for him the expression of a fundamental alteration of the way in which the subject currently and henceforth may understand itself. It is not meant then to be a literal expression of the origins of the identity of the subject, but a potential for how the subject *can* understand itself through the illuminative gaze of the Other. In this sense creation does not reveal the *origins* of subjectivity as such, but instead the possibility of its having been preceded by an Other to whom it owes an allegiance and debt.

Thus though this creation is *posited* as preceding the subject, one should not fail to understand that this position is a *logical projection* by the subject—a logical projection which follows the way in which its responsibility before another reorients its understanding of itself. The possibility of creation is not deemed by Levinas to be actually prior to the subject, but only logically prior. One always experiences oneself first and foremost spontaneously; one cannot experience nor understand one's own creation naturally. It is a position which must be derived posterior to the experience of oneself. Nevertheless, it is a posterior position which pertains to the anteriority of subjectivity. This curious relation is what Levinas refers to as the "posteriority of the anterior," a concept to which we first referred in chapter 1 (*TI* 54; cf. *BPW* 81–82).²

Though creation should in a sense naturally occur anterior to the subject's actual existence, it is only an occurrence to which someone can relate on the basis of their having already existed. It is, moreover, a possibility for understanding the past which may precede one's own existence which is only offered in the light of another's perspective. It is thus a possibility which arises only on the basis of the ethical encounter with an Other. Thus, though it seems as if the creative act must have happened *before,* it is actually only offered *after* one is already on the scene. In this sense creation is not so much an *act* which occurred at some point in time, but an *orientation* which one can take to one's own being concerning its relation to the Other. "The cause of being," Levinas writes, "is thought or known by its effect *as though* it were posterior to its effect" (*TI* 54). Creation is thus always only a logical possibility. In actuality, he claims, creation is something which is always yet to come, or still happening. It is thus more a transformative occurrence within the life of the subject than a preformative occurrence at the beginning of time. In other words, creation has more to do with what is to come in the life of the subject than from whence the life of the subject has come. In this sense creation is not so much a *fait accompli* but a promise. It is not then, an account of a *genesis,* but of a *covenant*—of the possibility of a reorientation of one's understanding of oneself. This claim has to do in part with how Levinas describes the procedure of creation itself.

CREATION IN LEVINAS: CREATION AS CONTRACTIO DEI

Levinas begins his account of the creative act by reformulating the traditional understanding of the creation as a process which occurs *ex nihilo*. Traditionally, claims Levinas, the *nihil* of creation has been figured as a pure and total absence, nothingness as such. The creative act then, proceeding from a God who has traditionally been understood as productive, has been formulated as God's positive expansion into nothingness insofar as that which is created thereby remains somehow contiguous and under the shadow of God. Such was its dependence. The danger of such an understanding, Levinas cautions, is that it denies any genuine independence to the created realm. Indeed, he claims, it implies a kind of "*pure* passivity on the part of the creature" (*EE* 2; italics mine).[3]

Though Levinas is certainly interested in illuminating the *relative* passivity of his account of the ego, indeed, as we saw in the last chapter—he insists on a passivity still more passive than the one offered by Fichte—he nevertheless does not want to deny the subject's agency and activity entirely. Were the ego entirely *produced* from nothing, thinks Levinas, its singularity and responsibility before another would in some sense be nullified. Indeed, were the subject entirely passive it would have no choice at all, neither for itself nor for the good. What Levinas must do then is provide a creation narrative that, while insisting upon the passivity of the subject, still maintains its absolute independence. In this way alone will Levinas be able to assert on the one hand the radical responsibility of the subject for an Other, and therefore its independence from the Other, while at the same time maintaining its creatureliness and dependence upon that Other: "What is essential to created existence is its *separation* with regard to the Infinite" (*TI* 105; italics mine).

In contrast to the traditional understanding of creation, then, Levinas posits a creation account that proceeds precisely from such a separation. This he does by referencing the traditional Kabbalistic account of the *contractio dei,* God's withdrawal from presence. For Levinas, the outset of creation should not be conceived of as an expansion of God into the nothingness, but as the contraction of God or withdrawal from presence into nothingness such that a space is opened up, a space wherein an independent existence may emerge. In the vacuum left by God's withdrawal the subject is able to emerge independently, is able to separate through enjoyment and representation, as dealt with in chapter 1. According to Levinas, "enjoyment separates by engaging in the contents from which it lives" (*TI* 147), while consciousness separates and distinguishes itself "in the form of an inner life, a psychism" (54). Indeed, "separation is the very constituting of thought and interiority, that is, a relationship with independence" (104). To be a thinking I, to have an inner life and to enjoy the world, is to be independent. But, interiority as a concept necessarily implies a separation from some exteriority; this is its logical consequent: if there is an inner, there must also be an outer from which it is distinguished. But enjoyment and interiority do more than merely signal the fact that some determinate separation exists; they are the very *effectuation* of that separation, its sufficient cause. Separation is effected through the interiority of enjoyment and thought—it is not merely "*reflected* in thought, but *produced* by it" (54; italics mine). In a sense, separation is produced by its product, namely interiority. This implies, however, that the effectuation of interiority is in some sense a self-referential occurrence—that is, it is something which occurs in radical independence, it is not assisted in any way from the outside, though, as we shall see in more detail shortly, it may be conditioned by the mutual and reciprocal separation of the exterior from it. Since this separation is effected by the interiority which is produced in it, human subjectivity should not be conceived of as something granted from the outside, like some benison from heaven, but as initiated from within the very being of human existence—it is a byproduct of the very way in which humans are. The interiority of the subject must first and foremost then be understood as a kind of independence.

Though the interiority of human existence is *effected* on its own, establishing its undeniable independence, this is an independence which is nevertheless *conditioned* by the simultaneous withdrawal and contraction of God. The creative act upon which the self-asserted independence of interiority arises, serves as the ground for the emergence of interiority. Yet, this is a ground which retreats so far from presence as to be all but invisible to the natural perspective. Indeed, Levinas seems to argue, in the creative act God in a sense becomes nothing—resists coming to presence such that individuals may emerge on their own authority and in their own light. So it is, he claims, that one need not betray the natural atheism of human subjectivity in asserting a creation narrative. That is to say that according to Levinas, though the assertion that the subject may be conceived of as created, this need not necessitate that the subject be somehow always internally aware of its indebtedness to God. Levinas's account of creation does not necessitate, nor even encourage for that matter, some sort of faith in God. Rather, almost paradoxically, creation is the precondition and requirement for any true expression of an authentic atheism.

The natural atheism of the subject, its natural propensity to consider itself outside of its relation to any possible creator, is not then, claims Levinas, the result of some fall from grace. It is instead the natural result of the very way in which human beings have been created, emerge as existents and are, as such. Atheism is not a deprived position then—it is not the result of the *loss* of some latent knowledge of the creator. Instead, it is the natural byproduct of the way in which creation occurs, and therefore a positive appearance. Indeed, it is consistent with the way in which creation is accounted for via *contractio dei*. Since the individual in Levinas's conception does not proceed from God directly, is not the result of some *production* or *expansion* of God, but rather emerges on its own by positing itself into the abyss opened up by the withdrawal of God, "one lives outside of God, at home with oneself, one is an I, an egoism," claims Levinas (*TI* 58). Atheism is not, therefore, the result of some active negation on the part of the individual, it is not a refusal to admit the presence of God nor the denial of God's existence. It is not a project by the subject—representative of some attitude or opinion held by the subject. Instead, atheism is the result of the self-negation of God; it is a possibility which is opened up by the self-erasure effected by God's contraction. Atheism is thus a kind of gift which is passively received by the subject in its very coming to be. If one is to maintain then that the self-effecting individual is to be understood as a creature, he or she must do so with trepidation. That is to say that, though such a creative act may occur, it is not natural to consider the interiority that emerges from it as a kind of creature. For, though the creative act may condition and ground the emergence of the individual, it is not a legacy which is felt in any positive way in the life of the individual as such. Creation accounted for via *contractio dei* is only a passive condition which allows for the active self-positing of the subject to occur. Actively then, the subject experiences itself as its *own creature*. Hence Levinas's claim that "the oneself is a creature, but an orphan by birth or an atheist no doubt ignorant of its Creator" (*OB* 105). The creative act, proceeding as it does via the contraction and self-abnegation of God, leaves the created entirely independent and severed from the ground from whence it arises. This inexorable independence is what gives birth to the subject's natural atheism. Thus atheism, far from being the active denial of some sort of faith, is in fact the only grounds from which any true faith as a positive assertion can arise.

In this sense, Levinas establishes atheism as a kind of condition to faith; for only an initially truly independent existence can decide to relate itself to God (see *TI* 77). Hence his claim that "the miracle of creation lies in creating a moral being. And this implies precisely atheism, but at the same time, beyond atheism, shame for the arbitrariness of the freedom that constitutes it" (89). By referencing an account of creation that proceeds not by the expansion of the creator, but by way of self-negation, Levinas is able to posit an entirely independent human existence on the one hand, while simultaneously maintaining, on the other hand, that this independence somehow bears the mark of a passive dependence. In other words, by Levinas's read, though human existence may affect its own emergence such that it is entirely severed from God and entirely independent, its existence cannot be taken as entirely autonomous. Instead, it must be understood as somehow conditioned by a God who refuses to exist such that others may exist. Thus, "creation leaves to the creature a trace of dependence, but it is an unparalleled dependence: the dependent being draws from this exceptional dependence, from this relationship, its very independence, its exteriority to the system" (104–05).[4]

Since creation allows for just such an independence, one established in interiority, the meaning and identity of such an emergent ipseity is not derived from its relationship to the external, but rather from the inside. Indeed, claims Levinas, the interiority of the subject is precisely "the refusal to be transformed into a pure loss figuring in an alien accounting system" (*TI* 56). Separation is thus the designation of an individual from some foreign totality or universal history in which all singularity is erased (104).[5] Instead, "separation designates the possibility of an *existent* being set up and having its own destiny to itself, that is being born and dying without the place of this birth and this death in the time of universal history being the measure of its reality" (55; italics mine). Though the subject may be conditioned by such a history wherein some notion of creation can be placed, the subject does not in a sense *live* in this history—does not take nor derive its meaning from this history. Instead, the subject lives from the inside, from its own interiority, and derives its meaning from the way in which it experiences its own being from that perspective. Thus though the life and death of any particular subject may be deemed insignificant from the *outside* perspective of some universal history, hardly anything will be deemed more important by the subject itself; hence Levinas's description of interiority as "the very possibility of a birth and a death that do not derive their meaning in history" (55). Instead, as emergent from that history, indeed, defined in contradistinction to it through the rupture of separation effected in interiority, the individual remains in its inception the locus of its own being. Hence Levinas's affirmation of Descartes's claim that one's primary identification is not with oneself as a *creature,* but with oneself as a thinking I, a *cogito* (54). This is in part why Levinas insists that one's identification with the act of creation can only be logically derived posterior to the actual chronological priority of one's self-identification, of one's experience of one's own being. The claim that creation *should* in a sense precede this self-identification can never amount to anything more than a merely logical claim—a claim which is, furthermore, grounded on the actual precedence of the *cogito.*

This distinction between the chronological and the logical understanding of time is the result, he argues, of the way in which creation proceeds via separation: "That there could be a chronological order distinct from the 'logical' order, that there could be several moments in the progression, that there is a progression—here is separation" (*TI* 54). One's separation from some external history and one's independent emergence as an interiority is necessitated by the very way in which such a separation occurs. Since time is experienced from the inside in the same way in which one experiences one's own being, the initiation of that being cannot be situated in some *prior* time. The separation which effects interiority simultaneously gives birth to the subject's time. Thus, says Levinas, "the psychism [of interiority] constitutes an *event* in being" (54). Separation, the birth of consciousness, and ipseity demarcates time for the subject into the present. "The present," Levinas writes, "is then a situation in being where there is not only being in general, but there is a being, a subject" (*EE* 71, cf. 78). The present, within which the subject lives, is thus not only distinct from some universal history; it is the negation of it. The subject lives only in his or her time, and in no other time. He or she lives only in a time which is initiated with his or her being and ends with his or her demise. If the subject is thus to be related to any creation, the creation from whence it emerges cannot be situated in any time other than its own. The logically assumed past in which such a creation could have occurred is not the expression of some actual time, some fixed or precise moment in history, even if that moment be the initiation of that history. Instead, Levinas seems to argue, it can only be thought of as having occurred in some *virtual* time—not a time which ever actually was, but a time which might have been or which might still be. Creation is an event which belongs to a "time immemorial." It is not an event then which has ever actually occurred in time, it has never actually come to pass; it is instead a logical possibility which is held out through the encounter with the Other. The past in which such a virtual event is situated then is never some point to which one can be related through any act of memory or retrograde. Nor is it something someone can pine for nostalgically, for it is not an event which has somehow been lost or covered over by the march of time. It is instead a past which is always situated before the subject through the ethical demand of the other as a possibility—as an option for the future, a way of considering oneself in relation to the Other.

This is in part why Levinas defines metaphysical desire, that desire which arises from the Other and is directed to the Other, as oriented not toward some distant past, like nostalgia, but toward the future, toward what is yet to come. Metaphysical desire is in some sense the feeling which accompanies the possibility of creation. It is the possibility of considering oneself as created which begins to stir within the heart of the subject through the ethical encounter with the Other. As such, the ethical appeal appears to emerge in the *trace* of the creative act; and, metaphysical desire, as one of the mediating phenomenon of this ethical appeal, likewise appears to testify to this creative act.

CREATION, THE TRACE, AND LONGING

Though creation is considered by Levinas to have occurred in a "time immemorial," a time which can have no real affect upon the subject it nevertheless leaves a kind of subtle trace, not in any way that directly references itself, but in such a way that can only be seen through the optics provided in the ethical encounter with the Other. The trace is not then some visual evidence for the creative act. "There is," after all, claims Levinas, "no natural religion" (*TI* 62). One cannot reason oneself to an understanding of God through any evidence provided for in nature and the "autonomy of the sensible in the world" (62). As we have just seen, the natural state of things appears devoid of any such reference to God; hence Levinas's insistence on the naturalness of atheism. The trace of creation is thus not some sort of heavenly fingerprint upon the world, but, as we have said, a kind of orientation one can take within the ethical exchange that signals the subject's dependence upon the Other. The trace is something which becomes apparent, for example, through the experience of shame and longing, phenomena which point away to the Other. It is, in a sense, a perspective offered on the apparent world made available through the ethical encounter with an Other—only after the appearance of the Other on the scene. In this sense, the Other introduces into the history of the subject something that was not there before: "The relation with the Other as a relation with his transcendence—the relation with the Other who puts into question the brutal spontaneity of one's immanent destiny—introduces into me what was not in me," namely the possibility of considering myself as one who has been created (203). The possibility of having been created is thus not in accord with one's nature, as we have seen, but is in fact, as Rudi Visker describes, "*against* nature."[6] The possibility of having been created opened up in the ethical relation is the *introduction of a new order into nature,* one that combats, the spontaneous naiveté with which the subject *naturally* understands itself.

By Levinas's reckoning, the trace is, in some sense, the absence left by the contraction of God in the creative act—it is the lingering mark of God's passing. It is a mark which can only be read, however, by the light provided for in the face of the Other in the ethical illumination (*CPP* 120). The face can signal the absence effected in the creative act because, he claims, it "is ordered out of *the absence in which the infinite approaches,* out of its *null site* [*Non-Lieu*], ordered *in the trace of its own departure;* it is ordered to my responsibility and my love, beyond consciousness, which it obsesses" (121). It is because the face operates in the aperture opened in the *contractio dei* that it has such a power over the subject to accuse it and call it into question: "it is because in the proximity of being is inscribed the trace of an absence, or of the infinite, that there is dereliction, gravity, responsibility, obsession and I" (124).[7] The face of the Other, in a sense, glows with the fallout of the creative implosion of God—as such, it harkens the subject to the possibility of this creation, to the possibility of a time which lies on the hither side of consciousness. According to Levinas, the face of the Other "comes enigmatically from the Infinite and its immemorial past, and because of this covenant between the poverty of the face and the infinite is inscribed in the force with which my fellowman is imposed for my responsibility before all engagement on my part" (*EN* 57). Hence his claim that in some sense "the other must be closer to God than I am" (*CPP* 56). Because the Other comes in the trace of God, in the wake of the *contractio dei,* it shines with the brilliance of God and illuminates with the light of the creative act such that in the gaze of the Other the subject can become opened to the possibility of thinking of itself as having been preceded, and thereby to the possibility of its having been created—its dependence.

The experience of shame and longing, by revealing to the subject the trace of its dependence upon another, introduces into the subject a kind of crib or hermeneutic by which to read and comprehend the trace left by God's contraction. Because the Other comes in the wake of this contraction, the ethical call harkens to the time immemorial of creation and, in a sense, gives voice to what in it was silenced by the very way in which it occurred. So it is that the light that would have shone from the creative act "lights up as the face of a neighbor, in the ambiguity of the one *before whom* (or *to whom,* without any paternalism) and *for whom* I answer" (*BPW* 118). The trace which becomes apparent in the illuminative gaze of the Other is thus in some sense "the presence of that which properly speaking has never been there, of what is always past" (63). It is through the experience of the face, of the ethical call and the shame it initiates, that we are presented with the impact of creation. Through the experience of shame and longing the power of the creation is evoked and awakened within the subject as a possibility by which the subject can reorient its understanding of itself to that which falls outside the bounds of consciousness.

It seems that longing, as an ethical desire for the Other which works to reveal our primordial dependency upon the Other, bears the mantel of the creative act. As the affectation of the idea of the infinite, longing testifies to the possibility of having been infinitely preceded. The presence of this infinite longing thus signals the fact that there is something greater at work in the depths of subjectivity than can be explained by reference to the subject's own history. It testifies to the possibility of the subject's subtle dependence upon another history, a history which includes the possibility of creation. Longing, as a kind of superabundant presence within the subject, as the presence of something which exceeds the limitation of the subject's being, signals the subject's dependence upon something outside of and beyond the bounds of its own being. It opens the possibility of considering the subject as having arisen and emerged out of another ground than itself. That is, it signals the possibility of having been created with longing appearing as a kind of vestige of the creative act. But since this creation cannot be situated in any determinate time which actually precedes the subject, but in one which only logically precedes the subject, this longing is never aimed backward, like nostalgia, but is aimed forward, onward to a future possibility contained in the face of the Other to a time which has *yet to come*.

CREATION IN LEVINAS: HYPOSTASIS AS CONTRACTIO HOMINIS

Levinas names the emergence of an individual through separation *hypostasis*. Hypostasis expresses for him the "upsurge of an existent into existence" (*EE* 25). It is the demarcation of an individual consciousness from the totality of being in general, the instantiation of being into the first person present: "I am, I think." It is, in fact, as we have just seen the very instantiation of the present as such. According to Levinas, "The present is the event of hypostasis. The present leaves itself—better still it *is* the departure from self. It is a rip in the infinite beginning-less and endless fabric of existing. The present rips apart and joins together again; it begins; it is beginning itself" (*TO* 52). But if the hypostatic act initiated and sustained through consciousness is figured as a separation and a rupture with the continuity of a totality, the question is begged: what is the hypostatic act a separation from? Since Levinas accounts for creation as the self-abnegation of God, the hypostatic act cannot be taken to be some Promethean act of rebellion against the heavenly order. If hypostasis is to be figured as some form of rebellion then, it must be a rebellion against some other force. And indeed, claims Levinas, the *refusal* implied in the hypostatic act is not against God, who willingly withdraws from the scene, but against another kind of totality, a totality that does not abdicate its claim over the subject but threatens instead to invade the subject on all sides and overwhelm its singularity. This threat is posed by the totality of being—of a neutral being without beings. The hypostatic refusal to be tallied as a part of an alien accounting system is thus the rebellion against the anonymous mass of being in general. Hypostasis, as the instantiation of a singular being, a *cogito,* an *I* present in its own *now,* signals a break in the homogeny and totality of being as such. It is the demarcation of being as a whole into separate and singular particular beings, beings who do not derive their meaning from their conjugation of universal being, but derive their meaning from themselves. In the formation of interiority effected through thought and enjoyment, the absolute indifference of *being in general* is transformed into the concrete existence of particular beings, individuals separate and distinct from the totality from whence they extract their being.

Remember from chapter 2, Levinas identifies this totality of being in general with the French verb infinitive *il y a* (see *EE* 52). *Il y a,* being in general, is for Levinas the state of being without any particular or singular beings—it is a being devoid of any indicators or demarcations. As such, the being of the *il y a* is not at all a neutral force for Levinas. It is instead, the very source of all evil, an evil so distinct that it cannot even be contrasted to the good, for therein no such determinations can be made. The being of the *il y a* is thus characterized by Levinas as a totalizing force, a force which rolls over any singularity or determinate possible good and does not allow for any difference or individuality—any determination of the ethical or the moral. It is the pure and total absence of any such differences, the utterly impersonal as such.

It is against this impersonal force that the hypostatic act rebels not against some other self, since the "existing [of the *il y a*] is not an in-itself [*en-soi*], which is already peace; it is precisely the absence of all self, a *without self [sans-soi]*" (*TO* 49); it rebels against the very denial of such a self. The hypostatic act, effected in thought and enjoyment, is the insistence of one particular being to demarcate itself from the totality of being in general. It is the insistence of a self to be *on its own terms* and *in its own way*. As the introduction of a self into an order than can admit of no such distinctions, the hypostatic act not only signals the birth of the individual, it also effects the demise of the *il y a*. According to Levinas, "Hypostasis, the apparition of a substantive, is not only the apparition of a new grammatical category; it signifies the suspension of the anonymous *there is*, the apparition of a private domain, of a noun" (*EE* 83). The emergence of a thinking consciousness, the conjugation of being into the singular form, "I am, I think," "is the rupture of the anonymous vigilance of the *there is*" (*TO* 51). It is the condensation and contraction of being in general into singular existents and particular beings, into determinate selves (53). Separation is thus the cognitive process through which an I is formed by concentrating the indistinction of being *en masse* around a particular point, a particular person, such that an inner can begin to be distinguished from an outer within being, such that my being can be distinguished from being as such. Hypostasis, as "the passage of going from being to some*thing,* from the state of a verb to the state of a thing," signifies a break with the totality and continuity of the anonymous being of the *there is* (*EI* 51).

The creative act, the contraction of God, should thus be figured as the initial separation which allows for the hypostatic act. God, concurrent with the totalizing being of the *il y a,* by refusing to exist, opens up a space within being wherein the hypostasis of the individual existence of human beings can proceed on its own. The contraction which lays the ground for the possible emergence of this interiority is the first break in the homogeneity of being. It is in light of this account of the creative act that the *nihil* of creation accounted for *ex nihilo* should properly be interpreted.

According to Levinas, the *nothing* out of which creation makes its way *ex nihilo* is nothing like the *nothing* of pure absence, absolute emptiness, or annihilation. It does not resemble then the Heideggerian presentation of the *Nicht* which is a negating negation—a negation that negates itself. It is instead the no-*thing*-ness retained in the indifference of the *il y a*. It is literally that domination of no-*thing* (see *EE* 5). Precisely the opposite of nothing figured as a kind of annihilative nonbeing, the *nihil* from whence the creative act emerges is in fact the *nihil* of pure being. It is maintained in a being that is so complete that it denies any difference and independence. It is, in a sense, absolutely everything. Not nothing, but a presence so complete that it forbids the contour of *any particular thing;* hence his insistence on an account of creation via *contractio dei*. God, by eschewing presence and withdrawing into nonexistence, by making himself *otherwise than being,* breaks with the totality of the *il y a,* rupturing its hold on everything and opening a space wherein human existence may contract its own being, wrench itself free from the anonymity of being, and condense and conjugate that being within the independent existence of a singular consciousness and interiority. It is only understood thusly that Levinas affirms an account of creation *ex nihilo* (see *TI* 63). "Creation *ex-nihilo*," writes Levinas, "breaks with system, posits a being outside of every system, that is, there where its freedom is possible" (104).

The contraction and condensation of the human being from being in general, the hypostatic act, comes in the wake of the creative act, the contraction of God. God's contraction provides an alternative to the pure being of the *there is* by opening a way out of existence—a way out of the totality of presence and being—by withdrawing beyond being. But, this creative act is only fulfilled when, in the space provided for by God's withdrawal, a definite "I am" is formed out of the formless *there is*. In this sense Levinas makes human beings coconspirators in their own creation.

Indeed, claims Levinas, creation occurs concurrent with the independent formation of the I. Hypostasis, our instantiation of being in consciousness, is in a sense the tain of God's contraction, its reverse side and reflective surface. The *contractio dei*, away from being, must be met by a converse *contractio hominis* of being into the conjugated "I am, I think," of consciousness. But, precisely because this latter contraction takes the form of a crawling inside oneself, of an independent interiority, the hypostatic act not only separates human existence from being as such, but also from the condition that allows it to separate. That is, because of the way in which the hypostatic act occurs, one not only becomes distinct from the totality of being, but distinct from the possibility of God—entirely independent and unaware of the ground from whence one arises. It is as if in stopping one's ears to the "rhythm" (*CPP* 4), "murmur" (*EE* 52), and "anonymous rumblings" (23) of the *there is* through the formation of interiority, one also shuts out the still, silent voice of creation, a voice which is muted precisely by the way in which it speaks by withdrawing from sound and presence. So it is that human beings are born atheists, ignorant of the subtle passivity implied in the very way in which they are independent—creation remaining always only a logical postulation held out by the Other who illuminates the trace of God's passing.

Thus, Levinas writes, "The I transcends the world of light—not to dissolve into the anonymity of the *there is,* but in order to go further than the light, to go *elsewhere*" (*TI* 268). And again,

"The marvel of creation does not only consist in being a creation *ex nihilo,* but in that it results in being capable of receiving a revelation, learning that it is created, and putting itself in question. The miracle of creation lies in creating a moral being. And this implies precisely atheism, but at the same time, beyond atheism, shame for the arbitrariness of the freedom that constitutes it" (89). Here is the great irony of the Levinasian account of creation: that it proceeds by erasing itself. In other words, the greatest testament to the act of creation is that there is not any testament. Its glory lies in its nonexistence, in the emergence of an entirely free, independent, and autonomous creation. This, thinks Levinas is the glorious paradox of creation.

CREATION THROUGH THE EYES OF SCHELLING

Levinas is not alone in his reliance upon an account of creation via *contractio dei* to assert the strange dependent independence of the life of the subject. Nor is he alone in connecting this legacy of this creative act to human longing and the human drive to exceed the limits of its own being and pursue the otherwise than being. Friedrich Wilhelm Schelling, a contemporary of Fichte's and a profound influence on both Heidegger and Franz Rosenzweig—arguably the two thinkers, along with Husserl and Plato, to whom Levinas is most indebted—also drew upon the notion of *contractio dei* to detail his understanding of the radical independence of human freedom and to inform his analysis of the significance of human longing.[8]

Schelling's problem at the beginning of his *Of Human Freedom* is the same as that of Levinas in his account of the autonomy of human identity; namely, how to maintain, on the one hand, the incontestability of human freedom while, on the other hand, upholding the absolute necessity of a highest being. That is, how to maintain the independence of human existence while asserting the existence of a ground upon which humans can be interpreted to be somehow dependent. According to Schelling, "Most people, if they were honest, would have to admit that in terms of their ideas individual freedom seems to be in contradiction to almost all attributes of a Highest Being" (*HF* 10). Since "absolute causal power in one being leaves nothing but unconditional passivity for all the rest," it seems that in upholding the former, one must necessarily deny the possibility of the absolute unassailability of the autonomous freedom of the latter (11). So it is that a dichotomy is typically established between the independence of human existence and the necessity of divine existence such that seemingly one need reject one of these two positions in order to uphold the other. But, he insists, neither belief need be sacrificed; both can simultaneously be upheld. In fact, not only are the two ultimately reconcilable; but, as we shall see shortly, internally inhere to one another as interdependent. By Schelling's read, "dependence does not exclude autonomy or even freedom" (18). The apparent conflict between the dependence implied by the existence of an absolute causal power and human autonomy is not the consequent of their inherent natures, but is instead the result of a failure on our part to comprehend them correctly. It is the failure of our ability to logically posit the nature of their relation.

According to Schelling, the apparent dilemma between maintaining both the existence of a highest being and the independence of human existence is "the consequence of an imperfect and empty conception of the law of identity" (*HF* 19), one which "confuses identity with sameness," by confusing the subject of a sentence which attributes identity with its predicate (14–15, n. 1). Thus, when one says, for instance, that humans are independent and that humans are created, and therefore dependent, which results in the seemingly illogical proposition that "there exists an independent entity that is dependent," the relation of the predicate therein to its subject, while identifying it, should not be taken to replace it. Though the predicate in such a proposition *gives an identity* to the subject, it *does not share its meaning* with the subject. Instead, it *informs* that meaning by giving it an identity.

The subject thus remains, according to Schelling, fundamentally irreplaceable by its identifier, by its predicate. When, for example, "one says: A body is body; he is assuredly thinking something different in the subject of the sentence than in its predicate. In the former, that is, he refers to the unity, in the latter to the individual qualities contained in the concept, body, which are related to the unity as the *antecedens* to the *consequens*. Just this is the meaning of another older explanation, according to which subject and predicate are discriminated as being the unexpressed and the expressed [*implicitum et explicitum*]" (*HF* 14). As a result, argues Schelling, the proposition that "an autonomous entity is dependent," or the claim that an entity can exist such that it is a "dependent independence," though seemingly absurd and contradictory, is not necessarily so since therein the subject and the predicate do not share the same meaning. On the contrary, he maintains that the two, precisely because they diverge in meaning, actually accord to one another in a kind of essential unity. That is each *identifies* its other. That is, though the two appear to essentially diverge from one another, in actuality each one lays the ground and horizon for its other, allowing it to appear. Each establishes the basis for its other as the statement "the room is illuminated," silently refers the room to a darkness which, in its contrast and absence, allows the room to be recognized and *identified* as illuminated. Light, by Schelling's estimation, needs the darkness to be itself—it must essentially inhere to its other to appear independent of it.

So too, Schelling argues, independence necessarily references a subtle kind of dependence to which it must essentially inhere in order to be itself. Thus, to uphold the absolute independence and freedom of human existence is already to presuppose a kind of latent dependence, for something or someone cannot be said to be independent without pronouncing the passive dependence that lies within it. According to Schelling, "Necessity and freedom interpenetrate as one being which appears as the one or the other only as regarded from various aspects; in itself it is freedom, but formally regarded, necessity" (*HF* 63). Human existence can be taken, it seems, as both dependent or independent depending upon the light in which it is illuminated, the angle in which one regards it. So it is that the necessity of God's existence as an absolute causal power and human freedom actually rely on, are grounded in and inform one another's meaning.

Following his interpretation of the law of identity to its logical conclusion, Schelling goes so far as to argue that what is truly contradictory is the artificial severing of one of these concepts from its other: "it would indeed be contradictory if that which is dependent or consequent were not autonomous. There would be dependence without something being dependent, a result without a resultant [*consequentia absque consequente*], and therefore no true result; that is, the whole conception would vitiate itself" (*HF* 18–19, cf. 62). Thus, it is not folly to maintain some sort of conception of creation while at the same time upholding the absolute autonomy of the human subject. Indeed, as we have just seen, for him the two accord and mutually imply one another in the logical law of identity: if God is the highest power, then God is also free and autonomous, creation being a spontaneous act; and if God creates in its image, then the result of this creation must resemble God, which necessarily implies the autonomy and freedom of the created such that it too can act in a spontaneous way; human existence, one can conclude, must therefore be somehow understood as both a created and dependent entity that is simultaneously autonomous and independent.

Schelling writes, "The procession of things from God is God's self-revelation. But God can only reveal himself in creatures who resemble him, in free, self-activating beings for whose existence there is no reason save God, but who are as God is"

(*HF* 19). In fact, he goes on to say, "immanence in God is so little a contradiction of freedom that freedom alone, and insofar as it is free, exists in God, whereas all that lacks freedom, and insofar as it lacks freedom, is necessarily outside of God" (20). God is in a sense the space wherein entities can act as they want and are free to do with themselves what they will. Being in God then is a way of being in freedom, in the openness of independence and autonomy whilst being apart from God is precisely to relinquish that openness and freedom.

Given this conception, a problem with which Schelling must contend is how to account for a creation in such a way as to allow for this interrelation between freedom, independence, and the divine. For, if human autonomy naturally accords to an account of its dependence upon the divine through a creative act, one must have a viable way of accounting for the process of that creation and the form it takes that does not betray either. Unfortunately, Schelling, like Levinas, finds the traditional Christian rendering of the creation account as *ex nihilo* somehow dissatisfying. He even seems to hint that it is, in some ways at least, part of the reason behind the confusion between the concept of identity and sameness, a confusion which establishes what he sees as the false dichotomy between autonomy and dependence (see *HF* 11). But, like Levinas, Schelling will not entirely deny the notion of a creation *ex nihilo,* but instead reformulate it to fit more smoothly into his system (see 49, n. 2; *AW* 14).

FROM BEING TO BEINGS

By Schelling's account, the story of existence begins *before* the beginning, before creation itself. In this before all of the potentialities which will be actualized in creation lie dormant. There is no necessity, nor freedom in this before. No individuality, nor identity. All is formless and vague, devoid of any determinative distinctions. There is not even light nor dark, good nor bad.

It is like the nothing of Michael Ende's *Die unendliche Gischichte* which threatens to overwhelm and consume Fantasia, except here of course, the nothing is so complete that there is not anything to threaten or be threatened. It is what Schelling refers to as the teeming *Ungrund* from whence creation springs.

The utter lack of determinacy present in the *Ungrund* should not be taken to imply an absolute absence, however, nor some kind of pure emptiness. Though the indeterminacy of the *Ungrund* does represent for Schelling a kind of nothingness, it is not the nothing of sheer lack. It is, on the contrary, a nothing which takes the form of a total presence. The *Ungrund* which precedes creation is a presence so complete that *no-thing* can exist within it, no I nor Thou, human nor God. According to Schelling, "As [the *Ungrund*] precedes all antithesis these cannot be distinguishable in it or be present in any way at all" (*HF* 87). The *Ungrund* is the state of undifferentiated being, being as such, a state of existence so thick that no determinate thing can actualize itself from it. It is, in this regard, similar to Levinas's conception of the *il y a* from which human consciousness distinguishes itself in the hypostatic act, as we shall see in more detail shortly.

Schelling characterizes the *Ungrund* which precedes creation as "complete indifference and indistinguishability" (SS 203). It is pure being obsessed with itself, entirely contained in its own being and admitting no opposition or individuality within it. It is, by Schelling's reckoning, a totality so complete that it denies the emergence of any particular beings: the *Ungrund* is "Being, as not *having being*" (*AW* 22). Though the Ungrund is posited as that which in a sense *precedes* creation, that from whence the creative act emerges, it cannot be understood to be actually prior, but instead only logically prior. This is because the totality of the *Ungrund* is so complete that it even admits of no distinction in time. In the *Ungrund,* there is no before nor after. The march of time, and the change by which time is identified and measured, can only be spoken of within the context of separate and distinct entities which can move and change. According to Robert Brown, "the *Ungrund* logically (not temporally) precedes the ground-existence distinction. It is not the identity of the two fundamental principles, but their indifference. Since it is ontologically prior to all distinctions, and nothing can be predicated of it, it is sheer *Nichtsein* (nothing in particular), but it is not sheer *Nichts* (nothing at all, mere emptiness)."[9] One cannot even say of the *Ungrund* that it *is* that which is before the demarcation initiated in creation. No such identifiers can be attached to it as it absorbs all that is into itself, like the primeval cosmic singularity from whence the Big Bang is supposed to have proceeded. The *Ungrund* is in a sense a superdense gravitational force which admits of no outside to its inside.

Schelling thus figures the *Ungrund* as the quintessentially *unruly* as there is nothing within nor without it by which to distinguish or limit it—no borders or structures to it by which to take hold of it—it is the *anarchy* of the absolute presence of pure being (*HF* 34). He also figures the *Ungrund* as a kind of *pure will*—a will purified of any actuality, of anything through which to determine or realize itself. Its purity, of course, is a kind of curse: the *Ungrund* is doomed to be *nothing more* than will—it can never raise itself past *potentiality* and into existence as such—can never interact with any other through which it can become an *actuality*. Thus the *Ungrund*, understood as an unruly pure will, is condemned by its very nature to the hovering indistinguishability of pure possibility. According to Schelling, because the *Ungrund* in its totality disallows by its very nature the emergence of any determinate beings it takes on the character of a nothing, a *Nichtsein,* a *nihil.* It is out of this nothingness that creation precedes *ex nihilo.* The *nihil* which precedes the creative act is not then a "*nihil privativum.*"[10] Creation for Schelling, as for Levinas, is not then the projection of being into a pure absence, as traditionally implied by the terms *ex nihilo*. Instead, creation is for him the separation and determination of particular/singular beings/presences from out of the fog of absolute presence.

Creation, by Schelling's count, does not then proceed in concert with the power of being preserved in the *Ungrund*, but rather manifests itself as the *rupture of this totality*. That is, creation proceeds by way of a separation and demarcation of this totality and homogeneity such that individuality arises. The anarchy of the *Ungrund* is abolished and the separation of creation begins as soon as one being wrenches itself free from being as such. This occurs not through any affirmation of being, but precisely though a negation of the indefinite possibilities it presents.[11] That is, the separation of one being from the *Ungrund* proceeds through a denial and refusal of the power of being contained therein. "Negation," says Schelling, "is therefore the necessary precedent (*primus*) of every movement" (*AW* 16). "[T]he negating force represses itself and precisely thereby intensifies itself into an independent being" (17). Creation begins with this initial negation of pure and indeterminate potential by discerning between possibilities, *choosing* between them, and thereby endeavoring upon one determinate pathway. God, by choosing to separate itself from the indeterminacy of the *Ungrund*, by choosing to say "no" to the continuity of pure being and pure potential, sets an initial limit within being as such, God divides the actual from the possible, what shines and illuminates from what grounds and supports, the kinetic from the merely potential. God's choice, by differentiating between the infinite possibilities contained within the being of the *Ungrund*, thus appears as a kind of initial negation—namely, a negation of the infinite, of the indefinite, of the merely potential as it is maintained in the *Ungrund*. It is this initial negation of the totality of being as such which sets the stage for and allows for the affirmation of singular and particular beings to be enunciated in human existence.

Hence Schelling's claim that "if there were not the No, then the Yes would be without force. No 'I' without the 'not-I' and in as much as the 'not-I' is before the 'I'" (18).[12] As Judith Norman puts it, "creation occurs when God *decides* to put chaos out of its misery, as it were, and grant it a relative stability."[13] God's decision, by making, separating, and determining between possibilities, brings an end to the indeterminacy maintained in the *Ungrund* such that it now can act merely as the *Grund* for the emergence of singular and particular entities.

This choice, which *cuts apart* the totality of the *Ungrund* of being such that it can give rise as a *Grund* to particular beings, is God's primordial choice for itself; it is God's self-election according to Schelling.[14] Slavoj Žižek puts it thus: "in a primordial act, God Himself had to 'choose Himself,' His eternal character—to contract existence, to reveal himself."[15] This choice to separate out from the totality of being, this definition of a particular space within the infinite possibilities held out, by bringing the anarchic rule of the *Ungrund* to an end, demarcates the initiation of the creative act. But, according to Schelling, given the nature of the *Ungrund,* God's self-distinction, self-election, as well as separation and sectioning of the totality of being, cannot proceed through some form of positive self-postulation or expansion into existence. It cannot be some expression within being. Were it to proceed in this way, God's choice would not truly be a negation of the power of the *Ungrund,* but a mere manipulation of it. Were God to affirm God's own existence in self-election, being itself would be affirmed merely sending a ripple across the plane of existence maintained in the *Ungrund.*

Remember that the *Ungrund* is characterized as the totality of being obsessed with itself (*AW* 22). As the operation of this obsession and the totality of being, the *Ungrund* was argued to be little more than a self-positing will. Understood thusly, were the determinate choice God affected in the creative act to occur as a self-affirmation, as a self-postulation into existence, it would immediately be rendered futile and meaningless. It would be a mere perpetuation of the continuity of being present in the *Ungrund*. This is why Schelling insists that the choice expressed in the process of creation is not an affirmation of possibility, but a form of negation. To differentiate itself from the presence of the *Ungrund,* argues Schelling, God's own choice must not affirm the power of being, but must instead negate that power and open a way out of it. To choose itself and separate out from the *Ungrund* God must then withdraw from being—God must contract from existence—move otherwise than being. Initiated thusly through the self-restraint of the divine, creation proceeds not as the expansion of presence, but as a retreat from it—creation proceeds through God's self-denial, refusal to be, and rejection of the indeterminacy and totality of the *Ungrund.*

Under the influence of the work of Jacob Böehme, Schelling names this creative movement, in line with what we have already seen in Levinas, a *contractio dei*.[16] Schelling writes, "When God restricts Himself to the first power, this especially ought to be called a contraction [*Contraktion*]. Contraction, then, marks the beginning of all reality. For this reason, it is the contracting rather than the expanding nature that possesses a primordial and grounding force. Thus the beginning of creation amounts indeed to a *descent* [*Herablassung*] of God; He properly descends into the Real, contracts Himself entirely into the Real" (SS 203–04; translation corrected). The *Ungrund,* as the totality of the possible, forbids the existence of the Real; for therein no particular entity exists to which the Real can adhere. The homogeneity of a being without beings exists merely as the potentiality for real existents. God, by cutting free from the infinite possibilities maintained in the *Ungrund* and by coiling inwards, projecting beyond being, *condenses* into a determinate possibility and thereby creates the ground for the emergence of the *Real.* But, to be able to make this choice, to be able to provide this ground, God must necessarily cut free from certain other possibilities—God's choice necessarily and by definition places restrictions upon God itself.

One such possibility God refuses, the one possibility God *must* in a sense refuse in order to differentiate from the *Ungrund,* is the possibility to be as such, to be a determinate manifestation and presence. Thus, although the divine chooses itself, elects itself at the outset of the creative act, this election is not for itself to be as such—God's choice is not for presence. Instead, this choice is to negate the possibility of God's existence as a determinate manifestation. It is the realization of this possibility which is negated in the first choice, and which opens up the way for actuality. According to Schelling, "That God negates itself, restricts its being, and withdraws into itself, is the eternal force and might of God...the negating force is that which is singularly revealing of God. But the actual being of God is that which is concealed" (*AW* 15). The *contractio dei* of creation is God's self-election *not to be,* to withdraw from presence and not to manifest as a determinate being. Thus, "God," Schelling argues, "in accordance with His highest self, is not manifest" (80). Instead, in the original creative act, God chooses to project beyond being. In doing so, God provides a space wherein other existents may emerge. God *is* in a sense this space, the absence—this withdrawal from being wherein determinate beings can live, and move, and have their being. It is only in the form of this absence, this negation, that God is therefore manifest. It is this fact which leads Robert Brown to argue that Schelling's God "is not 'nothing'—*überall nicht,* nor 'absolutely not existing'—*schlechthin nicht existent....* The contraction, which negates the separateness of the powers, is the first real being (Dasein) of God in the world."[17] God's being, his existence, is the *absence* that follows in the wake of the primordial self-election not to be, God's self-abnegation of presence. God, as the withdrawal from being, as the absence which allows beings to be, thus becomes for Schelling the "Supreme being, the purest Love, infinite communicativity and emanation"—being here conceived of as the horizon upon which beings appear (5).

Identifying this choice to not be as a choice of the purest primordial love through which all of existence is given birth, Schelling claims that all forms of determinate love between particular beings, following in the path of God's primal love, do not affirm the power of being, but, like God, reach out *beyond* it. By his read, "love does not reach Being [*Seyn*] from itself. Being is ipseity [*Seinheit*], particularity. It is dislocation. But love has nothing to do with particularity. Love does not seek its own [*das Ihre*] and therefore it cannot be that which has being [*seyend seyn*] with regard to itself" (*AW* 5–6). Particular beings, in as much as they love, and in doing so take up the primordial love from whence their being is preceded, seem to reach out beyond their particularity, their being, and into that absence, that withdrawal from being which allowed them to be in the first place. The procreation which results from this love is an affirmation in being of the initial withdrawal from being which conditions it. Love between determinate beings and its result thus appear to be a determinate reflection of the self-contraction of God in the creative act at the outset of existence.[18]

God, acting out of love, and thus, by definition for Schelling, stretching out beyond being, does not therefore emerge from the creative process as a determinate being, but rather as a determinate possibility—a determinate possibility which grounds the emergence of all actual beings. Thus, while God may never achieve the status of *actuality* in the same way that other determinate beings, like human beings, are actual; God must nevertheless be conceived of as *real*—for it is God's contraction into the *ground* of existence that ushers in reality as we know it. As we will see in more detail shortly, God's reality is manifest, as it were, as an ideal possibility for human existence—as a potentiality and promise held out for humans through which they can conceive and realize themselves more fully.[19]

The process of creation, the severing of the totality of the *Ungrund,* is not concluded with the *contractio dei* alone as no actual being emanates from it, only the nonbeing of God, God's existence as an *Ideal* (a product of ideation). God's withdrawal from being only lays the groundwork for the independent emergence of being, it allows for the existence of the world (*HF* 28). Schelling writes, "God yields the ideas which were in him without independent life, to selfhood and non-being, so that in being called from this into life, they may again be in him as independent entities. Thus in freedom the basis effects the separation and the judgment ($\chi\rho\iota\sigma\iota\varsigma$) and in this very way accomplishes God's complete actualization" (85). On the ground of the Real established in God's contraction and separation from the *Ungrund,* God's limitation of the indefinite possibilities maintained therein, human existence is presented as a *specific possibility* which can emerge as a determinate freedom. In other words, the absence opened up by God's withdrawal from being grants humanity the freedom to extricate itself from the totality of the *Ungrund*. This is a possibility which is actualized, like God's self-election, through a choice. But, unlike God's, this choice no longer takes the form of a negation, but of an affirmation.[20] In creation, human existence elects itself by *positing* itself, by projecting its specific and determinate being away from and into the emptiness left by God's withdrawal. Human emergence from the *Ungrund* is thus an autonomous and spontaneous act, but one which is, nonetheless, dependent upon the initial self-election of God—dependent upon the creative *contractio dei*. Thus though human beings and the world are entirely independent from God in their existence, this independence is nevertheless preceded and conditioned by God's self-negation: "That original negation is still the mother and wet-nurse of the entire world that is visible to us" (*AW* 30). Thus, concludes Schelling, "this act of restriction [*Einschränkung*] or descent on the part of God is spontaneous [*freiwillig*]. Hence the explanation of the world has no other ground than the freedom of God. Only God Himself can break with the absolute identity of His essence and thereby can create the space for a revelation" (SS 204).

The Mutuality of Independence and Dependence

The claim that human nature is free and independent on the basis of its dependence upon creation can be a bit misleading, however. For creation is not, for Schelling, what precedes this autonomous emergence, but rather precisely what is fulfilled by it. According to him, creation is therefore not complete until human existence emerges independently from the *Ungrund:* "the process of creation can rest only once consciousness has been awakened and created from the unconscious and from the depth of matter, namely, in man" (SS 208). Since creation is initiated by the withdrawal of God from being, actual *beings* are only differentiated and distinguished from the totality of the *Ungrund,* completing its destruction, once human beings posit themselves. Hence his claim that "only in man, then, is the Word completely articulate," the word which was at the beginning of creation (*HF* 39). The primordial "no" from whence independent being's obtain the freedom to posit their own existence only becomes fully articulate, and even there only silently, in the human affirmation of being, in the human "yes." This affirmation, this independence in which God's contraction as the creative act is fulfilled, is the work of human consciousness (SS 200). It is the life of consciousness then, as the self-positing of human existence, that ultimately signals the demise of the *Ungrund*. This conscious life, though hidden from observation from the outside, is evidenced in the functioning of reason. By his read, "the first effect of reason in nature is the separation of forces" (*HF* 36).[21] This of course logically follows from the account of creation given above, for if consciousness is the final separation of beings from being, then its concrete operation should also proceed by way of a separation. As a result, though creation is initiated by God, and human existence is thus made dependent upon another to whom absolute causal power can be attributed, it remains irrevocably and radically independent. So, concludes Schelling, "man's being is essentially *his own deed*" (63).

The self, which emerges from the totality of being effected through the life of consciousness, Schelling ties essentially to the human possibility of moral and ethical choice (*AW* 85). With the separation of human beings from the absolute being of the *Ungrund* other distinct possibilities arise concurrently, like the good and the bad, between which they must choose. Human beings, like God, though free and autonomous, are thus *not absolutely free;* they do not have access to an infinitude of possibilities. On the contrary, the very destruction of the *Ungrund*, as we have seen, implies the negation of a totality of possibilities. The possibility to choose to be good or to choose to be bad and other such definite possibilities presented to human existence are, in a sense, the shrapnel which result from the implosion of the absolute pure possibility of the *Ungrund*. The freedom which human beings posit themselves into, the absence provided by the *contractio dei*, is thus not an *absolute freedom,* but instead a *definite freedom*—it is the freedom to choose between definite possibilities, it is the freedom to choose between good and evil.

Human freedom is thus defined by Schelling as situated between these determinate possibilities; hence his claim that "the real and vital conception of freedom is that it is a possibility of good and evil" (*HF* 26). The real hard core of human freedom is always affected in a moral choice. He goes on to argue that the highest expression of the moral choice that is human freedom is to choose for the good. This choice is for him the choice to follow in the path of the *contractio dei;* it is the choice to follow the love that precipitated human existence. Thus, according to Schelling, "the highest moral act of man," is to separate and distance himself from his own being (SS 208). And, "whoever is unable to separate himself from his Being (i.e. whoever cannot become independent and free from it) but remains altogether entangled in it, and one with, his Being is completely trapped by his selfhood and unable to improve himself, be it morally or intellectually" (209). By grounding human existence in its own consciousness, by making it the initiator of its emergence as a singular being from the *Ungrund,* Schelling forges a path by which human independence can be tied to an account of creation and the two can be united. In fact, the two are so inexorably bound to one another for him that not only can human independence be deemed from one perspective to actually be a dependence upon God, but God's very independence can be deemed somehow dependent upon humanity. Indeed, as a determinate possibility which is held out to human existence, God's existence is only realizable through our orientation toward it as a possibility. Hence Alan White's observation that for Schelling, "God is the unity of his existence and the ground of his existence, but he can therefore come to be only as the human individual comes to be, only in a primal self-reflecting choice."[22] But, one must remember that for Schelling God does not come to be as any *actual existence,* but instead as an emergent determinate possibility—a possibility which is held out to determinate beings, and chief amongst them, human beings.

God's existence as a determinate possibility is therefore only present to human existence as a kind of eternal promise for the future.[23] In the present time in which human existence *is,* however, God *is not.* God's being, claims Schelling, cannot be conjugated in our time, but only in the future tense as an outstanding possibility, the possibility of a future period/age wherein God will be manifest in actuality.[24] God is in a sense the eternally *becoming*. "God is not manifest. God manifests himself. He is not actual. He *becomes* actual" (*AW* 80; italics mine). God's actuality is only as a promise, as something which is eternally on its way, always not-quite-yet, always on approach without ever fully arriving.[25] This argument has led Robert Brown to observe that for Schelling "God's being is a life, not an abstract *Sein*. Therefore it implies a process of becoming and development."[26] Thus, though human existence is dependent upon God, God's existence is for us never fully manifest or clearly present—it is always somehow unfulfilled. And, God's coming to be into existence, as a life and manifestation which is actualizing through the independence of the created world, is somehow dependent upon that creation.

Since God's being is never something which is wholly present within the world, its possibility—the recognition of the existence of God as a determinate possibility for human existence—is something which can only be concluded posterior to and on the basis of the independence of human existence and the world in which it dwells (SS 200).[27] Again, Robert Brown claims that for Schelling God's existence is thus "not an existence that can be anticipated, prescribed, or deduced, but only one to be acknowledged *a posteriori*, within history."[28] Thus, though God arises from the indifference of the *Ungrund*, the possibility of God immediately "sinks back down into the unfathomable depths," repressing manifestation, becoming little more than the ground of existence and a promise held out for the end of time (*AW* 80).

According to Schelling it is, in fact, on the basis of God's self-concealment at the inception of creation that the beginning of human existence and time can even proceed. He writes, "By virtue of restricting Himself to the first power—by being spontaneously only *One*, although capable of being *all*—God affects a beginning of time (*nota bene:* not *in* time)" (SS 203). God's self-negation at the outset of creation initiates the flow of time, the actual occurrence of this act, however, cannot therefore be placed within time. It is the condition of time, and not, therefore, present in time. "God's self-restriction," writes Schelling, "implies a beginning *of* time, though not a beginning *in* time. God himself is not, therefore being placed in time" (204). The creative act, then, also cannot be placed at any moment within determinate human history, for time and history only begin with the procession of being initiated in the human contraction of being into conscious life, the act which concludes creation. Thus creation, though the foundation of human existence and universal history, cannot be made a part of that history, cannot be conceptualized as ever actually having happened, as it were. Creation is thus that which *never was,* it never *actually happened,* as it cannot be contained in any temporal past. Creation instead belongs to a sort of logical past—a logically posited past which precedes all time, which precedes time itself. Creation belongs then to what Schelling names the *eternally past,* a term which indicates for him a time before time—a happening before any happening (*AW* 39). It does not then belong to any past which has merely been sucked down through the ages to reside in a time immemorial to any creature. It is beyond any possible memory, as such. It is, by its very nature, atemporal.[29]

Elsewhere, Schelling names the creative act the *eternal beginning:* "The beginning in [God] is an eternal beginning, that is, a beginning that was as such, from all eternity and still always is and one that never ceases to be a beginning" (*AW* 17).[30] As an eternal beginning, it is a beginning which is still happening now, as it were. Creation is not only relegated to the eternally past then, but is also included in the eternally happening—the realm of the never full, completed, or finished. It is in a sense still continuing in the life of independent existence. It is becoming alongside the existence of God. Creation, then like God, is something which is always held out as a possibility to human beings which comes from the future. It is a possibility contained in the being of God which approaches from a distant horizon opening human existence one up and reorienting its understanding of its own being.

The coming to be of existence initiated in creation and perpetuated and maintained in the becoming of God thus never *was* as some occurrence in history, but instead always *might be* as a determinate possibility for one's own understanding of what preceded and conditioned that possibility. Creation is thus for Schelling the expression of a kind of *ideality,* an idea which resides in the consciousness of the human subject for how it can conceive of itself. It thus expresses not any actual past, but rather a purely ideal past—not a past which was ever present, but a past which has always already occurred, or is always already occurring.[31] This explains Schelling's insistence that "creation is not an event but an *act*" (*HF* 75; italics mine). Creation then, and along with it God's existence, is never something fully manifest, present in time, but rather something which, in the words of Slavoj Žižek, "can be described (narrated) only *post factum,* after it has already taken place."[32] In this sense, creation, though logically prior to our existence, actually more appropriately and chronologically belongs to a time posterior to human independence. Creation is a logical conclusion formulated on the basis of a thorough observation of the nature of human existence. Thus, though independent existence is established and dependent upon creation as an *act,* creation as a *narrative,* as a *concept,* is somehow grounded in and dependent upon the nature of human existence. A convenient formulation can be made as follows: creation is the logical ground for the actuality of human existence and human existence is the actual ground for the logical conclusion of creation. Given the way the happening of the creative act is derived on the basis of human existence, and the way that it continues in human history, and even the way that, in Schelling's narrative, creation is only concluded in the human instantiation of its own being, human existence can be seen as somehow participatory in their own creation (64). Again, human beings are coconspiratorial in their own creation. By existing, human existence carries creation from out of the depths of a possible time that never was and into the actuality of living history. So it is that God and creation, as it were, ride into actuality on the back of human history.

The eternally becoming beginning of existence, the possibility of "a true beginning, a beginning that never ceases to be a beginning," is grounded in the way in which God contracted into nonexistence and projected into a beyond being that is situated on the distant horizon of human history as a future possibility (*AW* 85). According to Schelling, "The beginning is only the beginning insofar as it is not that which should actually be, that which truthfully and in itself has being. If there is therefore a decision, then that which can only be posited at the beginning inclines, for the most part and in its particular way, to the nature of that which does not have being" (13). Were the possibility of creation and the existence of God to actually take on being and presence in history, the emergence of either one as a determinate actuality would be so complete and overwhelming as to eclipse the emergence of any other independent being, thus nullifying any true beginning and plunging any possibility of distinction, even its own, back into the indefinite chaos of a being without beings—it would signal the return of the *Ungrund*. For God to truly initiate a beginning in the creative act then—a beginning which precedes all beginnings—God must recede into the shadows of nonexistence, appearing only as a determinate possibility for a future beyond all time.

SCHELLING AND LEVINAS: A MISSED CONNECTION

Clearly there are a number of similarities between Schelling and Levinas's respective accounts of the origin, procession, and result of the creative act, a similarity duly noted by Fiona

Steinkamp in her article "Eternity and Time: Levinas Returns to Schelling."[33] By Steinkamp's read, Levinas and Schelling's mutual accounts of "the philosophic problems of consciousness, the nature of what is prior to both consciousness and being, and how eternity and time are related" are so similar that in many ways Levinas's work could even be read, as the title of her article indicates, as a "return" to Schelling.[34]

Steinkamp begins her comparison of the two authors with a description of Levinas's *il y a* as a "field of forces," an idea she cribs from pages of *Time and the Other* (*TO* 46).[35] This "field of forces," she contends, is described by Levinas as preceding being. Understood as such, she describes the *il y a* as "that to which beings and persons *return;* it is itself *neither a being nor consciousness* but presumably is *prior to either* of them."[36] What Steinkamp seems to fail to notice here is Levinas's resort to the Heideggerian distinction between being and beings, already referred to as the ontological difference.[37] For, while it is true that the *il y a* precedes *beings,* it is not true that it precedes *being as such.* Just the opposite, for, as we have seen, the *il y a* is being as such, it *is* being without any determinations. Thus while the *il y a* may manifest as a "field of forces," this field should not be placed beyond or before the realm of being. Granted, in as much as the *il y a* precedes the emergence of beings, and therefore seems to betray any real meaning implied in the ontological difference, and seemingly with it the possibility of asserting its existence as being as such (i.e., how could there be a being without any beings to presence it), this is precisely Levinas's claim. In fact that is what makes it so unique. For Levinas, the *il y a* which precedes creation is precisely such a being without beings. Failing to note the singularity of Levinas's account of the *il y a* and how it ruptures the traditional logic of ontological separation, Steinkamp forges ahead comparing her description of Levinas's *il y a* to the field of forces described by Schelling as residing within what he names "the oldest of all beings," namely God.³⁸ In doing so she sets up a problem which plagues the rest of her argument, for, given what we have just seen concerning Schelling's account of God as precisely that which breaks with the totality of being, it is a grave mistake to compare God with Levinas's *il y a*.³⁹

Nevertheless, this is precisely the comparison that Steinkamp makes. According to her, Schelling's God contains within its being both the principal of affirmation and negation, and the unity of these two principles, thus God too contains within a "field of forces" similar, in her eyes, to the one described by Levinas as present in the *il y a,* both suggesting, she claims, a totality from whence there is no escape. Furthermore, she argues, since this field of forces encapsulated in Schelling's God serves as the foundation of all beings, as that "which underlies all being," then it too can be seen as "prior to" being.⁴⁰

What Steinkamp fails to see is that by describing God as holding in unity the principles of negation and affirmation, Schelling has already established this God as a break with the indifference implied in Levinas's use of the phrase "field of forces," for negation and affirmation are already two distinct forces from one another, and thus *not* representative of the kind of absolute homogeny implied in Levinas's descriptions of the *il y a*.⁴¹ Indeed, quite in contrast to Steinkamp's argument, if a corollary to Schelling's descriptions of God is to be found anywhere in Levinas, it is to be found in his own descriptions of the divine. God for both thinkers is accounted for as that self-nugatory will that separates itself from the totality of indifference by projecting itself otherwise than being. This negation is even described by both as initiating in the contraction of God such that an absence or space is opened up wherein independent beings may project themselves into being, emerging on their own recognizance. Thus, though it is true that Schelling posits God as the unity of the principle of affirmation and negation, the unity implied therein does amount to a totality or an indifference akin to the *il y a*.⁴²

This is evident, first and foremost, in the fact that, according to Schelling, this unity does not happen *before time,* in the time of indifference, but is rather a promise held out for the end of time. In this way again we see a parallel between Schelling's God and Levinas's. Since both account for the initial rupture with the totality of indifference with a kind of primordial negation, God for both must not be understood as some kind of *being,* present in the now. Instead, the being of God in both Schelling and Levinas's respective accounts is somehow a projection of that which lies *beyond* time as a promise for a future ever more distant. God, they both seem to argue, should thus not be understood as something which *is,* nor ever really *was* in some distant past before time, but only as a potentiality and a promise for the future. The unity of forces that is promised in Schelling's descriptions of God, far from resembling the *il y a,* seems more akin to Levinas's hope for the messianic first enunciated in *Totality and Infinity* (see *TI* 285) but not fully explored until the later works, a hope which expresses for him the idea of an eternal time—the eternal approach of the Other/God.

Furthermore, the unity promised in Schelling's God should not be confused with Levinas's *il y a* as it does not imply a totality. In contrast to Steinkamp's read, the unity of principles promised in God's coming to be is not the promise of some sort of dialectical resolution such that a new totality is borne of their reconciliation. Quite the opposite, according to Schelling, the unity of forces promised in God's becoming is in a sense the final balancing of the principles within God such that though they must forever rival one another, this rivalry will finally appear as part of the same movement instead of appearing as two conflicting movements. Their unity is thus one wherein their singularity is maintained, and not one wherein it is erased resulting in some kind of homogeny, as implied by Steinkamp.

By comparing the unity promised in Schelling's God to the totality contained in Levinas's descriptions of the *il y a,* Steinkamp seems to have made precisely the same mistake that Schelling warns against at the beginning of *Of Human Freedom,* that of failing to see the difference between the law of identity and the law of sameness. It is, as we have seen, thoroughly misguided to compare Schelling's conception of the divine with Levinas's understanding of Being as such, especially when there is already something within Schelling's system than can serve this purpose, namely the *Ungrund*.

Schelling's descriptions of the *Ungrund,* as the indifference out of which and in contrast to which existence must define itself, seem to be much more suited to comparison with Levinas's account of the *il y a* than anything else. For both Schelling's *Ungrund* and Levinas's *il y a* describe a totality so complete that no independent existence can arise within them. Furthermore, both thinkers identify the power of this indifference with the totality of a being without beings, a power which must be disrupted for the procession of independent entities to occur. Finally, both situate this indifference and its negation in a time eternally past.

This notion of the eternally past and the theory of temporality implied in it is yet another point of contention with Steinkamp's failed comparison. By her read, both thinkers, by describing what is "prior to being" draw upon a notion of eternity.[43] Both, she also claims, making reference to Levinas's account of hypostasis, also posit the interruption of this eternity as the initiation of time in the form of the present and the accompanying beings which instantiate it.[44] Thus, she argues, both account for the initiation of time in a decisive and free act, one which she explores in Schelling as God's nugatory procession. But here again Steinkamp seems to miss a crucial point. While it is true that time commences for Schelling in the negation of the indifference maintained in the *Ungrund* of existence and thus also of a kind of eternity, we must remember that God's negation is not directed at either the being of the *Ungrund* or the continuity of time maintained therein, but at itself. God's rupture with the power and continuity of the *Ungrund* does not proceed via a restriction against the being of the *Ungrund,* but in God's existential self-denial. It is a negation directed self-ward, as it were. The actual progression of time instantiated in the existence of independent entities thus does not begin with God's decision, but with its counterpart, the spontaneous decision of free and independent beings. In this sense it is not God who is the author of time, but human beings. God's relation to time in both Schelling and Levinas is as the promise which lies at the end of it—God for both of them is in some sense the promise that time may eventually be redeemed.

On the basis of her claims that both argue for a notion of an eternity which precedes being, the interruption of that eternity signaling the initiation of time and the birth of the present, Steinkamp argues that both Schelling and Levinas maintain a link between time and that eternity in the form of the "trace." Thus, the fact that Schelling's preceding principles can be "'traced' in our present,"[45] she argues, can be compared to "Levinas's remark that the trace leads to 'an absolute past which writes all time.'"[46] But here again Steinkamp's comparisons miss their mark, as she fails to distinguish between the notion of eternity and the notion of infinity, a mistake wrapped up in failing to understand the difference between the logically prior and the chronologically prior. Remember that for Levinas the trace present in the face of the Other, though presenting the creative act, is not a reference to the *eternally* past, and most certainly not to the indifference which precedes the present, but instead signals that which is *infinitely* in the future. Thus though creation precedes human existence, it is experienced not in that which lies temporally *before* that existence, but in that which is *situated before* (i.e., *in front of*) it, that is, the other, the ethical demand of the face, the infinite, and the future. The eternal, on the other hand, is precisely what is ruptured by this existence in the hypostatic act. It is not at all then what is signaled in the trace.

By initially confusing the meaning of that which logically precedes being in the work of Schelling and Levinas, and then drawing parallels between the two on the basis of that confusion, Steinkamp fails to grasp what is really vital in the comparison she hopes to draw. Still, despite some the equivocation in her analysis, Steinkamp should be commended none the less for sniffing out a comparison that seems to have been almost entirely overlooked by the scholarly community thus far. For, it is true that a number of apparent comparisons exist between the work of Schelling and Levinas, even though Steinkamp's article is one of the two or three published on this link, and certainly the most exhaustive of the lot. While it is clear that Levinas and Schelling's work shares a number of significant insights, they are probably not enough to warrant describing the former as little more than a "return" to the latter. To invoke Schelling's understanding of the law of identity, perhaps it is best to say that while his work can be *identified* with that of Levinas's, the two cannot be taken to say the *same* thing.

THE LEGACY OF CREATION: ETHICS AND LONGING

One of the crucial differences between the work of Schelling and Levinas rests in the ethical value they ascribe to the indifference which precedes creation. As we have seen, Levinas, for his part, given his identification of the good with difference and the otherwise, aligns the indifference of the *il y a* with evil. Since the *il y a* affords no room for ethical choice, it traps existents in a palpable moral insipidity so complete that any possibility for the election of the good is entirely suffocated. Thus, the possibility of the good appears only with the interruption of this totality. The good is in fact for him that very force which rips apart the totality of the *il y a* and allows for the separation of singularity.

Now, while Schelling, in his turn, does associate the division of the indifference held together in the *Ungrund* with a moral value (i.e., human existence's emergence as situated before the choice for good or evil only out of the rupture of the *Ungrund*), he does not go so far as Levinas in ascribing a negative ethical value to the *Ungrund* itself. The *Ungrund* for Schelling expresses nothing more than a simple total presence. A presence so complete, moreover, that it allows for no such distinctions between good and evil. The *Ungrund* cannot then be ascribed an ethical value for Schelling as it is in Levinas. It is instead, he claims, "neutral towards both," good and evil (*HF* 88).[47] Were one to postfactually ascribe some value to the *Ungrund*, one would have to see it as a somehow beneficiary force for "*without* indifference, that is, *without* the groundless [*Ungrund*], there would be no twofoldness of the principles" (88). The *Ungrund*, as that which eventually gives way to the ground of existence, and therefore also to the singularity of human existence and the possibility of good, must somehow be appreciated. Its neutrality is thus precisely what recommends it for Schelling, whereas it is this same neutrality which condemns it for Levinas. Thus though it need be wrought asunder for the emergence of singularity and the good like the *il y a,* the *Ungrund* is not ethically equivalent to it by Schelling's descriptions.

Perhaps one of the most interesting differences between the work of Schelling and Levinas, in as much as we have explored them here, lies in how they respectively account for the legacy of the creative act. As we have seen, for Levinas the chief legacy left by God's *contractio dei* is the ethical situation. Indeed for Levinas there is no real break between the two. Creation is, after all, the rupture with a totality which in some ways, as the first act, defines the realm of the ethical. Thus, just as creation is initiated by God's self-contraction which gives way and opens a space for human beings passage into existence, so too, thinks Levinas, must human beings give way to the Other by checking their natural mode of projecting into the world such that the Other can have room to be, as we saw in the last chapter. This is the ethical legacy of creation. So it is for Levinas that the ethical act is exemplified in the "after you, sir" that one addresses to the Other when one finds oneself in competition with the Other, an act which, for him, follows in the wake of God's "after you, sir" addressed to determinate existents at the dawn of creation (see *OTB* 117; *EI* 89).[48] For Levinas, in creation God hold's itself back such that human existence has room to pass through, just as one must hold him or herself back when confronted with the existence of the Other and the demand to be issued in the face of that Other. The ethical act for Levinas thus harkens back to the time of creation, it serves as a kind of window to creation such that it can appear before us as a possibility for how we understand ourselves. So it is that according to Levinas the creative act is only fully articulated in the ethical act. The ethical act is that which carries the meaning and the trace of creation into the now of human existence.

Schelling would certainly not disagree with Levinas's linking of ethics and creation. Indeed, for Schelling the ethical choice placed before human existence, the choice by which that existence is in fact defined, is most certainly the legacy of creation. And too, humanity's choice for the good is modeled, as for Levinas, on God's self-election *not* to be. Thus, says Schelling, as we have suggested, the greatest moral good can only be achieved by humans through a self-initiated movement away from their own being (SS 208). Similarly, human beings are not alone in the world but are with others (226) and are furthermore only fully realized through these others (*AW* xxxvi). Thus, the human movement toward the moral good defined as one's self-initiated distancing from one's own being is only achieved through the intervention of others. Indeed, says Schelling, a being's liberation from itself can only be effected through the other (23). Clearly, he sees in this ethical movement a legacy of the creative act in much the same way that Levinas does. But, for Schelling, this is not the main way in which the legacy of creation is felt by human beings. Thus, while ethics does carry a trace of creation, as indeed, all emergent entities do, the ethical encounter is not for Schelling the phenomenon in which this trace is most felt. Instead, argues Schelling, and this is where his work becomes especially illuminative for the study at hand, the legacy of the creative act is most pronounced for human existence in the experience of longing (*Sehnsucht*).

According to Schelling, creation, as the rupture of the *Ungrund* which proceeds out of God's self-abnegation of being, is the concrete demonstration of God's longing for being, God's longing for self-realization (*HF* 34, 74; *AW* 21).[49] This longing is in fact, according to some readers, God's primal nature.[50] Remember, however that given the way in which God's nature is projected out beyond being, and displaced onto to an eternally distant past and an always approaching future, the self-realization longed for can never be fulfilled. It is the mark of God's nonexistence striving eternally within the heart of what arises in the wake of God's self-contraction—that which reflects and completes the creative act, namely human existence. So it is that, according to Schelling, God's longing for being, a longing which by the very nature of God and creation can never come to completion or be satisfied, is somehow displaced, sublimated as it were, into human life. This is why human life is so deeply marked by a protracted desire and longing which stretches out beyond the horizon of the furthest future and seems to be irrevocably insatiable.

Longing is for Schelling the legacy of our patronage by God and the trace of God's contraction; and therefore, the primary way in which we primordially experience God. So it is, claims Schelling, that human longing establishes a "rapport with God"

(SS 232) such that the image and *idea* of the possibility of God is made available to us. God is in a sense *seen* and felt, through human longing: "Man's will is the seed—concealed in eternal longing—of God, present as yet only in the depths,—the divine light of life locked in the deeps which God divined when he determined to will nature. Only in him (in man) did God love the world,—and *it was this very image of God which was grasped in its center by longing* when it opposed itself to light. By reason of the fact that man takes his rise from the depths (that he is a creature) he contains a principle relatively independent of God" (*HF* 38–39; italics mine). Thus, whereas ethics is the primary way in which the metaphysical existence of God and the legacy of creation is expressed according to Levinas, for Schelling the seeds of these metaphysical possibilities are contained in human longing. Hence, claims Schelling, while human existence may remain eternally consciously ignorant of its dependence upon a creative act grounded in the nonexistence of the divine, the soul will always be somehow "conscientious of creation," through its deepest longings (*AW* xxxvi).

According to Schelling, the creative act is not directly signified in human longing, but indirectly. That is, since the creative act proceeds by way of a projection beyond being it cannot be strictly present within being. The evidence and trace of the creative act maintained in human longing is not therefore the contraction of God as such, the absence which flows from his contraction, but the totality and abundance which is destroyed thereby. In other words, what longing retains is, in a sense, a shard of the *Ungrund* which implodes with the contraction of God. Though the *Ungrund* is itself the indifferent totality of pure being, it is also the expression of a kind of pure will, a will that cannot actualize itself precisely because of its purity, precisely because it is not contaminated by any determinate beings through which it could realize itself. God's longing for beng is in a sense what congeals out of the indeterminate and unruly will of the *Ungrund,* which, in a play on the etymology of longing, Schelling also names an obsession or addiction.

According to Schelling "the obsession [*Sucht*] [of the *Ungrund*] abates into longing [*Sehnsucht*], wild desire turns into a longing to ally itself, as if it were its own true or highest self, with the will that wills nothing, with eternal freedom" (*AW* 28). Longing is the desire for a specific being, a specific self, namely the being and selfhood of God, which is resolved from the sickly desire of the *Ungrund*.[51] But, since such a selfhood and being cannot be actualized as such, as it is a being that would be just as absolute as the *Ungrund* and therefore indistinguishable from it, the only way in which it can at least be separated and made somehow determinate is by renouncing the claim to being in actuality and reducing itself to an existence as a determinate possibility, a possibility held out and projected into the ever distant future. This possibility, precisely because it is determinate however, already demarcates a separation and independence of the divine from the indeterminate totality of the *Ungrund*. Still, the longing to be as such remains unfulfilled and thereby eternally present in that which arises in the space opened up by the contraction of God, namely human existence. This longing, as the result of the condensation of the unruly willing of the *Ungrund* thus signals the conversion of the *Ungrund* into the *Grund* of human existence. Still, it ever retains the mark of its origins—ever signals the unruly depths from whence it sprung, and thereby, only negatively and logically signals the creative act which allowed stability to emerge from it.[52] Hence Schelling's now infamous declaration that through the order of creation "the unruly lies ever in the depths," as "the *irreducible remainder* which cannot be resolved into reason" (*HF* 34; italics mine).

Since the contraction of being into the definite and independent entity that is human existence is primarily effected through the use of consciousness and reason, its dependence upon the creative act is that which in a sense exceeds the bounds of its finitude and thought. It is that which eternally overflows definite representation and can only be *felt* in the affectivity of longing. So it is for Schelling that though human longing signals the absence of God, it is actually the expression of a kind of abundance, a kind of too-much-ness from whence all existence springs. Longing is thus the expression of the absence of God and the abundance of the *Ungrund,* it is the uneasy union of the twin opposing primeval forces (*Penia* and *Poros*) which gave birth to human existence. Longing is thus much more than any merely subjective emotion. It is instead the determinate way in which God's existence is manifest and expressed—the very way in which the possibility of God's being is presented. Longing emerges as the expression of the curious presence of the divine in human life—the presence of that which is beyond being and presence, the presence of a god who withdraws from being.

Given the fact that this longing is directed out toward the eternal future seemingly promised in the possibility of God's being, but also emerges out of the eternally past from whence this possibility arises, longing seems to be experienced as simultaneously the drive to proceed further than the now and the desire to return to another time—this is perhaps why longing can so easily be confused with nostalgia. Schelling himself when describing the affectivity of longing characterizes it as a kind of desire to return (*HF* 36). Indeed, he has even named it a curious kind of melancholy (*Schwermuth*) which seemingly "mourns a lost good" (SS 230). What is important to remember here, however, is that this lost past or good to which one may attach their longing is a past which never was, it is the desire for a good which never presented itself, but instead projected itself out past the horizon of the now. Thus, though longing can be felt as the desire to recuperate the existence of the divine which is lost in its self-abnegation and contraction, this recovery is one which is properly directed not backward but forward, toward the eternally future in which the existence of the divine now resides as a promise.[53] According to Schelling, though longing may be inappropriately understood or experienced as directed backward, it is not properly a retrograde, but a progression, a movement beyond the now and toward the eternally distant future in which the being of God is projected as a kind of eternal promise.

The work of longing, this propulsion toward the beyond, is effected, thinks Schelling, by way of an internal division within human existence. Just as God's longing for being was meted out through the division and separation in the creative act, so the work of human longing births an inner division within human existence (*AW* 89–90). Indeed, as the direct expression of the creative act, longing manifests as precisely that force which effects a distance within human existence such that human beings can separate and divide themselves from their own being and interests and pursue another path is the birth of ethics and of erotic love. It is this distance, this possibility which is opened through it whereby one can choose otherwise than one's own interests, which is for Schelling one of the determinate features of human longing. It is this feature of longing which fundamentally distinguishes it from other forms of desire.

Like Levinas, Schelling characterizes most forms of determinate human desire as a variation of a "hunger" for and "addiction" to being (*AW* 231). By his read, most forms of human desire are the expression of the human interest in pursuing and ameliorating its own goods or alleviating and avoiding that which threatens it as bad. As such, they are all the expression of the power and urgency of the call of being upon human existence and the expression of a force which drives it inward on itself and resembles, albeit on a small scale, the *Ungrund*'s will for itself, as mentioned before, Schelling also identifies as a kind of obsession and addiction (*Sucht*). Longing (*Sehnsucht*), on the other hand, as the expression of God's contraction of that will into a determinate desire to be, which, pursued by way of God's self-projection into nonexistence and converted into the desire for an eternally distant future, is not bound to the realm of being, but expresses precisely the separation from that being such that something else may *come to be*. Longing, for Schelling, is thus not the province of being, but of *becoming*: "Longing [*Sehnsucht*] has no relation to that pure spirit except that pure spirit is the freedom *to be* and in as much as it *is*, in comparison with all else, *has being* (τὸ ''ON). In contrast, longing has in itself the *possibility to come to Being,* to subject (understood in the authentic meaning of the word), to the stuff of actualization" (28; italics mine, translation modified). The "rapport with God" (SS 232) mentioned earlier, which is established in human longing, is in part grounded in the fact that longing bears within it this intrinsic connection to the realm of becoming—a connection that evidences a break within human existence from the pull of being. According to Schelling "this cision, this inner divergence, the work of true longing [*Sehnsucht*], is the first condition of every rapport with the divine" (*AW* 28; translation modified).[54] In this way, Schelling unites the work reason and function of longing: "Reason, in the light which has appeared in the beginnings of nature, rouses longing (which is yearning to return into itself) to divide the forces (to surrender darkness) and in this very division brings out the unity enclosed in what is divided, the hidden light" (*HF* 36). Reason, the product of consciousness, and longing, as an affectivity which expresses that which overflows and cannot be contained by consciousness, thus work in concert to illuminate the nature of human existence, and thereby the silent potentiality of the existence of God contained therein. Affectivity and reason are not in opposition for Schelling, but two expressions of the same movement, one collecting that which cannot be contained by its other.

CONCLUSIONS

Schelling's work aids our investigation by illuminating the metaphysical depths and implications of what we have discovered thus far concerning the nature of human longing. That is, it casts much of what we have already seen in a particularly metaphysical light. For example, throughout our study longing has repeatedly been examined as a curious kind of presence and surplus that can appear as and is felt as a kind of absence. In chapter 1 we saw how Levinas drew from Plato's account of Eros as the result of the perfect union of *Poros,* abundance, and *Penia,* poverty, in his account of longing such that it could be understood as expressing something akin to the presence of a super abundant absence. Chapter 2 sought to further illuminate this element of Levinas's thought by examining his relationship to Heidegger's account of authentic Eros, which he named a *primordial longing,* as simultaneously an authentic *striving* for Being, which, as we saw there, represented for him a kind of absence that lay beyond all determinate manifestations of being, and an authentic having of that Being, a having which had without possessing. This led us to reflect that ultimately the crucial difference of Levinas's account of longing lay in his analysis of its ethical significance, which we then sought to explore in more detail in chapter 3; which, in turn, led us to realize the metaphysical power of the experience of longing. Now, by examining the connection between Levinas's thought and Schelling's, the metaphysical depths of longing as the avenue toward a kind of creature consciousness have emerged. Longing, it seems, functions as the present manifestation of the primordial absence of God, an absence which allowed for all presence and existence to proceed. In this sense, longing seems to function for Levinas as the conduit through which God flows through determinate existence. It is the presence of the ghost of God haunting human experience—a superworldly presence which overflows determinate existence with the trace of a being who never properly was.

This also illuminates the distinction we made in chapter 1 between longing and other forms of desire which Levinas characterized as need. Need, we said there, arises out of the interests of the subject and revolves around the limitations of his or her being. As such, it circulates entirely within the realm of the ontic. Longing, on the other hand, as we saw in chapter 2, concerns itself essentially with that which lies *beyond being*—it is essentially metaphysical. Through Schelling we discovered that the break with being manifest in longing, its inherence to the metaphysical proper, is established in its connection to a God who is not a part of the realm of being, but who has instead always already projected into the metaphysical *beyond being*, choosing to manifest only as that which *could be*, or which *could be coming*. This further illuminates Levinas's insistence that longing, unlike nostalgia, is not directed backward toward some past to which it hopes to return, but instead toward the eternally distant future, wherein the promise of God resides.

The connection drawn by Schelling between God's contraction before time and human longing in time also further illuminates Levinas's claims that longing seems to express a kind of passivity within human existence. As the expression of the presence of the nonexistent God therein, longing does not originate nor arise from any determinate activity within human existence, but instead grows from the primordial creative *act* effected by God through self-contraction—an act upon which human existence is passively dependent. Thus, though human existence may be the product of God's active contraction of being, human longing betrays a passive dependence upon this contraction away from being. Longing is thus an essentially nonsubjective experience which slips into the human heart like a thief in the night. It is, in this sense, not unlike a disease which is contracted through

God's primordial creative contraction into nonexistence precipitating the dawn of time.[55]

So it seems as if any investigation into the nature of longing necessarily contends with questions concerning the nature of the metaphysical, questions which, as we saw in the last chapter, are only mediated for Levinas through an ethical encounter with the Other. But, we cannot conclude yet, for if the power of longing emerges from its inherence to this metaphysical reality, then the nature, function and power of this relation must be further examined.

FIVE

Longing and the Numinous
Levinas and Otto in Dialogue

LONGING AND THE BEYOND

Over the course of our investigation of Levinas's dialogue with the history of philosophy a clearer picture of his understanding of the nature of human longing has slowly emerged. As we have seen, longing is for him a kind of insatiable and interminable movement within human nature—one which is not circumscribable by any conceivable satisfaction. Indeed, it is not only perpetually *unsatisfied,* but is, in fact, *unsatisfiable* as such. Longing thus does not accord to any determinate object of possible satisfaction—neither one which is beyond us, in a time outside of our own, nor one that has been lost through time and can be reflected upon nostalgically. Unlike these kinds of desire—desires like the yearning for God and nostalgia, respectively—longing cannot be understood as the result of some determinate lack or absence within human nature. Rather, it is the expression of some sort of presence or surplus therein—a surplus, moreover, which has been repeatedly understood as exceeding the bounds and natural limits of human finitude, or at least calling them into question and regrounding them. As such, Levinas and others identified human longing with the *in*finite, with that which overflows and explodes the borders of the finite—with that which lies on the hither side of human finitude. Though the nature of the surplus expressed in human longing has varied between authors, each in his own way has understood the tie between human longing and this surplus as somehow signaling a break or rupture in the traditional understanding of the human subject as something whole and complete unto itself—in absolute control of its own existence. Each has understood, in his own way, how human longing signals the presence of a kind of passivity within human existence and testified to its dependence upon something or someone else, a passivity which ultimately, Levinas claims, attests to its dependence upon a ground which is not its own, but which is established in the Other.

Identified with the surplus of the infinite, Levinas identified longing as a positive force or power within human nature and not the manifestation of some privation. Longing seems to have a momentum and trajectory all its own—not one guided by some insufficiency, but one which carries within it the trace of an excess. Longing, he argued, is not like hunger, thirst, nor any other determinate desire, therefore, but functions in its own way. As such, as we have seen, longing cannot be understood as a species of some genus desire—but should instead be posited on its own, as a vigorous energy sufficient unto itself. If anything, longing could be made in Levinas the silent or hidden urgency behind many other determinate desires, as that which runs in and through them, motivating their appearance.

This understanding of the relation between longing and other determinate desires begs a reevaluation of the traditional understanding of human desire—for, if determinate desires are to be taken as situated upon the explosive current of human longing, then their operation, like longing's, should not be deemed the result of some privation, but should instead be understood as the expression of a kind of excess within human nature. In this perspective many determinate desires could no longer be taken, like hunger or thirst, to be the expression of some nutritive lack within any particular person, but would instead be seen as the expression of some unsettled positive power therein. And indeed, there is something to the nature of our determinate desires which seems to reflect this orientation. When one wants a new car, for example, one is not generally *in want of* a new car—one is not generally *lacking* a new car. One's desires very rarely correspond to some determinate absence or *need*, but instead seem to reflect some sort of driving force within. Typically, moreover, one's desires for these sorts of consumable objects are the result of not having taken one's longing seriously enough—as an experience which is particular unto itself and different from the experience of other determinate desires. Typically one wants to consume more when one has failed to recognize that the insatiableness and incompleteness within is not the result of some determinate absence, but is concupiscent with one's very nature. One is driven to consume when one fails to recognize that the seeming emptiness one feels does not correspond to any determinate object of possible satisfaction, but is instead part and parcel with the very way in which one *is*. So much of consumption today is the result of taking longing to be some sort of determinate desire and failing to recognize its alterity. So much of what motivates human beings to eat more, drink more, buy more, and own more lies in this failure to allow the insatiability of human longing to stand on its own and to hold sway in human life as an indeterminate insatiability.

Though perhaps the motivating force behind so many other determinate desires, longing itself remains, claims Levinas and others, forever *indeterminate*—remains unattached to any determinate object or aim. It is, in fact, the prevailing indeterminacy of human longing which makes it so easily confused with other determinate desires. There is something within human nature which resists the indeterminacy of human longing, which wants to concretize it by tying it down to some specific object (a new job, a bigger house, a different spouse, and the like) and, in so doing, end its restless power. It is even perhaps this attempt which gives rise to certain determinate desires—their appearance on the scene the expression of the failure to take longing on its own terms. This failure is understandable, of course. After all, there is something profoundly unsettling in the nature of human longing—for, it carries within it the prospect that the reason that we are so perpetually unfulfilled has to do with who we *are* as such, and not with what we *own* or what we *do*. It is unnerving to consider that regardless of how hard one works or strives, or how much one achieves, one will still find oneself longing for something else, something other than can be had or grasped.

It is the nature of longing, it seems, to always push out beyond the immediately graspable. Indeed, longing pushes beyond the immediate as such. This is why Levinas concluded with his interlocutors that longing is that force or power within human nature which is forever drawing it out, beyond the limits of its own being. Perhaps more than any other trait by which we have identified the nature of human longing, it is this trajectory beyond the bounds of being which is most uniquely its own. It is, in fact, this aspect of longing which gives rise to its sundry other phenomenal attributes. Longing was deemed insatiable, for example, because it moves beyond the realm in which the satiable can be found, beyond the realm of being; and, longing is indeterminate because that which lies beyond the horizon of being is unavailable to phenomenal intuition. As the expression of an excess which overflows the bounds of being, and appears, as a result, as some sort of absence of being, longing seems to belong inherently to the realm of the metaphysical—to that which lies beyond, *meta,* the realm of determinate beings, *physis*.

From all of this we can now understand the depth and richness of Levinas's identification of longing as a truly *metaphysical desire*. As such a metaphysical desire, longing serves as the phenomenal expression in the immediate of that which lies beyond the immediate—of that, moreover, which conditions and lays the ground for the immediate. Thus, though longing may appear in a certain phenomenal way, there is something about it which is tied to that which does not appear, to that which could never appear, and thereby, to that which is unavailable to phenomenological study. In the attempt to get a handle on the way in which longing functions as an expression of the metaphysical we sought to explore the tie between longing and ethics in chapter 3. This study, however, revealed that in order to understand the relation between longing and the metaphysical we had to examine its tie to the metaphysical considered on its own and not merely in so far as it operates within the physical realm of intersubjectivity. So it was that we uncovered the tie within Levinas's work between longing and the beyond being that is the being of God in chapter 4.

Longing, we discovered there, is, for Levinas, inherently metaphysical because it *inherits* the power of a God who chose not to be. As such, it is the expression in being of the superlative force of a God who lies beyond being—of a God who has passed from being and thus remains *wholly other* than being. Thus, though longing is the expression of this overwhelming creative force, it can be felt, as we have consistently detailed, as a kind of absence—for, it testifies to the absence of God as a determinate being. Longing, it seems, is the feeling of a God *without being*—of a God who is not now, who never was, and who can only be related to and understood as this longing.[1] As we said at the end of the last chapter, longing is, for Levinas, the feeling of the wholly otherwise—it is the feeling within being of that which is beyond and otherwise than being. Longing is thus the determinate expression and experience of a God who, by nature and choice, lies beyond expression and experience. Longing is not then merely the *path* to God, as it was deemed by Augustine and is perhaps still deemed by people like Marion, but *is* God, in as much as God is at all—it is how God *is* in the world; God is the affectivity of the beyond which we name human longing. God's passing beyond being is absorbed by and contained in human longing. It is for this reason that longing has been characterized with words typically held in reserve for the experience of God: infinite, insatiable, excessive, overwhelming, and so on.

In order to further understand the nature, function, and operation of human longing in Levinas's work then, especially in terms of its inexorable tie to the metaphysical, we must examine the way in which the experience or feeling of God has traditionally been accounted for.

The Beyond and the Numinous

The concept of the *feeling of God* as the wholly other is one which has been extensively explored over the past century. Indeed, perhaps never in history has this concept been as expounded upon as it is today, especially as it appears in relation to the so called "theological turn" in contemporary French thinking. Still, the concept of God as the wholly other has never been as clearly and determinately written about as was done by Rudolf Otto in his seminal work *The Idea of the Holy* (*Das Heilige*). According to Otto, the feeling of God, or holiness, like the beyond being pursued by longing, must be understood as a category set apart from the realm of "the Rational" as it remains "inexpressible—an $ἄρρητον$ or *ineffable*—in the sense that it completely eludes apprehension in terms of concepts" (*IH* 5). This ineffableness, this resistance to the powers of ratiocination, claims Otto, is the most significant aspect of the experience of God or the idea of the holy.

Though the concept of holiness may be commonly taken to express something akin to the "completely good" or to represent an "absolute moral attribute, denoting the consummation of moral goodness...this common usage of the term is," for him, "inaccurate" (*IH* 5). The Good is not, thinks Otto, the primary referent to the idea of the holy—it is not the primary way in which the transcendence of the beyond inhibited by God is felt or experienced. According to his read, the concept of the Good is, rather, secondary to the concept of the holy—an *attribute* or *evaluation* applied to the experience of the holy only after the fact.[2] Primarily and immediately, the holy is experienced, he claims, as the wholly irrational and inexpressible. Thus, he argues, though it may be "true that all this moral significance is contained in the word 'holy,'...it includes in addition—as even we cannot but feel—a clear *surplus* of meaning" (5; translation corrected, italics mine). The idea of the holy is initially and primarily the experience of this excess or overabundance, this surplus. It is this "surplus of meaning" which, he claims, makes up the hard core of the experience of the holy.

According to Otto, "'holy,' or at least the equivalent words in Latin and Greek, in Semitic and other ancient languages, denoted first and foremost *only* this surplus," the attribution of any moral value to this surplus coming only later and secondarily, and certainly not necessarily (*IH* 5–6; translation corrected). Like the beyond being sought by longing, the holy is that which lies beyond the realm of the rational and remains forever ineffable. And, like the beyond being sought by longing, the ineffableness of the holy is not the result of some deficiency of meaning—the holy is not inexpressible because it somehow falls *short* of attaining some thematizeable meaning. Instead, the holy is ineffable, because it falls *beyond* the meaning—because it expresses a too muchness, as it were, a surplus and excess of meaning that explodes the borders and limits of the rational. The experience of the holy is described by him as an overwhelming abundance of meaning—one which exceeds the capacities of the rational structures of thought and language. The object of this experience is thus deemed by him a kind of mystery—indeed, it is the *mysterium tremendum*. According to Otto, "the truly 'mysterious object is beyond our apprehension and comprehension, not only because our knowledge has certain irremovable limits, but because in it we come upon something inherently '*wholly other*,' whose kind and character are incommensurable with our own, and before which we therefore recoil in a wonder that strikes us chill and numb" (28; italics mine).

Note Otto's claim that the object of the experience of the holy is something which is deemed to be "inherently '*wholly other*.'" Because that which is intuited in the experience of the holy so far exceeds the bounds of the intelligible it is deemed wholly other. The experience of the holy is thus a kind of intuition of "the '*wholly other*' [θάτρον, anyad, alienum], that which is quite beyond the sphere of the usual, the intelligible, and the familiar, which therefore falls quite outside the limits of the 'canny,' and is contrasted with it, filling the mind with blank wonder and astonishment" (*IH* 26; italics mine). Though Otto characterizes this experience of the wholly other as an experience of a *mysterium,* a comparison which Levinas, for one, would take issue with, there can be little doubt that Otto's descriptions of the holy as the wholly other do not accord, at least in part, with not only Levinas's descriptions of the beyond being, but with Heidegger's as well.[3] In fact, there is cause to argue that it is from Otto that the language of the wholly other first emerges in the discourse of Western thinking informing the work of both Heidegger and Levinas.[4]

Given the way that it manifests as the experience of something wholly other, holiness, claims Otto, can only be thought, first and foremost, as an expression of "the 'Beyond' [ἐπέκεινα]"

(*IH* 29). It is this superlative element to the experience of the holy that Otto seeks to isolate and explore in his work. Famously, Otto coins the word *numinous,* which he takes from the Latin *numen,* typically translated as divine presence, "to stand for this element in isolation, this 'extra' in the meaning of 'holy' above and beyond the meaning of goodness" (6–7). The numinous thus expresses for him an experience, a state of mind not unlike Heidegger's *Befindlichkeit.* It is that state of mind that connotes the feeling one has when under the sway of this kind of presence—when intuiting the presence of that which lies beyond presence. "This mental state," he claims "is perfectly *sui generis* and irreducible to any other; and therefore, like every absolutely primary and elementary datum, while it admits of being discussed, it cannot be strictly defined" (7). It is not his goal in *The Idea of the Holy* to therefore define the experience of the holy, but rather to describe it as best he can using a combination of historical, theological, and protophenomenological investigations, much as we have done in our attempt to detail the nature of longing, an experience equally as elusive. Otto thus proceeds in his investigation by detailing the various ways in which the numinous has been expressed and understood over the history of religious thinking.

One of the most significant traditions that Otto draws from in informing his picture of the feeling which accompanies the holy is the mystical tradition. Otto's interest in the mystical tradition seems to stem from the fact that it is one of the few Western traditions that has sought to experience the holy precisely as he describes it, as that which signals the Beyond, exceeds the Rational, and expresses the wholly other. The attempt within mysticism to understand the object of this experience on the basis of such an experience yields for Otto a number of significant intuitions concerning the nature of the numinous and the numinous object—most significant amongst them, he seems to think, is the characterization of the object of the numinous experience as *beyond Being.*

According to him, "Not content with contrasting [the wholly other object of numinous experience] with all that is of nature or this world, Mysticism concludes by contrasting it with Being itself and all that 'is,' and finally actually calls it 'that which is nothing'" (*IH* 29–30). And yet, he claims, "the 'void' of the eastern, like the 'nothing' of the western mystic," is nothing more than "a numinous ideogram of the 'wholly other'" (30). Citing Jacob Böehme, Schelling's philosophical mentor, and Meister Eckhart as examples (111), Otto claims that "the felling of the 'wholly other' gives rise in Mysticism to the tendency to follow the 'via negationis,' by which every predicate that can be stated in words becomes excluded from the absolute Numen—i.e. from Deity—til finally the Godhead is designated as 'nothingness' and 'nullity,' bearing in mind always that these terms denote in truth immeasurable plenitude of being" (201–02).

Though most elaborately formulated by the mystics, this tendency to ascribe to the numinous an object which, as wholly other, somehow *is not* can even be observed in something as simple as the traditional ghost story. A ghost story, claims Otto, inspires feelings not unlike the numinous "not because [a ghost] is 'something long and white' (as someone once defined [it]), nor yet through any of the positive and conceptual attributes which fancies about ghosts have invented; but because it is a thing that *'doesn't really exist at all,'* the 'wholly other,' something which has not place in our scheme of reality but belongs to an absolutely different one, and which at the same time arouses an irrepressible interest in the mind" (*IH* 29; italics mine). There is something about the wholly other intuited and felt in the numinous which seems to belong out beyond being—beyond presence, beyond all that is as such. As the experience of that which lies beyond conception, as that through which the inexpressible is felt, the numinous, though a phenomenal occurrence, seems to reach toward that which exceeds the phenomenal realm—it is the feeling of a presence of that which cannot present itself as such. As a result, the object signified by the numinous can appear to be a kind of nothingness—that which *is not,* that which lies beyond determinate presence. The superlative plenitude felt in the numinous, like the beyond being pursued by longing as described by Levinas and others, though an excess and overwhelming presence within human experience, seems to signal that which is profoundly absent, that which is precisely nothing. That which is signaled by and felt in the numinous, this appears as a kind of "nonabsent absence," to borrow a phrase from Blanchot—it is a power which is so transcendent of our everyday experience that it appears wholly absent.[5]

Though the numinous expresses that which seems to lie beyond being, and certainly beyond the realms of human conception, as is made clear in the mystical tradition, Otto still sees it as a firmly phenomenal occurrence. As such, the numinous signals a breach within the phenomenal realm through which a new conception of that realm can be formulated. That is, as the tie within being to that which lies beyond being, the numinous seems to cast the phenomenal realm in a new light—it seems to make available a new conception of the phenomenal realm, one forged in the fires of the beyond being. One of the intuitions this light makes available, as Otto details it, is the possibility of conceiving of the phenomenal realm as the product of a creation.

According to Otto, the numinous inspires a "feeling of dependence" which can endow a kind of "creature consciousness" (*IH* 10). The numinous experience, as the experience of something "objective and outside the self," beyond the realm of that which is the self, opens one up to the possibility of conceiving of that self in relation to the beyond (11). This "creature-feeling" which arises in the numinous, can displace the self from its centre evoking within it a new self-consciousness—one not based on its understanding of itself as experienced from the inside, but instead as related to and dependent upon something outside and objective. Still the primary referent of such an experience is not the self, but precisely that outside, that object which lies beyond the self. Thus, though "the 'creature feeling' is itself a first subjective concomitant and effect of another feeling-element, which casts it like a shadow," nevertheless, "in itself [this feeling] indubitably has immediate and primary reference to an object outside the self" (10).

Since the object intuited and felt in the numinous is deemed so superlative and wholly other to the one who experiences it, Otto characterizes the numinous as somehow overwhelming and overpowering (*IH* 20). It is a feeling which is daunting and frightening (31). The numinous thus carries within it an element of the *awful,* he claims—the object which it expresses is one of "horror and dread" (31). Otto thus associates it with "the monstrous" (82) and understands it as the source of something greater than fear, a trembling before the beyond which he calls a shuddering (15). The numinous is thus experienced as "the feeling of 'something uncanny,' 'eerie,' or 'weird'" (15; cf. 130).

Clearly, a number of similarities exist between the numinous and the synoptic account of longing emergent through an analysis of Levinas's dialogue with the history of philosophy. Both longing and the numinous appear to function as phenomenal expressions of that which lies beyond being. Both, furthermore, in intuiting this beyond, somehow tie the realm of determinate beings to that which is wholly otherwise than them. Indeed, both are the way in which this wholly otherwise is felt and experienced in the here and now. As such, both make available a conception of the here and now as reflected in the light of the beyond. That is, both open up the possibility of conceiving of the self as the result of a kind of creation. Both, therefore, inspire feelings of dependence and creature consciousness. Furthermore, both have been described as the manifestation of something which is superlative and excessive—something which, nevertheless, appears as nothing. That is, both express a transcendence so transcendent that it risks being confused with a pure absence. This comparison of longing to the numinous is even suggested by Otto himself who at two points in his text seems to consider that there might be something of longing or yearning to the experience of the numinous, though precisely how he conceives of such a longing is not discernable (see *IH* 32). According to Otto, the numinous, like longing, "shows that above and beyond our rational being lies hidden the ultimate and highest part of our nature, *which can find no satisfaction in the mere allaying of the needs of our sensuous, psychical, or intellectual impulses and cravings*" (36; italics mine). But there is another element to the numinous as Otto describes it which complicates our comparison of it to Levinas's account of longing.

According to Otto, in addition to expressing something *daunting* and *overwhelming,* the numinous also expresses something which is *fascinating*. Thus, he claims, that just as the "daemonic-divine object [intuited by the numinous] may appear to the mind [as] an object of horror and dread;...at the same time it is no less something that *allures* with a potent charm, and the creature, who trembles before it, utterly cowed and cast down, has always at the same time the impulse to turn to it, nay even to make it somehow his own" (*IH* 31; italics mine). This attractive element of the numinous, claims Otto, "bewilders and confounds," it "captivates and transports...with a strange ravishment, rising often enough to the pitch of dizzy intoxication" (31). So it is that the numinous becomes associated for him with the "magical" and the "shamanistic" (33). It is this description of the numinous as a kind of fascination bordering on the frenzied which gives way to the magical and the shamanistic which troubles our attempts to establish a concrete tie between it and Levinas's account of longing.

Levinas and the Numinous—The Ambiguity of the Infinite

The trouble with Otto's descriptions of the beyond being, for Levinas, is that by uniting in it both the "daunting and the fascinating" (*IH* 31), Otto creates a dangerous equivocation that not only blurs the nature of the way in which the beyond being is, as it were, but also combines in such a way as to threaten the assertion of the radical independence of the subject. Concretely, this equivocation, for Levinas, is between the idea of the holy as the daunting and the idea of the sacred or the divine as the fascinating.[6] In contrast to what he sees as the equivocation in Otto's phenomenology of the beyond, Levinas aims to account for the beyond by first distinguishing between what he calls "the holy [*le saint*] and the sacred [*la sacre*]," the latter being what he claims Otto identifies with the numinous (De 225; cf. *NR* 152).[7] The sacred, in its attractive power, represents for Levinas the false promise of magic and shamanism—of mystical union with the beyond. It expresses for him a power which is shrouded in mystery—as menacing as it is attractive. But, he goes on to argue, this is not a true expression of the profound and infinite otherness of the beyond pursued by metaphysical desire, it is instead its opposite. The sacred is, claims Levinas, "the 'other side,' the reverse or obverse of the Real, Nothingness condensed to Mystery, bubbles of Nothing in things—the 'as if nothing is happening' look of daily objects—the sacred adorns itself with the prestige of prestiges" (*NT* 141).

Regaled and adorned in its own assumed splendor, the sacred attracts unto itself with the promise of a mystical union and participation in occult secrets and mysteries known only to a few. According to Levinas, "This way of existing without revealing itself, outside of being and the world, must be called mythical. The nocturnal prolongation of the element is the reign of mythical gods. Enjoyment without security" (*TI* 142). Levinas identifies this form of enjoyment in the mythical with the indeterminate infinitude of the *there is* as it was detailed in chapter 2 (142). The sacred thus expresses for Levinas a form of the infinite, but not the good infinite of the beyond being as it is experienced in metaphysical desire. The infinite contained in the numinous or the sacred is for Levinas an infinite without bounds, an infinitude which threatens the singularity of the subject, whose identity is established in finitude. Levinas thus distinguishes the kind of infinitude present in the sacred from that one contained in the idea of the infinite. This infinitude of the sacred and the *il y a* is for Levinas, a "bad infinite," a concept which he draws from the work of Hegel (196–97; cf. *OB* 193, n. 34).[8] The bad infinite contained within the sacred is characterized by Levinas as the perpetuation of the indeterminate being of the *there is*.[9] It is, he claims, a mode of existence "without limits, and thus in the form of an origin, a commencement, that is, again, as an existent. The absolute indetermination of the *there is,* an existing without existents, is an incessant negation, to an infinite degree, consequently an infinite limitation" (*TI* 281).[10] It is thus the sacred, as the manifestation of this bad infinitude, thinks Levinas, which should properly bear the title of the numinous, as it is the sacred which in its attractive power and totality presents a kind of threat to the subject. It is the "sacred which appears as the magical and the numinous," he claims (De 225).

As an infinitude established in and maintained through the perpetuation of and continuity with a Being without distinctions or individuations, the sacred expresses for Levinas not a force for the Good, like the idea of the infinite and metaphysical desire, but rather, in fact, a force for evil (*le mal*). The bad infinitude of the sacred is evil for Levinas because it is maintained in a plenitude of being which, in its totality, has no room or space for any otherness or determinate identity or singularity. It is, in a sense, an unbounded and limitless infinitude, an infinitude which allows for no differentiation or separation and thus mitigates the possibility of a free choice for the good or the ethical. The bad infinite thus expresses for Levinas a kind of excess, but not one like the excess experienced in metaphysical desire. Instead, the excess of the bad infinite is an excess of Being, as opposed to an excess of the otherwise. It is this tendency toward excessive presence that establishes its moral value for Levinas; for, he argues, "evil is an excess in its very quiddity" (*CPP* 180).

In sharp distinction to the numinosity of the sacred and the bad infinite, Levinas establishes what he deems the *holy* in the face of another who is separate and distinct from us and represents the good infinite of ethical responsibility. He writes, "Man as Other comes to us from the outside, separated—or holy-face" (*TI* 291). Harkening back to chapter 1 you will remember that for Levinas the beyond being sought by metaphysical desire is only initially deemed good by him because, by his read, it deflects the pull of its own attraction onto the other such that one's only invitation into the beyond is offered in the ethical. As Rudi Visker puts it, "The Good [in Levinas] is only good because it breaks that sacred spell—that desire to touch what we have always already lost and which, by that very fact, attracts us—and reorients the course of the dynamic thus awakened, inclining it towards the others."[11] Thus for Levinas, "metaphysics is [only] enacted in ethical relations," it is only in this relation that any idea of the holy can be thought (79). It is in the infinite responsibility for the Other that the holy resides. The ethical demand of the Other thus expresses for him the "exigency of holiness" (*EI* 105). "Everything that cannot be reduced to [this] inter-human relation represents," for Levinas, "not the superior form but the forever primitive form of religion," it represents the rule of the mythical and the sacred (*TI* 79). It is, moreover, according to Levinas, what "all of the Bible struggles against" (De 225).

Situated as it is within the relation with another who is separate and distinct from me and, moreover, situated on a height above me, far from promising the kind of mystical union held out for in the sacred, the holy is established and maintained, according to Levinas, through distance and the rupture initiated within me through the ethical call (*EI* 117–18; *GDT* 164). One never relates to the divine power of the beyond face to face, as it were, but only through the face of the Other, through the ethical, as in a "relation without relation" (*TI* 80).[12] According to Levinas, "The dimension of the divine opens forth from the human face" (78).[13] Herein, God, the holiness of the holy, is understood as retreating, in a sense, behind the neighbor such that a "desacralization of the Sacred," occurs (*DF* 18). One does not relate to the beyond sought in metaphysical desire therefore as a devotee of the mystical or as a frenzied believer consumed and possessed by the charm of the sacred, but as an atheist. God is fundamentally *invisible* and, as such, can only be intuited through the ethical relationship with another. Remember from chapter 3 that for Levinas "ethics is the spiritual optics" (*TI* 78). God is presented through the face of the neighbor—only therein can the reign of God be seen. One's access to a holy God is not offered straightforwardly as the sacred is to the mystical believer, but via the determinate need of the neighbor presented to an ethical atheist—to one who is concerned with the affairs of the other. "To relate to the absolute as an atheist," claims Levinas, "is to welcome the absolute purified of the violence of the sacred. In the dimension of height in which his sanctity, that is, his separation, is presented, the infinite does not burn the eyes that are lifted unto him" (77). As such, the holy expresses for Levinas a kind of good infinite, an infinity mediated through responsibility and guilt (see *OB* 142).

This infinite, which appears in the ethical relation to another whose demand I cannot satisfy because it extends infinitely beyond my power, is not, for Levinas, the numinous as it is detailed by Otto, but the holy—encountered in the wholly other. According to Levinas, the other to whom I must respond in the infinite ethical relation "is not numinous: the I who approaches him is neither annihilated on contact nor transported outside of itself, but remains separated and keeps its as-for-me" (*TI* 77; cf. 215). The transcendence experienced through metaphysical desire is thus not the "apostasy and ecstasy" (42) of the shaman, but the moral rigor of the ethically oriented person. In this relation, this "metaphysical relation, the idea of infinity, [one] connects with the noumenon which is not a numen;" one connects to the beyond without being swept up by it and participating in it (77). This mediation of the Good beyond being through the ethical, through the idea of the infinite and metaphysical desire, "is a protection against the madness of a direct contact with the Sacred that is unmediated by reason."[14]

It is important to note here that this protection, this preventative power, operates through the movement of metaphysical desire and the idea of the infinite. Metaphysical desire, as an ethical desire which draws the subject not toward the beyond as such, but toward the beyond as it is mediated through the determinate other, as we saw in chapter 3, functions as a kind of shield protecting human singularity against the overwhelming threat of the sacred. Longing thus appears to be for Levinas a holy desire which mitigates the temptation of the sacred and the numinous (see *TI* 50). It provides for him a channel through which the metaphysical beyond being can be related without risking annihilation.[15] It presents, in other words, a kind of bound infinity—an infinity that is under control, as it were—one that does not veer into the unmanageable and indeterminate realm of the *there is*. Longing thus functions simultaneously as a kind of sign or phylactery marking the demise of the *there is,* and as a kind of vaccination protecting against its return.

There is a problem here however. Despite Levinas's deliberate attempts to purge the concept of the numinous from his account of the beyond being pursued by metaphysical desire by distinguishing between the infinite as it appears as the sacred, and therefore bad, and the infinite as it appears as the holy, and therefore good, there is cause to argue that a touch of the numinous still remains in his work. This is the case because, against Levinas's best efforts, the subtle line he establishes between these various expressions of the infinite is easily blurred, lending itself to possible confusion.

This is a danger that Levinas himself famously admits, confessing that the infinite transcendence of the Good, of a God who withdraws behind the neighbor, is in fact "transcendent to the point of absence, to the point of a possible confusion with the stirring of the *there is,*" that is, to the point of possible confusion with the reverie of the sacred and the totality of the bad infinite (*BPW* 138). The problem with this "possible confusion" however is that Levinas himself seems to occasionally, albeit unwittingly, tumble into it, resulting in an obfuscation of the real difference between the holy as the good infinite and the sacred as the bad infinite. For example, Levinas describes the good infinite pursued in metaphysical desire and present in the ethical encounter as *monstrous* (*GDT* 220; cf. *BPW* 138)—a term which seemingly belongs more properly to the concept of the numinous as detailed by Otto and opposed by Levinas.

Elsewhere, when discussing the infinitude of the ethical responsibility, Levinas describes the good infinite with the same language he uses to identify the bad, naming the infinitude of responsibility a kind of "*perpetuity,*" though in this case not of being, but instead of the ethical command (*CPP* 136; italics mine). There he even suggests that it is from this perpetuity that the idea of the bad infinite is "extrapolated," which seems to imply that one's experience of the sacred is in fact a derivative experience of the encounter with the holy—that it is through the infinitude of the beyond being misapprehended as the sacred that the idea of the bad infinite arises. This of course suggests that both the good infinite and the bad infinite are merely differing conceptual determinations of the same experience—that there is in fact only one infinitude either experienced in the ethical call or experienced in the incessant murmur of being. This is also suggested in *Otherwise Than Being* where Levinas compares the otherness of the plenitude of being, the *il y a,* with the otherness and alterity of the beyond being sought by metaphysical desire. There he writes that "the *there is* is all the weight that alterity weighs supported by a subjectivity that does not found it" (*OB* 164). Levinas goes on to suggest there that the only difference between the alterity of the beyond being and the alterity of the *there is* is that the latter does not allow for the existence of a subject who can support itself under such a weight. Indeed, he even seems to claim, that were a subject able to somehow bear itself up under the weight of the *there is,* the *there is* would immediately become something akin to the *otherwise than being,* seemingly suggesting that the only difference between the two lies in how a subject can relate to them—the former allowing for such a relation and the latter annihilating the subject such that no relation can occur. So it seems that the determinative difference in Levinas's work between the good infinite and the bad infinite lies in how a subject exists, or does not exist as the case may be, in relation to it. The good and bad infinite do not seem to express two qualitatively different powers, but rather two different orientations to the same power, the power of the infinite apprehended by the subject in two different ways.

Whether this interpretation of the ambiguity in Levinas's work is accurate can be debated; it cannot be debated, however, that such a sincere ambiguity does exist concerning the status of the infinite as it is accounted for therein. This ambiguity is in fact well documented and extensively commented upon by everyone from John Caputo to Rudi Visker.[16] It is perhaps best expressed, however, in the words of Levinas life-long friend Maurice Blanchot who wrote that: "The *there is* is one of Levinas's most fascinating propositions. It is his temptation, too, since as the reverse of transcendence it is thus not distinct from it either. Indeed, it is describable in terms of being, but as the *impossibility* of not being, as the incessant insistence of the neutral, the nocturnal murmur of the anonymous, as what never begins (thus, as an-archic, since it eternally eludes the determination of a beginning); it is the absolute, but as absolute indetermination."[17]

The existence of such an ambiguity, the possibility of such a confusion between the good infinite of the holy and the bad infinite of the sacred within Levinas's work, only concerns us here because of the way it seems to lend support to our claims that longing, as that drive which is inexorably bound to the beyond, is somehow intrinsically related to the experience of the numinous. For such an ambiguity allows us not only to continue our investigation of the relation between longing and the beyond as the numinous, as is supported by our synoptic account of its attributes, but it also directs our focus in how it is that longing may relate to such a manifestation of the beyond. That is, perhaps this ambiguity in Levinas's work concerning the nature of the beyond points to an ambiguity in the nature of the beyond itself, an ambiguity, moreover, which may inform our investigation into the nature of human longing. Perhaps, as we have seen, it is the nature of the beyond itself to appear alternatively as either a profound good, what Levinas names the holy, or as a deceptively attractive bad, what Levinas names the sacred. In the case of the latter, as is suggested by Levinas's work, perhaps it is the function of longing to protect us from the potential threat in the beyond thereby allowing us to relate to it as a good. That is, perhaps it is the function of longing to protect us from the sacredness of the beyond such that we can be in touch with its holiness. Longing seems to allow us a dose of the infinite without becoming overwhelmed by it—it allows us to be in touch with the infinite as good and supportive instead of being overwhelmed by the infinite as bad and destructive. This is a suggestion which is supported by Schelling and Heidegger's respective analyses of longing. Indeed, perhaps nowhere is the relation between longing and the numinous more deeply explored than in Schelling's *Of Human Freedom* and Heidegger's respective interpretation of it. To understand this connection, however, we must first understand the way in which these two thinkers treat the nature of the beyond pursued by longing as numinous.

HEIDEGGER AND SCHELLING ON THE NUMINOUS — GOD IN THE DOCKS

Schelling was perhaps the first thinker in Western philosophy to treat the nature of the beyond as a potential threat to the life of the subject. Writing in 1809, over 100 years before Otto's groundbreaking publication, Schelling had already detailed the nature of the monstrous threat contained in the existence of the divine. His discovery came through the course of his attempt in the *Philosophical Inquiries into the Nature of Human Freedom* to derive a new conception of God, one that did not think of Him simply as an *actus purissimus* or as the foundation of a moral order, but instead as a vital force, one active in the manifestation of both good and evil. "God is more of a reality than is a mere moral world-order," Schelling argued there, "and he has in him quite other and more vital activating powers than the barren subtlety that abstract idealists ascribe to him" (*HF* 30; translation corrected). United to the created order as that which becomes through it, God should be identified and understood, argues Schelling, in the mode in which that order presents itself. In other words, God's being, as the one who now *is not,* but who is, nevertheless, always coming in and through the now, must be understood in such a way that it can include within it the potentiality not only for good, but also for evil — since, after all, both appear in the now as determinate options for human existence.

Evil, claims Schelling, is an essential and vital part of existence. It is in fact for him, as we have seen, part and parcel with the freedom that defines the nature of human existence, that existence which for him lies at the center of all existence itself. This evaluation by Schelling of evil as a real and vital force within existence of course goes against the traditional conception of evil. Traditionally evil has been defined not as the positive expression of some determinate force within being, but as the privation of the good of being, being having traditionally been linked to the Good. Indeed, the so called "problem of evil" has most commonly been dealt with over the history of Western philosophy by denying evil any real existential power and by defining it as a purely negative force and which is by nature a solely nugatory and annihilating force. Schelling's reformulation of the nature of the divine thus initially comes through his revaluation of the existential status of evil. Indeed, in many ways it is this commitment to conceiving of evil as a real and vital force within being from whence most of Schelling's insights flow. His analysis of the nature of evil is so vital to his rendition of both human freedom and the nature of the divine in *Of Human Freedom* that, according to Heidegger, it can in many ways be seen as "the keyword for the main treatise" (*GA* 42: 168 / 97).

Schelling begins his revaluation of the nature of evil by discounting the way in which it has traditionally been dealt with. According to Schelling, it is folly to claim, as has traditionally been done that: "in evil there is nothing at all positive, or—otherwise expressed—that evil does not exist at all (not even in connection with or through something else which is positive) but that all actions are more or less positive, and that the difference between them is a mere plus or minus of perfection" (*HF* 27). Heidegger, in his reading of Schelling's *Freiheitsschrift,* expresses the absurdity of this view by giving voice to "the blind man who has lost his sight," who, he claims, "will argue vigorously against the statement that blindness is *nothing existent* [*nichts seindes*] and *nothing depressing* and *nothing burdensome* [*nicht Bedrängednes und Lastendes sei*]" (*GA* 42: 177 / 101; italics mine). Simply because a determinate form of human suffering or evil such as blindness may manifest through the negation of some other power, sight in this case, should not be taken as a simply nugatory power. Instead, both Heidegger and Schelling claim, evil should be conceived of as a rival positive power—as the expression of another mode of being. This tendency to see the absence by which an evil such as blindness may present itself as a kind of simple privation, and therefore as nothing real or containing any ontological force, is, according to Heidegger, the result of a general confusion within the history of philosophy between the notion of *lack* and *privation,* on the one hand, and the notion of *nothingness* proper, on the other hand. According to him "a lack," such as the lack of sight, "is a not-being-present. Nevertheless, this absence is not nothing [*Der Mangle ist als Fehlen zwar ein Nichtvorhandesnsein; gleichwhol ist dieses Fehlen doch nicht nichts*]" (177 / 101). The absence of sight is not nothing—it is not something simply privative. The nothingness which manifests itself in blindness and evil is, he claims, "not nugatory [*das Nicht nicht Nichtiges*]; but, rather, something *tremendous* [*Ungeheures*], the most tremendous element in the nature of Being" (177 / 101, italics mine).

According to Heidegger, by establishing evil as a determinate mode of Being, by recognizing it as a tremendous element in Being, Schelling is able to treat it not only within "the sphere of mere morality…, but rather in the broadest sphere of the ontological and the theological fundamental question, thus a metaphysics of evil" (*GA* 42: 168 / 97). Only once evil is conceived of in this "broader sphere," as a force within being, thinks Schelling, can any real conception of the nature of human freedom be maintained as the power to choose between these two ways of being. For, according to Schelling: "either real evil is admitted, in which case it is unavoidable to include evil itself in infinite Substance or in the Primal Will, and thus totally disrupt the conception of an all-perfect Being; or the reality of evil must in some way or other be denied, in which case the real conception of freedom disappears at the same time" (*HF* 26). Committed to establishing an understanding of the divine based on the concrete manifestation of the world, and not one which manipulates our understanding of the world in order to maintain some metaphysical conviction concerning the nature of the God, Schelling clearly opts for the former, embracing a metaphysics of evil and thereby forcing a reconstruction of the idea of God.

Schelling begins by defining evil as a positive phenomenon in its own right, and as such a phenomenon which is established and maintained in the way in which beings emerge on the grounds provided by God's self-denial (*HF* 44–45). As such, claims Schelling, God's being must somehow be implicated in the emergence of evil, certainly at least, in its appearance as a determinate option for human beings. Moreover, since God is understood by him as that force which is always becoming through real existence, evil, as a determinate mode of that existence, must in fact be seen as somehow *necessary* for God's self-revelation through being (50). Indeed, claims Schelling, evil must be conceived of as a condition for God's emergence in and through existence, as God who is always becoming therein. According to Schelling, "in order that evil should not be, God himself would have not to be" (83). "Not only does something positive lie in evil in general," claims Heidegger in his reading of Schelling, "but the *most positive* element of nature itself, the ground's willing to come to itself, 'is' the negative here, 'is' as negation in the form of evil" (*GA* 42: 250 / 145). Now, while it is true that God is not in any real way now, God, for Schelling, nevertheless is a possibility for the now—God is as one who is becoming through the now and who may eventually be. God's being thus seems somehow inexorably tied to the presence of evil in the world for Schelling.

We must be careful to guard against confusion here, however. It is not Schelling's intention that God be made somehow the author of evil. After all, were this the case, human freedom as the potentiality for good and evil would find itself threatened once again, though this time from other quarters. The choice for evil is always made by human beings, it is the outworking of their freedom, thinks Schelling. God does not therefore determine the existence of evil, we do. But God, as the indeterminate grounds for existence and the freedom for good and evil, and as a possibility held out for that existence, must be implicated in any evil which appears. God cannot be absolutely identified with the existence of evil, after all the existence of evil is in some ways more real than the existence of God according to Schelling; nevertheless, God must be understood as inexorable from the appearance of evil. Both good and evil, as permutations within existence, are thereby determinates of the God who is becoming through existence. In this regard, claims Schelling, "good and evil," can be viewed as "the same, only regarded from different aspects," for both are part of God (*HF* 80). It is this unity of the good and evil which is precisely what is forgotten, according to Heidegger's read, in the "moral interpretation" of the existence of evil, the interpretation in which evil is defined in contrast to the good and being. According to Heidegger: "in the moral interpretation we forget that good and evil could not strive apart from each other if they were not intrinsically striving against each other and that they could never strive against each other if they did not mutually thrust into each other and were not together in the ground as they are" (*GA* 42: 273 / 157). What is interesting to us here, however, is the not the way in which good and evil inhere to one another in the being of God, but the way in which, according to Schelling, evil distinguishes itself from the good in the operation of the ground, and how this relates to our conception of the beyond as the numinous and informs our understanding of the movement of human longing toward such a beyond. What is interesting, then, is the way in which Schelling accounts for the relation between God, evil,

250 Longing for the Other

LONGING AND EVIL

As we saw in the last chapter, Schelling identifies God as not only the ground which withdraws into nonbeing in order to allow for the procession and emergence of independent beings, but also as the force which is always approaching through the movement of human history—that which becomes through the independence of the created order and the radical independence and freedom of human existence. This force expresses a kind of *will* (*Wille*), namely God's will to be—God's will to emerge and appear through the created order, God's *self-will* (*HF* 34, 24). It was this will which Schelling characterized as a longing within creation, that is, the longing of the absolute "to give birth to itself. This is not the One itself, but is co-eternal with it. This longing seeks to give birth to God, i.e. the unfathomable unity, but to this extent it has not yet the unity in its own self" (34). As the will of God to come to actualize through creation, the will working its way out through creation is a will toward the absolute, toward this promised unity. It is thus a universal will, a will toward a universalization wherein everything will be assumed within the totalizing being of an absolute God. "It is God's will," writes Schelling, "to universalize everything, to lift it to unity with light or to preserve it therein" (58). The expression of this will, as the approach of God in and through creation, Schelling names God's revelation (*Offenbarung*) (52). The revelation of God, which one can only take to express the way in which God appears to man, is thus experienced as the approach of a totalizing universalization, as an approaching consummation which aims to envelop and appropriate everything into itself.[18] The approach of God thus signals the possible return of the *Ungrund,* of that state of Being so complete that it disallows any distinction or demarcation of particular beings. God's self-revelation, God's approach as this will to universalize everything, thus appears as a kind of threat to humans whose existence is defined through their particularity as singular beings.

Though we may be attracted to the possibility of God as our origin and ground (see *GA* 43: 261 / 151), the object of this attraction threatens to overwhelm and destroy us. Schelling thus compares it to "the ancient tale," of Odysseus, where "the irresistible song of the sirens sounded out of the deep to draw the passing mariner down into the whirlpool" (*HF* 59). Elsewhere, he describes the approach of the being of God as a "consuming fire" which in its purity and absoluteness threatens to burn away every distinction in its path. The possibility of God's existence proper is, explains Schelling, a "horrifying" prospect for humanity (*AW* 104). It is the approach of the numinous object. Heidegger characterizes the threat posed in the approach of the divine as the *look* of God.[19] "This look," he contends with Schelling, "is a consuming fire for every particular will. The sundered self-will of man is threatened by this fire. It threatens to extinguish all self-will and every being-a-self" (*GA* 42: 263 / 152).

The ever looming threat within the created order presented in the possibility of the numinous engenders, claims Schelling, an eternal "veil of sadness which is spread over all nature," and creates, "the deep, unappeasable melancholy," which accompanies human existence (*HF* 79; cf. SS 230). Heidegger characterizes the experience of this threat present in the revelation of God as a kind of dread (*Angst*) which he names a "life-dread" (*Lebensangst*) (*GA* 42: 263 / 152). This "life-dread," claims Heidegger, "is a metaphysical necessity and has nothing to do with the little needs of the individual's intimidation and hesitancy" (263 / 152). In this way it resembles the anxiety (*Angst*), in contradistinction to fear (*Furcht*), detailed in *Being and Time* (see *GA* 2: ¶ 40). Life-dread, it seems, is not something one feels about any *particular* experience. It does not arise before any *determinate* possibility. It is instead the amorphous dread one feels at the approach of the universalizing and totalizing gaze of the *absolute* and the *indeterminate* which is announced in the being of God.

The revelation of God and the initiation of this life-dread, thinks Schelling and Heidegger, provokes a reaction within human existence. Overcome with anxiety by the possible annihilation of this existence, the revelation of God as the universal inspires human beings to seek shelter in the singularity of their own being, to counteract the universal will of the divine by burying themselves in what is particular and singular about their being. So the approach of the will to universalize inflames the human will to particularize, to section itself off from the universal. According to Heidegger's reading of Schelling, as "the ground becomes the more powerful in man, the flight to self-craving [*Eigensucht*] becomes the more urgent because this craving (*Sucht*) is that through which the will of the ground striving for darkness wants to remove itself from the luminosity of the divine look of light" (*GA* 42: 263 / 152).[20] In the face of the divine look human beings turn inward. This movement, claims Schelling, throws human existence off balance: "The terror of life drives man out of the center in which he was created; for being the lucid and pure essence of all will [the will of God] is [a] consuming fire for each particular will; in order to be able to live in it man must mortify all egotism, which almost makes necessary the attempt to leave it and to enter the periphery in order to seek peace for his selfhood there" (*HF* 59). Determinatively, this will to particularize, this attempt by human beings to shore up their existence against the annihilating threat of the coming of the divine, is manifest in the way in which we take our longings, that force which, according to Schelling, expresses "the most obscure and thus the deepest aspect of human nature" (SS 230). By his read, faced with the totalizing threat of the revelation of God, human beings are driven to a supererogation of their longings, and, in doing so, reinforce them somehow in the attempt to strengthen what they feel is the core of their singularity and existence. This is done, claims Schelling, by attempting to treat one's amorphous and indeterminate longings as determinate desires with specific attainable ends, which results, he argues, in the reversion of human longing into a "mere craving [*bloße Sucht*] or desire [*Begierde*], that is blind will" (*HF* 38).

At the approach of the divine felt in revelation, human longings, as the expression of God's desire to be, begin, in their indeterminacy, to appear, like God, as a kind of threat. Their indeterminacy thus begins to loom ever larger and appear overwhelming and unmanageable. The appearance of the possibility of God, in a sense, incites human longings—it stirs it up as heat and pressure excite the movement of molecules, or like wind makes a loose sail flap. In the attempt to tie themselves to the mast of their own being in order to survive the luring threat presented in the being of God, human beings begin to tie their longings down to determinate objects and, in so doing, begin to convert the indeterminacy of their longings into simple terminable desires. In doing so, longing becomes confused with any other mere hunger or craving—something which, tied to the determinate realm of being, appears to be satiable and emergent from some determinate absence or need.

Schelling goes to great lengths throughout his treatise on the nature of human freedom to distinguish longing, as an expression of God's desire for being, from the craving, blind passion and hunger that result from an imbalance within human nature (see *HF* 49). Heidegger too recognizes this distinction in his reading of Schelling, as we first saw in chapter 2, describing "addiction [*die Sucht*]," as "a striving [*Streben*] and a desiring [*Begeheren*], indeed the addiction of longing, of being concerned with oneself [*des Bekümmertsein um sich*]," which he identifies as a kind of sickness (*Krankheit*) and disease (*Seuche*) (*GA* 42: 125 / 217).

When longing is reverted into this kind of desire by the human will to particularize, claims Schelling, it is no longer the expression of the human tie to the beyond, but instead becomes a manifestation of "the hunger of selfishness [*Hunger der Selbstsucht*] which, in the measure that it deserts totality and unity becomes even needier *begieriger*] and poorer [*dürftiger*], but just on that account more ravenous, hungrier, more poisonous" (*HF* 69). Since longing is originally for Schelling an expression of the infinite and eternal desire of God to appear, once it is tied to the realm of the finite and determinate it rages out of control. Converted into a kind of hunger by the human dread which arises in the face of the indeterminate, longing becomes an insatiable drive to have and consume more. It thus reverts into what Schelling calls a kind of "addiction" to and "hunger for Being" (*SS* 231)—it becomes a kind of "obsession [*sucht*] with Being" (*AW* 21; cf. *HF* 41). In the attempt to protect itself, human existence thus becomes a slave to itself, captivated by its own being and wants. As a result, it loses the very thing by which its being was determined: namely, a radical freedom from and in being.[21] This freedom can only be restored, claims Schelling, once this "obsession [*sucht*] [with Being] abates into longing [*Sehnsucht*], [and] wild desire turns into a longing to ally itself, as if it were its own true or highest self, with the will that wills nothing, with eternal freedom" (*AW* 28; translation modified).

According to Schelling, this will to particularize, this tendency to take one's longings as determinately achievable desires and to seek out their fulfillment and satisfaction, is what provokes the emergence of determinate evil. "The general possibility of evil," writes Schelling, "consists in the fact that, instead of keeping his selfhood as the basis or the instrument, man can strive to elevate it to be the ruling and universal will, and, on the contrary, try to make what is spiritual in him into a means" (*HF* 68). When one seeks to elevate one's own self-will over and above the will to universality presented in the coming of the divine by treating his or her longings as determinate desires, when one strives to make a universal principle of one's own self and innermost being, evil results.

Evil, claims Schelling, is this "very exaltation of self-will" (*HF* 41). In the words of Slavoj Žižek, "in human Evil, the *Selbstheit* of the Ground is self-illuminated, elevated to the Spirit, it takes over as the *spiritual* principle of egotism which strives to instrumentalize and subordinate to itself every otherness."[22] As a manifestation of an imbalance within human nature, the evil that results from the supererogation of longing and its conversion into a determinate desire, like the cravings that result, manifests as a kind of disease claims Schelling; for just as disease "occurs only because some entity whose freedom or life exists only so that it may remain in the whole, strives to exist for itself....Just so is the case of evil" (42).

Since this reversion of longings into determinate desires and hungers, which results in the emergence of evil, is originally inspired through the revelation of the divine, claims Schelling, the approach of God can in some ways be understood as the "general cause of temptation, a solicitation to evil" (*HF* 50). But, this solicitation and temptation can occur in another way as well. It can also occur through the sheer willfulness and pride of humanity. Evil, for Schelling, is always the result of the improper treatment of longing which occurs through the elevation of self-will into a universal principle. But, he thinks this elevation need not occur initially as the result of the appearance of God, it may simply appear on its own, as an expression of the radical freedom of human existence. When this occurs, when one attempts to make of oneself a universal principle, treating that which is properly only an indeterminacy as a determinate actuality, one begins by attempting to actualize the possibility held out in longing, and in doing so treats it improperly as any other kind of determinate desire.

But, since longing is distinguished from other desires as the expression of and drive toward the beyond being that is the being of God, when it is treated improperly what is pursued as a determinate object is God itself. As a result, the normally indeterminate being of God begins to appear larger and more determinately, it begins to take on reality. Taken as a determinate object, God begins to take on an actual appearance as opposed to a merely potential one and, hence, begins to shine as a numinous object. When this occurs, as we have already examined, human nature is thrown off balance and evil results. But it is important to note that this possibility exists for Schelling. The improper treatment of longings which results in the manifestation of evil thus need not be *initially* occasioned by God's revelation, but may in fact arise from an improper employment of human freedom. In either case, longing is always tied to the way in which the being of God appears as the numinous object. Longing, it seems, functions as a kind of ballast for the infinite being of the beyond which it moves toward and manifests. When longing is treated properly and maintained as a distinct phenomenon, that is, when it is held in a proper relation to the beyond, then it functions properly by allowing a way to experience the beyond without being overwhelmed by it—to experience it as a possibility, rather than a threatening actuality. On the other hand, when longing is treated improperly and made a kind of determinate desire with specific ends, the beyond toward which is directed begins to loom menacingly through it, appearing as a threatening and numinous object. This causes the equilibrium of human existence to be thrown off balance casting into headlong into evil action. To use another metaphor, longing seems to serve for Schelling as a kind of filter through which the light of the divine beyond being may shine within being without burning or consuming it—the divine only appears as the overwhelming and threatening when that filter is tampered with and treated improperly.

CONCLUSIONS: LONGING AS THE VACCINATION OF THE INFINITE

If we are to take all that we have discovered through Levinas and his historical interlocutors concerning the nature of longing as correct, a very clear, albeit unusual picture begins to emerge. Longing, it seems, as that movement within our being which carries within it the trace of that which lies irrevocably beyond our being, seems to serve a determinate function in relation to that beyond: namely, it serves to dole out the metaphysical into the created order in such a way that it can be experienced concretely without threatening the destruction of the one who perceives it affectively. In this regard, and in contradiction to the traditional theological analysis, longing does not appear to be, for Levinas, that which carries us to God, and which, if we follow diligently, promises to conclude in God's presence, as is conceived by Augustine; but precisely that which protects us from the divine by maintaining a regulated distance from God. Indeed, as we have seen, longing appears to be a kind of defense against the beyond—a way of encountering it without being overwhelmed by its otherness. Longing is thus, in a sense, a discrete expression of the absolute otherness of the beyond—a way in which we may, like Moses's bush, appear within the illuminative sphere of the divine without being consumed by it.

Figured in terms of its manifestation as a kind of disease or sickness, as was evoked in the introduction by Shakespeare, C. S. Lewis, and Goethe and was seen to be pregnant in the original meaning of the word, longing appears to be a kind of *vaccination* against the infinite. Though a disease, it is not debilitating; it is instead a kind of protection. Figured as the infection of the infinite within the finite, longing appears to be a way of warding off wholesale contamination by the beyond—an epidemic which would threaten the very nature of independent existence. Longing thus appears to be a small dose of the infinite contracted at the very outset of creation; indeed in the primordial contraction of God, the immemorial explosion of the divine—the glow of which serves as the illuminative clearing for determinate existence. Understood thusly, longing emerges as a protection within us against the return of this prehistoric bad infinite, of a presence so complete it disallows any differentiation.

Understood as the symptom of this contraction, longing evidences the fact that we have always already been tainted by the touch of the beyond, pricked and infected by God. In fact, it is due to this infection that we have first and foremost been *empowered,* as Heidegger noted, as free and independent creatures. Far from debilitating us then, the infection of the infinite felt in human longing manifests itself as an insatiable drive and power. Longing is not, as has traditionally been thought, borne out of some determinate absence, but is instead the expression of a radical overflowing and abundant presence within human existence. The reason this presence seems to have been so easily misapprehended for so many and for so long as some form of absence or lack, is the result of the way in which the presence it bears is; for, as we have seen, longing is the present expression of beyond as the withdrawal from being.

As the expression within being of that which lies beyond being, the divine, the lack seemingly affected in longing, the fact that it is never fulfilled, is thus not the expression of an absence proper, but rather of the way in which the super abundant being of God which it mediates appears. As we have noted, longing is the expression of a kind of superabundant absence, a transcendence which is transcendent to the point of absence. Though the expression of a kind of absence, longing is not privatively motivated. It is instead evidence of something extra within us—something which comes from outside.

Longing is not nostalgia nor a determinate hunger or craving. It is never a desire to return to something lost within our own past or the desire to restore something that has been evacuated through use. It is instead, the expression of a kind of profound passivity—the desire for something that never belonged to us, nor could ever be possessed by us. Longing is the mark of our own belonging in and dependence upon something else—something otherwise. It is the expression of the fact that our radical freedom and independence is situated on a ground which is not our own, but which is provided by the Other who first chose not to be in order to enable our own being. Longing's relation to the past is to a past still further and more distant than our own past—to a past which is situated on the hither side of time, to a past which is always already past.

Though longing arises from this immemorial past, it is not directed toward this past, but instead always reaches out beyond us into a future still more future—to a future time which lies beyond our own. It is thus partially fulfilled in the birth of a child, in whom we see ourselves extended beyond the time allotted to us, as Levinas details in his account of fecundity, and experienced as an ethical drive toward the determinate other who commands our responsibility. But longing reaches still further than fecundity and ethics, it reaches into the time of the messianic, into the time of the ever approaching God who becomes through longing.

We have defined longing, in its pursuit of the infinite, as the expression of a kind of infinite within the finite realm of human existence. It was for this reason that Levinas identified human longing with the idea of the infinite, with an *ideatum* which overflows its *idea*, and that Plato recognized its endlessness as a voyage in the course of the gods, a recognition which has been supported by Heidegger, Fichte, and Schelling, who have all recognized the infinitude implied by longing's insatiability. Understood in its function as a kind of defense against the numinosity of the beyond, longing can thus perhaps also be understood as the expression of something resembling a bound infinitude, if such an idea can be conceived. Bound within the discrete realm of human finitude as longing, the pure infinitude of the beyond becomes somehow manageable—still profoundly other, but not threateningly so. Longing thus appears to be an operation by which the bad infinitude of the sacred, to use Levinas's term, is converted into the good infinite of the holy, of the beyond being and the Good, and thereby the basis for ethics. It is an operation by which the infinite can express itself within the finite without exploding its limits, by which a God beyond being can manifest in being without unraveling the fabric of existence, which is defined through its finitude.

Given its link to the infinite, however, though longing may function in a protective role, it also presents a kind of temptation; namely, the temptation to resurrect total presence of the primordial *il y a*. Misinterpreted and mistreated as a determinate desire, a desire which demands actualization through the consumption of present objects, longing, the vaccination of the infinite, quickly transforms into a ravenous all consuming disease giving way to all kinds of determinate evil. Perhaps this is the explanation behind the mindless consumption of late capitalism and all of the war and destruction it has spawned: a misinterpretation of the meaning and nature of our longings. For, indeed, when we take what is, by definition, an infinite and unsatisfiable longing, as a determinate desire which, one thinks, can be eventually satisfied, all attempts to achieve satisfaction inevitably lead to excess, the kind of excess all too apparent in the West in the last century. This transformation of longing from a good infinite, serving as a vaccination against the return of a presence so complete it absorbs all determinate existents, to a bad infinite, which attempts to actualize a complete presence through the consumption of all determinate entities, transfers longing's ethical potency into evil. Hence the ambiguity of Levinas's infinite.

But, longing need not be treated in this way. Understood properly, longing need not pose a threat, but may instead offer a kind of promise—a promise of liberation from the constraints of being, a promise that our true fulfillment can be found, not by attending to our own being, but by attending to the ethical demands of the Other. Only when understood and treated thusly can we begin to perceive the true nature of longing: to be both a human and a truly divine phenomenon.

NOTES

NOTES TO INTRODUCTION

1. Arnold, "The Buried Life," italics mine.
2. Hemingway, *A Moveable Feast,* 56–57.
3. Lewis, *Surprised by Joy,* 73, 78; italics mine.
4. Ibid., 176.
5. Ibid., 16.
6. Shakespeare, "Anthony and Cleopatra," act 5, scene 2, lines 281–82.
7. *American Heritage Dictionary of English,* s.v. "long."
8. *WordNet 3.0 (Princeton University, 2003),* s.v. "longing," http://wordnetweb.princeton.edu/perl/webwn?s=longing.
9. *Oxford English Dictionary,* s.v. "longing," 1131.
10. Ibid., 1131.
11. Ibid., 1131.
12. Ibid., 1131.
13. Ibid., 1131.
14. This reference to the infectious genesis of longing and its manifestation as a sickness will be developed in more detail later, especially in chapters 1, 4, and 5.
15. Herbert "The Temple," old English spellings maintained.
16. Shakespeare "Sonnet 147."
17. Lewis, *Surprised by Joy,* 17; italics mine.
18. *Wildhagen and Héraucourt German-English Dictionary,* s.v. "Sehnsucht," 1106.
19. Ibid., 1106.
20. Ibid., s.v. "Sucht," 1175.
21. *Deutsches Wörterbuch,* s.v. "Sehnsucht," 157.

22. Ibid., 157.
23. Ibid., 157.
24. *Wildhagen and Héraucourt German-English Dictionary*, s.v. "sucht," 1175.
25. Ibid., s.v. "siechen," 1116. As we shall see, this etymology is also noted by Heidegger.
26. Goethe, "Selige Sehnsucht," 240:
>Tell a wise person or else keep silent
>For the masses will mock it right away
>I praise what is truly alive
>And what longs to be burned to death.
>In the calm waters of the love nights
>Where you were begotten,
>Where you have begotten,
>A strange feeling comes over you
>When you see the silent candle burning.
>Now you are no longer caught in this obsession with darkness
>And a desire for higher lovemaking sweeps you upward.
>Distance does not make you falter.
>And now, arriving in magic, flying
>and finally, insane for the light
>You are the butterfly.
>And you are gone.
>And so long as you haven't experienced this,
>To die and so to grow,
>You are only a troubled guest on a dark earth.

27. See Nietzsche, "On the Uses and Disadvantages of History for Life," 61.

Notes to Chapter One

1. As an interesting side note, Adriaan Peperzak reads Levinas's phenomenological account of need here, and the distinction he will subsequently make between it and metaphysical desire, as in part a response to the concept of economy established in Kant's practical philosophy ("Some Remarks on Hegel, Kant and Levinas," 213).

2. Richard Cohen provides a rich read of Levinas's employment of the Odyssian/Ulyssian narrative, especially as it pertains to the ethical life, and offering some interesting suggestions as to how it relates to many of the current conflicts the world is embroiled in today in his "Notes on the Title of *Totality and Infinity*," 125.

3. Whether or not this is an accurate reading of the Odyssian tale is yet to be seen. One must remember that at the end of the *Odyssey*, though Odysseus has returned to Ithaca, he has not yet returned "home," as expressed in Tennyson's poem Ulysses wherein our "aged king" declares that he "cannot rest from travel." Remember that at the end of the *Odyssey* Odysseus cannot yet settle in Ithaca, but must still travel on in a seemingly impossible journey to plant an oar in a land the inhabitants of which have never heard the name of Poseidon in order to appease his wrath. This is a seemingly impossible task of course, because to the Greeks the inhabitable world is circumscribed by the ocean making Poseidon's realm global in proportion. This seemingly eternal delay of the eventual return home in the *Odyssey* gives it an entirely different meaning, one not so much about homecoming as about exile.

4. Spinoza, *Ethics,* 126.

5. Though examinations of nostalgia like that of Rudolf Bernet's (see "Heimwee en Nostalgie") would complicate this conclusion, indeed for Bernet nostalgia seems to contain a similar movement, we must remember that, for Levinas, nostalgia is a technical term. It is to the specificity of his use that we are referring here.

6. It is curious to note that, despite Plato being one of the most frequently and overtly treated of Levinas's interlocutors, relatively little secondary literature has been written on this interaction (especially when compared to how much has been written on Levinas's interaction with Heidegger). Two notable exceptions are, of course, Adriaan Peperzak's *To The Other,* which constantly goes back to Levinas's interaction with Plato in order to explain his work, and Stella Sandford's article, "Plato and Levinas: The Same and the Other." See also Sarah Allen's very recent *The Philosophical Sense of Transcendence.*

7. Stella Sandford even suggests that not only does Levinas's language of being, nonbeing, and beyond being come from Plato, but that in fact even his concepts of same and the other emerge from an interaction with Plato's *Sophist* ("Plato and Levinas: The Same and the Other").

8. Derrida famously characterized Levinas's troubled interaction with Plato as a kind of strange patricide. He claims that Levinas's curious ambivalence to Plato is because while both Levinas and Plato sought to overcome the logic of the Parmenidean One, Plato did not go far enough, leaving Levinas no choice but to ultimately go beyond him ("Violence and Metaphysics," 89).

9. For a survey of these differences in interpretation see, for example, *Levinas and the Ancients,* ed. Brian Schroeder and Silvia Benso.

10. This point has been thoroughly documented by Adriaan Peperzak in *To the Other*.

11. Again, Peperzak notes that Levinas's divergence with Plato here rests upon his reading of the power of Eros to mediate the soul's dialogue with itself in anamnesis (*To the Other,* 50).

12. Not all are convinced, as I shall address, by the contrast Levinas draws between metaphysical desire and Eros, much less this distinction between metaphysical desire and need. Deborah Achtenberg, for one, has argued that upon closer analysis these seemingly divergent accounts may share much more in common than Levinas would admit (see, for example, her "The Eternal and the New").

13. Here is, once again, the intimate bond between sickness and desire. As will be shown soon, this connection is fleshed out even more by Socrates in the *Phaedrus*. There he even suggests that Eros can be understood as a kind of infection. This suggests, on first glance, that there is perhaps some connection between Eros and the English term longing.

14. One must remember that in Greek Πόρος, resource, has two different meanings. It not only expresses resource in terms of abundance, but also in terms of ways and means. As such, Πόρος can also be used to express a kind of passage or "way across," hence its antonym aporia (ἀπορία) meaning stuck, blocked, or finding no way out (*Liddell and Scott's Greek-English Lexicon*, s.v. "Πόρος").

15. Understanding the way in which Eros is the movement between absence and presence which unites the two in its being is a significant key to understanding how it is that Plato accounts of *erotic* mania. We shall return to this idea in greater detail later in the chapter.

16. Mitchell, *The Hymn to Eros,* 129.

17. Adriaan Peperzak, for one, sees in this account of Plato's something similar to Levinas's contrast of the Odyssian journey to the Abrahamic journey noting that, by his read, Eros seems to, at least in this regard, fulfill Levinas's expectations of the Abrahamic movement of ethics (*To the Other,* 67–68).

18. Rosen, *Plato's Symposium,* 217.

19. Hyland, *Finitude and Transcendence,* 108.

20. Peperzak, *To the Other,* 43–44.

21. See Gonzalez, "Levinas Questioning Plato."

22. According to Levinas, "the Good declines the desire it arouses while inclining it toward responsibility for the neighbor" (*OB* 123). Also note that credit must be given here to Rudi Visker from whose language I draw in naming this break in the power of the Good an *interruption* ("Dis-possessed," 126).

23. Clearly this discussion has a profound impact on how one interprets Levinas's claims concerning the nature of the divine, which will

be explored in more detail in later chapters, most directly in chapter 4 on Levinas and Schelling. For more on the impact of Levinas's claims concerning the displacement of the power of the Good onto the mantle of the other in a religious context see Kosky, *Levinas and the Philosophy of Religion*.

24. See Purcell, *Levinas and Theology*, 62.

25. Robert Bernasconi notes this well showing that though Levinas sets off looking for metaphysics, his winds up discovering that it is only present in the social realm of ethics: "[Levinas] was not looking for ethics, but for the meaning of transcendence, and yet when he discovered the meaning of transcendence, it turned out that it was indeed ethics" ("No Exit," 101).

26. The relation between longing and the concrete ethical relation to another will be explored in greater detail in chapter 3 on the relationship between the work of Levinas, Fichte, and Schelling.

27. For an interesting read of Levinas's critique of the role of vision in the formation of the subject and an analysis of how this critique affects his thought as a whole see Jay, *Downcast Eyes*.

28. This recognition resembles an episode recounted by Freud in a footnote to his *Three Essays on the Theory of Sexuality*. There he writes that "[I once heard] a three-year-old boy...calling out of a dark room: 'Auntie, speak to me! I'm frightened because it's so dark.' His aunt answered him: 'What good would that do? You can't see me.' 'That doesn't matter,' replied the child, 'if anyone speaks, it get light'" (90). Though Freud analyzes this passage as testifying to the fear which erupts at the child's loss of his love object/mother, it could equally be read as further evidence in the Levinasian account of the Other as the illuminative principle.

29. For a more complete rendering of this story and investigation into its implications see Visker, *The Inhuman Condition*.

30. The way in which the Other invites the subject to arise to its true self will be developed in more detail in chapter 3 on Levinas's dialogue with Fichte.

31. Simon Critchley notes this powerfully, reading in Levinas an account of a kind of rebirth of subjectivity through the ethical encounter, one where in the subject is refounded on a ground no longer its own, but belonging to the other (*Infinitely Demanding: Ethics of Commitment, Politics of Resistance*, 57).

32. This "way out" should remind the reader of the Πόρος provided in Eros. The Other's appearance and solicitation through metaphysical desire offers a way out of the enslavement to being just as Eros provides

a way out of the limitations of temporal beauty and into the stability of divine beauty.

33. Peperzak, *To the Other*, 22; Peperzak, *Beyond*, 164–65.

34. Cf., Visker, *The Inhuman Condition*, especially chapter 4, "The Price of Being Dispossessed: Levinas' God and Freud's Trauma." Also, see Fabio Ciaramelli, "The Posteriority of the Anterior." We will return to this concept in chapter 4.

35. For more on the idea of the infinite and how it is employed in Levinas's concept of transcendence see Cohen, "Some notes on the Title of Levinas's *Totality and Infinity* and its First Sentence," 121.

36. We should note here Levinas's ambivalence toward the word *possession*. Possession seems to have for him both a positive and a negative ethical value. It is positive as used above in as much as it indicates the entrance of the other and the freedom from our attachment to ourselves introduced therein—that is, in as much as it signifies the subject's having been made the possession of the Good. But, in as much as possession can express the way the subject's domination of the world through reason, *possessing* what is other to it and reducing that otherness to its self (*BPW* 9; *TI* 46, 158); or, in as much as possession expresses the loss of independence, which he associates in *Difficult Freedom* with pagan ritual, Levinas disdains it to the point of condemnation.

37. By claiming that the idea of infinity is "within me," Levinas is not trying to invoke the mysteries of Zeno's paradox (the possibility of reasoning an infinite contained within a finite). This would require reading the word *in* as a containment. But it is precisely this idea that Levinas is set against. The idea of the infinite is not "contained" inside of the finite, but overflows the finite—explodes the borders of the finite in such a way that it becomes irrevocably opened to the radically exterior (see *BPW* 136–38; *EN* 219–22).

38. This reference to disease and the contraction of the infinite by its subject/host is not only an attempt to reference, in part, an internal reference to sickness present in the old meanings of *to long*, but it is also a foreshadowing of our analysis to come in chapters 4 and 5.

39. It is interesting to note here that the next major section of the *Phaedrus* concerns itself with both the notion of infection and disease as well as with the concept of cure or *pharmakon* present in the act of writing, as is so rigorously explored by Jacques Derrida in "Plato's Pharmacy." Perhaps, the act of writing could be read as a possible *pharmakon* suitable to treating the kind of infection manifest in erotic transcendence. This is a relation, however, which cannot be explored suitably in this investigation, but nevertheless warrants further study.

40. Theaetetus's questions may indeed be the expression of a kind of erotic movement for Plato. See, for example, the *Cratylus* where Plato describes how the nature of a Hero emerges either from his or her birth as a result of the Eros which binds gods to men, or as a result of his or her being brave enough to ask the tough questions (398c–d). More on how Plato examines the nature of Eros there will be said near the end of this chapter.

41. It is interesting to note here that the word Plato uses to describe the pains of labor here, ὠδίνουσι (*odinousi*), is the same word that he uses in the *Phaedrus* (251d) when describing the pain the soul feels when its wings are inspired to grow by erotic striving after the beyond. We will return to this relation in more detail later.

42. We must remember that Theaetetus has not been made "pregnant" by Socrates' questioning. Socrates is not the philosophical father of Theaetetus's intellectual pregnancy. Instead he figures himself merely as a philosophical midwife helping Theaetetus to deliver a healthy baby—a child he had growing within him long before he met with Socrates. Socrates' only "children" then are those he helped into the world, not those he fathered himself.

43. Plato also references the subject's passivity in regards to his or her inception upon the philosophical path in the *Parmenides* (130e), where Parmenides mentions to the young Socrates that his troubles with the subject matter are a result of the fact that "philosophy has not yet taken hold upon you." Philosophy, it seems for Plato, is an endeavor which is initiated not by the subject, but one which *takes a hold* of the subject—moves in and through a subject from outside.

44. Peperzak, *To the Other*, 132.

45. We must be careful to distinguish what Levinas examines here as the erotic from Plato's account of Eros as such. Though Eros references the sexual, it does not pertain exclusively to the realm of sexuality, as is so often misconceived. Thus, what Levinas examines as the erotic here is not the same as what he addresses in his condemnation of Platonic Eros. He is instead merely using the parlance of our times to connote the sexual.

46. It should be noted here that in his earlier works, *De l'évasion*, *Time and the Other*, and even *Existence and Existents* for instance, he uses the term love, and even makes direct reference in some cases to erotic love, to relate ideas he will later associate exclusively with metaphysical desire. But, we cannot be so strict as to fail to see that what he explores as erotic love in his later works differs radically from what he terms love in his early works. To conflate these two accounts would be to do a serious injustice to Levinas and result in grave confusion.

47. In his exploration of the concept of the caress in Levinas, Richard Cohen shows how Levinas's concept of Eros mediates in some essential way the ethical relation given birth to in metaphysical desire ("The Family and Ethics," 2).

48. For a wonderfully rich and intriguing read of the nature and role of Levinas's account of erotic love in *Totality and Infinity* see Moyaert, "The Phenomenology of Eros."

49. Luce Irigaray has fleshed out in prose to wonderful end an evocative rendition of the Levinasian relation of metaphysical desire, Eros, and fecundity in "The Fecundity of the Caress."

50. Cohen, "Family and Ethics," 2.

51. The especially curious relation between erotic desire, fecundity, and metaphysical desire suggests that there is some sense in which, though fundamentally and eternally insatiable, metaphysical desire can somehow be, at least temporarily, slated through the sexual and the relation to its product, the child. That perhaps the sexual and the child serve as a kind of resolution to metaphysical desire that satisfies it without satisfying it. Thus, they express the possibility of relating to the end of metaphysical desire, the Other as such, without having a direct relation to it, a possibility Levinas names "a relation without relation," (see Cohen, "Family and Ethics," 4). The way in which metaphysical desire is resolved in this way (without being entirely resolved) will be further explored in chapters 4 and 5.

52. This notion of the other's possession of the world is thus like Sartre's reading of the way in which the world bleeds toward the other in his *Being and Nothingness* (see chapter 1, "The Existence of Others," of part 3, "Being-for-Others"). There, however, the other steals the world from me in his possession of it, whereas in Levinas, it is I who steals the world from the other. In any case, it is this notion of a determinate other to whom the world belongs that is referenced here, not the holy Other, God.

52. More on the withdrawal of the Other and its role in the establishment of an independent world will be said in chapter 4.

54. The genesis of the subject as a separated being will be detailed in chapters 3 and 4. For now it is sufficient to recognize that enjoyment, and with it other desire, differ from longing in the way in which they remain entirely separated from and opposed to the Other.

55. Of course there are a number of ways in which one can approach the difference between Levinas and Plato, and indeed there are disagreements amongst Levinas scholars on how to read his relation to the ancients as a whole. Whereas some, like Adriaan Peperzak and Deborah Achtenberg,

seem to see much more in common between Levinas and Plato, others insist on their ultimate difference. For more on this debate, again see *Levinas and the Ancients,* ed. Schroeder and Benso.

56. *Liddell and Scott's Greek-English Lexicon,* s.v. "'Επιθυμία."
57. Hyland, "'Έρως, 'Επιθυμία, and Φιλία in Plato," 32.
58. Ibid., 40.
59. We must, of course, be careful when using the explorations pursued in the *Cratylus* to present a purely Platonic view since everything Socrates investigates therein he does under the adopted assumption that beings are in motion, and thus that being itself is motion, which is an assumption which he denies near the end of the dialogue. Nevertheless, his analyses of desire, when taken to establish a kind of taxonomy, are not affected by this later denial. Thus it is not his definitions of them that are questionable in light of this denial, but the way in which these definitions are employed in the attempt to say something about the nature of being.
60. The way in which longings are perpetually reverted into desires, and the consequences of such actions, will be explored in more detail in the final pages of this work.

Notes to Chapter Two

1. For a more detailed analysis of the number of ways and places in which Levinas openly contrasts his work to Heidegger's see for example: Peperzak, "Phenomenology—Ontology—Metaphysics."
2. Though the beyond being so much a part of Levinas's later thought is not yet fully articulate in the early work, his condemnation of the Heideggerian conception of being, the condemnation which led him directly to the embrace of such a beyond being is present already in his earliest work (see *EE* 4–5). Robert Bernasconi has even suggested that the reason Levinas turned more toward the beyond being in his later work was the result of a failed attempt in early work to truly distinguish and distance his thought from a Heideggerian ontology (see Bernasconi, "No Exit," 104). Levinas's problems with the Heideggerian position will become clearer as this chapter goes on.
3. This is in contrast to Levinas who figures his thought, as we saw in the last chapter, as a kind of qualified return to *Platonism,* a "return to Platonism in a new way" (*BPW* 58). But while Heidegger and Levinas's language may differ then in their mutual return to Plato, the former rejecting Platonism on behalf of Plato himself and the later embracing some form of Platonism but in a way which takes it away from its traditional rendering, both approach the platonic texts in a similar way. Namely, both

attempt in their treatment of Plato to return to the origin of Western thinking and illuminate it in such a ways as to reveal the hidden underpinnings and assumptions of that history, and in some cases, to thereby undermine that history. This will become more evident shortly.

4. Also in *"What Is Metaphysics?"* Heidegger lists the joy one feels while in love as one of the fundamental attunements between human Dasein and Being. But, there again, when attempting to elaborate on the nature and function of those fundamental attunements he quickly leaves love behind focusing the bulk of his investigation into the nature of anxiety (*GA* 9: 8 / 87).

5. Vedder, "Heidegger on Desire," 353.

6. This is a difference which, as we will see shortly, has a profound impact upon how we understand the operation of Eros in contradistinction to other forms of desire, such as needs.

7. The Wildhagen and Héracourt German-English Dictionary alternatively translates the word *eigen* as "individual (style)" and "particular." It even notes that it can be used to denote something that is "special" or "private" clearly indicating its reference to that which is personal or "one's own" way of doing something—one's way of being—what Levinas refers to as one's ess*a*nce.

8. Heidegger's characterization of the nature of truth changes after his turn toward the Being of the *es gibt* in the later works as can be seen in his essays "On the Essence of Truth," and "Plato's Doctrine of Truth" (*GA* 9). There truth (*aletheia*) or disclosure, as a negative term, references for him the sway of untruth (*lethe*) or closure in the primordial essence of Being. Being thus becomes for him in the later works not that which is revealed and appears through Dasein's disclosure of entities, but that fundamental withdrawal from presence, that fundamental closure, which allows beings to appear at all and be disclosed. As we shall shortly see, it is this latter notion of truth and Being which is at work in his analysis of the function of Eros.

9. See Gans, "Ethics or Ontology," 117–21.

10. See Taminiaux, "The Early Levinas's Reply to Heidegger"; and, Keyes, "Evaluation of Levinas's Critique of Heidegger."

11. Though Heidegger would object to the language of passivity and activity as it still relies too much upon a conception of a subject, a conception which he persistently tries to do away with, it is nevertheless useful to employ such language here to underscore the fact that for Heidegger Eros is not a project, either consciously or unconsciously of human existence. Humans are caught up in the movement of Eros—a movement which seems to originate in something outside of them and

move toward something equally beyond them. This should become clearer as our examination of the text continues. In any case, we must be careful to note that human existence for Heidegger is not some thing which can be acted on or act, either passively or actively respectively, by some other object. These sorts of distinctions are intentionally blurred in the later Heidegger.

12. Heidegger's attempt to overturn the traditional account of human subjectivity is even more articulate in his 1942 lecture on the *Parmenides* (*GA* 54) and in his famous 1946 *Letter on Humanism* (*GA* 9). Unfortunately, a more complete rendering of this argument will carry the study at hand too far adrift at present. For more on Heidegger's interaction with and deconstruction of the notion of human subjectivity see, for instance, Raffoul, *Heidegger and the Subject*.

13. It is interesting to note here that according to Heidegger, that which is had in authentic having, that which is held before one through authentic having, is not presented by means of a recollection. According to Heidegger, "this having-before-oneself of something not immediately present is not necessarily a recollecting" (*GA* 34: 297 / 211). In this sense Heidegger's analysis of that which is present in and through longing and which occasions it is in line with Levinas's claim that the idea of the infinite which is expressed through metaphysical desire could not be the product of our own anamnesis, but instead signals the presence of a strange alterity within them. The way the alterity signaled in this presence is worked out by Heidegger will be seen shortly.

14. We see in this account of the erotic phenomenon something which already begins to approach our understanding of human longing. As we shall see more shortly, Heidegger, like Lewis, seems to see Eros as a correlate or manifestation of a deeper longing for things "a long way off."

15. In the text on *Schelling's Treatise on the Essence of Human Freedom* (*GA* 42) Heidegger characterizes this kind of need, which he contrasts with longing, as an "addiction" (*Sucht*) which, he claims, "has nothing to do with searching [*Suchen*] etymologically—[but] primordially means sickness [*Krankheit*] which strives to spread itself; sickly [*siech*] disease [*Seuche*]" (217 / 125). He thus contrasts it to longing which is concerned with and pursues the beyond as a kind of "being concerned with oneself" (217 / 125). This connection between need and addiction, as two movements opposing the nature of longing, is grounded in the fact that in both personal satisfaction and power is sought to the occultation of the real/authentic object of primordial longing. So it is that in both one's own being eclipses the transcendent Being pursued by longing. That

this transcendent Being is the proper object of longing for Heidegger will become apparent shortly.

16. This distinction seems to reflect and repeat the various modes of Erotic transcendence we identified in Plato at the end of the last chapter, authentic Eros resembling Eros ordered under the rubric of *Himeros,* and inauthentic Eros, respectively, resembling Eros ordered under the guise of *Epithumia*. This comparison is immediately supported by Michael Zimmerman's claims concerning Eros quoted above.

17. Zimmerman, "Ontical Craving Versus Ontological Desire."

18. Ibid., 511. Though Zimmerman identifies authentic Eros as situated within the realm of the ontological to distinguish it from seemingly lesser desires that tarry on a merely ontic level, as we shall see in more detail shortly, Heidegger's claims concerning the nature of authentic Eros establish it within the realm of the properly ontological, a realm which Heidegger seems to identify as the metaphysical, as that which is truly ontological, and not merely ontical, lies for Heidegger, as we shall see shortly, out *beyond* being (see *GA* 34: 106 / 77).

19. Vedder, "Heidegger on Desire."

20. The influence of Schelling's work on Heidegger is an important realm of scholarship almost wholly ignored. Heidegger drew from Schelling almost as deeply, if not as deeply, as he did from Nietzsche, especially in formulating his later thought. This is commented upon by Hans-Georg Gadamer in his remembrance of Heidegger where he writes that: "Schelling's profundity must have resembled more closely his own innermost philosophic motivations. I had already heard Heidegger read in a seminar on Schelling the following sentence from the *Freiheitsschrift,* 'The *Angst* of life drive the creature from its center,' and then he went on to add, 'Gentleman, show me a single sentence out of Hegel's work that has such depth.' The later Schelling began to loom larger and larger behind Kierkegaard and, later, Nietzsche as well. He frequently delved into Schelling's *The Essence of Human Freedom* in his class" (Gadamer, *Heidegger's Ways,* 163). More on Heidegger and his reading of Schelling, in particular his reading of this *Angst* will be presented in the final chapter.

21. We will examine the nature of both Schelling's account of longing and Heidegger's analysis of this account more completely in chapters to come, but I must recognize the excellent reading of Heidegger's interaction with Schelling's conception of desire done by David Clark in his "Heidegger's Craving Being-on-Schelling."

22. Heidegger's relation to National Socialism has of course been endlessly speculated: was he really a Nazi or did he see himself as a reformer of the Nazi party, and so on? For more on Heidegger's interaction

with the Nazi movement see, for example: Neske and Kettering, *Martin Heidegger and National Socialism;* and, Tom Rockmore's excellent book *On Heidegger's Nazism and Philosophy.*

23. Heidegger himself often makes this stress choosing to italicize the *becoming* of this journey home (i.e., Heimisch*werden*) in order to emphasize the fact that it is the *becoming* that is import to him, and not so much the attainment or arrival at any assumed end or home, though one may be pursued (*GA* 53: 60 / 49).

24. It should be noted that though this sentence seems to refer to human beings in general (*der Mensch*) Heidegger immediately follows it with a sentence referring to a "particular human kind" (*eines Menschentums*) situated in a particular history which he names a few pages onward as "Western humankind" (*abendländischen Menschentums*) (*GA* 53: 65 / 52). It is a way of being which excludes the "Anglo-Saxon world of Americanism," which he contends is "resolved to annihilate Europe" which is for him the "homeland" and the "Western World" (68 / 54). These occasional geopolitical rants are not uncommon in the texts of this period (see the beginning of the 1936 lectures on Schelling [*GA* 42] which begins by situating Schelling's work within the political history of Germany). Still it is my contention that though revealing Heidegger's turn toward a more particularistic account of the manifestation of Being, these rants should not detract from allowing his work to be taken up by others, if not generally, then at least instantiated within other particular people groups. In any case, Heidegger's particular reverences to the fate of the German people should not distract from the fact that these same insights might extend even to those living in the "Anglo-Saxon world of Americanism."

25. This claim that not-being-at-home is not merely an inauthentic modification of man's way of being-in-the-world goes all the way back to *Being and Time* where Heidegger links "anxiety" (*Angst*), wherein "one feels '*uncanny*' [*unheimlich*]" (*GA* 2: 188 / 233) with the Dasein's possibility of pulling itself out of its inauthentic "absorption in the 'world'" and into a more authentic expression. This "'uncanniness,'" claims Heidegger, "also means 'not-being-at-home' [*das Nicht-zuhause-sein*]" (188 / 233). Not-being-at-home is thus not an inauthentic expression of human existence, but the truest expression of the way in which it is in-the-world. It thus expresses for Heidegger a kind of *superlative* mode of existence, a mode which has pulled itself out of the mire of the seemingly homely in the world and into the real of its true essence and possibilities—a mode, therefore, which recognizes the inherent *excess* sought in authentic erotic striving and primordial human longing.

26. Heidegger's observation of the *namelessness* of human longing confirms Matthew Arnold's poetization of it, quoted in full in the introduction and referenced near the end of the last chapter, that longing somehow constitutes an *unspeakable* desire.

27. The namelessness of longing would extend even into the work of art for Heidegger. Poetry and the visual arts, operating as sister endeavors to the philosophic enterprise, complement philosophy's attempt to frame being and its phenomenal manifestations. But, claims Heidegger, in his essay on "The Origin of the Work of Art" (*GA* 5), not only do the plastic arts operate like the language employed by philosophy, opening a clearing wherein being may shine, they are also grounded upon the true use of language, namely poetry. Hence Heidegger's claim that the essence of all art is poetry, and thereby to language. Thus though a piece like Van Gogh's depiction of a peasant's shoes may not formally employ language, it too is ultimately dependent upon language and restricted by its limits. Thus though longing may seek expression in it, and though the beauty of the Van Gogh's work can most certainly can inspire longing, longing itself can never be fully articulate in any work of art—can never be fully exposed or laid bare therein. Just as one can never name nor speak longing, neither can it be painted.

28. See Vedder, "Heidegger on Desire."

29. Note the play on the French word *Regard* that Levinas employs in his use of the word "regard." *Regarder* in French not only means to look at, but also means to be concerned. Thus, for Levinas, the other who looks at me is the other who concerns me, whom I am forced to be concerned about.

30. This "bad infinite" stands in contradistinction for Levinas to the "good infinite" expressed in metaphysical desire, presented in the face of the Other, and demanded in the ethical encounter as responsibility. It is in contrast to this bad infinite then that Levinas explores Descartes's idea of the infinite. This difference between a bad and a good infinite will be revisited in chapter 5.

31. Levinas's conception of the *il y a* will be revisited in chapter 4 where it will be examined in relation to and illuminated by Schelling's notion of the *Ungrund* of existence.

32. The way in which this distinction occurs, the hypostasis of a particular being from out of the totality of a being without beings, will be made more clear in chapter 4 when Levinas and Schelling's notion of creation will be explored.

33. One should perhaps be cautious here not to understand Heidegger's reference to a soul as a betrayal of any essentialist tendencies. Heidegger's

employment of the term soul is merely in keeping with Plato's own analysis of human nature. It should not be taken then to express some deep essence in human existence for Heidegger, nor some separate entity therein with which its true nature can be identified. Instead, Heidegger employs Plato's reference to the soul in his own way to express the way in which human beings *are* in their own most being. Soul thus appears to be another way of saying *Dasein* for Heidegger—another way of referencing the being of human existence—the way in which humans *are*. Thus when Heidegger defines the soul as a *striving,* he also establishes what it means for humans to be. Human beings *are* their *striving* according Heidegger. When we examine the nature of striving, then, we simultaneously reveal the nature of human existence. And likewise, when we say something about the nature of human existence or the soul, we reveal something about the nature of striving.

34. From this point on, and in keeping with the traditional English rendering of Heidegger's works, the word being will be capitalized (Being) when referring to being in its own right and will remain un-capitalized (being) to refer to determinate beings/entities. This is merely to clarify what is being discussed as we chart Heidegger's conception of the ontological difference.

35. It is interesting to note here that this statement by Heidegger concerning the nature of the Being pursued by longing resembles Levinas's now infamous statement concerning the nature of that transcendence which is sought in metaphysical desire, that transcendence which is "transcendence to the point of absence, to the point of a possible confusion with the *there is*" (*BPW* 141). As we shall shortly see, there may be grounds to argue that the transcendence sought in Levinas's metaphysical desire is the same one sought as Being in Heidegger's characterization of longing and authentic Eros, and that perhaps Levinas's problems with it has to do with his own confusion of it with the *there is*—a confusion resulting from an possible obfuscation of the importance of the ontological difference between Being and beings in Heidegger's work.

36. It is in recognition of this *nothing* at the heart of Being that Heidegger elsewhere refers to as the essence of Nietzsche's so called nihilism, the *nihil* of his nihilism (see "Nietzsche's Word: 'God Is Dead,'" *GA* 5). There he writes that "the *nihil* of nihilism means that there is nothing going on with [B]eing. Being does not come to the light of its own essence. In the appearance of beings as such, being itself stays away. The truth of [B]eing escapes us. It remains forgotten" (264 / 197; cf. "What Is Metaphysics?," *GA* 9: 105–08 / 84–85).

37. Steven Ganz has suggested that this element of Heidegger's thought,

this concept of the Being beyond all beings appearance as a mystery, resembles Levinas's own thought on the beyond being, despite his desire to distance himself from Heidegger ("Ethics or Ontology," 119). The possible overlap of Levinas and Heidegger's thought here is a topic which will be treated in more detail shortly.

38. O'Connor, "Being and the Good."

39. It should be noted here that Heidegger grants no ethical power to his conception of the Good. It thus does not serve for him as a discerning power which establishes a way in which agents can make moral choices. Such conceptions, he thinks, are absolutely foreign, he thinks, to the ancient, and specifically Platonic, conception of the Good. This, as we will shortly see, is a major source of contention between his and Levinas's respective accounts.

40. The different positions on this relation can be seen from Robert Manning's book *Interpreting Otherwise Than Heidegger*, which traces both the points of divergence and convergence between Heidegger and Levinas asserting all the while that what we find in Levinas is a kind of nuanced critique of Heidegger's thought which works within its overall logic, and Tina Chanter who finds in Levinas a kind of corrective to some of the Heideggerian excesses (*Time, Death and the Feminine*) to Richard Cohen (*Height of the Good in Rosesweig and Levinas*) who insists on the almost absolute difference between their two projects.

41. C. D. Keyes embarks on a similar project in his "An Evaluation of Levinas's Critique of Heidegger," listing what he sees as the four major differences between Levinas and Heidegger's respective positions, but it seems to me that on closer analysis those four can be collapsed even further to the two examined. Bettina Bergo has suggested that these respective accounts of transcendence establish one of the fundamental differences between Levinas and Heidegger's thought ("Ontology, Transcendence, and Immanence in Levinas"). While I am convinced of her point, a through analysis of this difference here would be beyond the point as it has been so well treated by her before, and as it would distract from the major difference between their work which emerge in our overall study of the nature of longing.

42. Of course there is even an ambiguity here, as has been famously pointed out by Maurice Blanchot ("Our Clandestine Companion"). More will be said on this curious ambiguity in chapters 4 and 5.

43. Levinas's concept of illeity, of the face of the third person who is beyond the difference between being and nothingness and who convicts me with responsibility will be explored more in the following chapter on Levinas and Fichte on the birth of the ethical subject.

44. This is not the first time in this chapter that we have seen Heidegger distinguish what he sees as the original Greek meaning of particular words from what he sees as the "harmless meaning suitable for aunties." What is interesting to note however, is that the other time he was referring to the conception of Eros which, as we saw, he claimed would not "be suitable for bigoted old aunties" (*GA* 34: 216 / 155). Though perhaps a silly point, this again underscores the intimate connection between authentic Eros and the Good understood as the Being beyond all being.

45. Rosen, "Heidegger's Interpretation of Plato."

46. This definition of the Good as the "orderliness of an order," is what Heidegger explores more thoroughly in other texts, for instance his text on *Schelling's Treatise on the Essence of Freedom* (*GA* 42), *An Introduction to Metaphysics* (*GA* 40), and the *Parmenides* lectures of 1942–43 (*GA* 54), and as the *fit, order,* or *jointure (Fug)* of being, which he relates to the Greek word for justice *(δίχη)* (cf. *GA* 40: 123 / 160–61; *GA* 42: 86 / 50; *GA* 54: 137 / 92–93).

47. Jacques Taminiaux has provided a wonderfully rich reading of the difference between Levinas and Heidegger's respective reads on the nature of the Good beyond being in his "The Early Levinas's Reply to Heidegger."

48. Derrida, "Violence and Metaphysics," 138.

49. Robert Bernasconi, like Bettina Bergo, has suggested that one of the fundamental differences between Heidegger and Levinas's respective phenomenologies is their accounts of transcendence especially with regard to the ethical in his "No Exit," 102.

50. Again, Steven Ganz has pointed this difference out wonderfully on his "Ethics or Ontology," 117.

NOTES TO CHAPTER THREE

1. Remember that, for Levinas, the metaphysical is always a social/ethical power. For more on this see, for example, Bernasconi's "No Exit," 101.

2. This idea is first introduced in chapter 1 in the section entitled "Plato and Levinas Reconciled?" As will become immediately clear, this concept is key to our study of the nature and function of human longing. As such it will be explored in more detail in this chapter and eventually examined in terms of its implications upon the concept of creation in the next chapter.

3. Bernasconi, for one, has called into question this apparent division between Hegel, at least, and Levinas claiming that there is much more

of a similarity between their two works, especially in terms of how the ethical relation with another is figured, than Levinas would at first admit (Bernasconi, "Levinas Face to Face with Hegel").

4. Though Levinas rarely mentions Fichte by name, he remains nevertheless one of the main targets for his attack on the idealism present in Western philosophy, as we shall see in more detail later.

5. This is because, according to Levinas, the I is *always already* broken open by the Other—always already called away from itself. Levinas's descriptions of the natural tendencies of the I then should in some sense be understood as precisely that, a description of *tendencies*—of the potentiality toward which the I naturally careens. After all, the otherwise is always otherwise for the subject—it is always a movement contrawise to its natural state even if that movement has always already been introduced.

6. There is nothing resembling a clear *kehre* in the Levinasian oeuvre. Thus this distinction between the early works and the later works is made exclusively with regard to his descriptions of shame. To this end, and for our purposes here only, we will designate all texts written prior to *Totality and Infinity* as early (i.e., *On Escape, Time and the Other,* and *Existents and Existents*). This distinction is not meant, therefore, to account for any subsequent changes in Levinas's thinking, as if often noted between *Totality and Infinity* and his latter work *Otherwise Than Being,* a change of which more is often made than should be.

7. It is useful here to return briefly to Levinas's contentions with the Odyssian story as it is a perfect example of precisely this ability. Though Odysseus is certainly beset by the otherness of the world in any number of forms, so much so that his entire project is severely delayed and nearly abandoned: never once is the thread of the narrative broken, never once does Odysseus stop being himself—stop being the *I* that is at the center of this unpleasant adventure. The wrath of Poseidon though strong enough to separate Odysseus from his home and crew, is not strong enough to separate Odysseus from himself. This requires an otherness further abroad that the otherness of the pagan gods in their link to the earth.

8. Robert Bernasconi has expounded this discovery in Levinas as part of the way he overcomes Heidegger's fundamental ontology by showing that the excedence of human freedom does not attain to the heights of ethical freedom offered in responsibility for another (Bernasconi, "No Exit," 107).

9. For a thorough analysis of this (im)possibility—this possible perpetuation of the ties of being after death—see Rudi Visker's, "Is There Death after Life?"

10. Fichte often referred to his work as an egoism or an ego-ology in reference to the fact that what was primarily under investigation therein was the ego. Egoism, as described by Fichte, should not be confused therefore with some sort of ethical system, but rather as a mere description of what is of interest to him for investigation. See, for instance, section 12 of the second introduction to the *Wissenschaftslehre* (1797) where he refers negatively to his system as an egoism by describing what he deems false systems of philosophy that masquerade under the label of egoisms but actually fail to properly represent this title.

11. An example of this is, for instance, in *Totality and Infinity* where Levinas uses the Fichtean language of opposition (A vs. non-A) to contrast his account of the presentation of the face in its otherness to the notion of contradiction established in a more idealistic account of interaction (*TI* 150), or in *On Escape* where Levinas discusses the need to escape and the revolt of being against itself as more profound than the opposition of an I to a non-I (*OE* 52–53).

12. It is a difficult task to write on Fichte or even on the *Wissenschaftslehre* alone, for both Fichte and his main text, much like his presentation of the "pure I" therein, seem to exist only in theory. The actual empirical existence of both is thus a much more complicated matter. Over 15 different versions of the *Wissenschaftslehre* alone exist (see Lumsden, "Fichte's Striving Subject," 123), and this is far from Fichte's only account of the nature of the I. Nevertheless, a remarkable consistency exists both between texts and between versions of these texts on the core issues pertaining to the nature of the I. The differences, though quite profound in some places, are relatively marginal to what it is that will be of interest to us here. Therefore, for the sake of our investigation, we can safely limit our study of the Fichtean system to the 1794–96 version of the *Wissenschaftslehre* with minor variations included from the subsequent 1802 versions, its two 1796 introductions, and the 1796–97 version of the *Grundslage des Naturrechts* to obtain a fairly cohesive and expansive understanding of the ideas at issue in Levinas's critiques. References will be made to their English translations listed in the bibliography and noted in the list of abbreviations.

13. Fichte's claims here could be seen as the philosophical forerunner to Heidegger's insistence upon ontological difference and the attempt to read being not as an entity, but as a movement, as a kind of activity. Fichte's "self-positing" I is merely an I which has no substance other than its activity in intuiting itself. It is its self-consciousness, it is as that consciousness of a self. It is not however, as we shall see in more detail

shortly, necessarily self-originary, nor entirely turned inward—but is in fact dependent upon the outside and directed toward an outside itself.

14. Fichte explores the possible "passivity" of the self in the *Wissenschaftslehre* (*SK* 130–60) insisting that just as much as the I can exert an influence on the world so too can an influence be exerted upon it, can the world influence it. This affectivity before the world could be expressed as the perspective through which the self-positing being is understood as a being-posited as a self by another. This is something which will become more clear as we continue.

15. Check may strike those more familiar with the German language as an unusual translation of the word *Anstoß*, its typical German connotation being a kind of nudge or bump, as in two billiard balls. But, the English word *to check* evokes not only this literal meaning but also the richer contextual meaning contained herein. For, in English the verb *to check* contains within it two different meanings. Firstly, it means to bump up against forcefully, as in ice hockey, "to *check* an opponent against the glass"; but it also means to limit and hold back, as in the phrase "to keep one's feeling in check." It is these two meanings that the translators are drawing upon in their use of the word *check* for *Anstoß*, and it is with these two meanings in mind that the term should be understood in its philosophical relevance.

16. Hohler, *Imagination and Reflection*, 59.
17. Zöeller, *Fichte's Transcendental Philosophy*, 31.
18. Hohler, *Imagination and Reflection*, 89.
19. Williams, *Recognition*, 51.
20. Ibid., 68 n. 43, 53.
21. Ibid., 49; italics mine.
22. Scribner, "Levinas Face to Face with Fichte," 151.
23. Lumsden, "Absolute Difference and Social Ontology."
24. See Hohler, *Imagination and Reflection*, 19.
25. Lumsden, "Fichte's Striving Subject," 137.
26. See Hohler, *Imagination and Reflection*, 31.
27. For more on the reciprocity of this relationship see Robert R. William's *Recognition: Fichte and Hegel on the Other* and Stephen Houlgate's article "Hegel and Fichte: Recognition, Otherness, and Absolute Knowing."
28. See also "Martin Buber and the Theory of Knowledge."
29. Zöller, *Fichte's Transcendental Philosophy*, 24.
30. Scribner, "Levinas Face to Face with Fichte," 157.
31. Quoted in Zöller, *Fichte's Transcendental Philosophy*, 37, from an incomplete and untranslated text by Fichte, *Neue Bearbeitung der Wissenschaftslehre* (GA II.5:347).

NOTES TO CHAPTER FOUR

1. Visker, *The Inhuman Condition*, 93.
2. See the end of the section entitled "Plato and Levinas Reconciled?" in chapter 1.
3. It is not Levinas's aim to entirely reject an account of creation *ex nihilo* but rather to reform it. As we shall see in more detail shortly, this will come for Levinas through a reevaluation of the meaning of the *nihil* of creation, one which works against this traditional interpretation.
4. This reference to a *trace* of dependence is an idea to which we will return in more detail shortly. Nevertheless, it is important to indicate it here as it signals an important move in Levinas's thought. Though the subject is entirely independent from exteriority in its ipseity, there is still some vestige of its dependence, a vestige which is only made apparent through the ethical interaction with the Other (i.e., through shame or Desire). Thus, though the subject is first and foremost understood by him as entirely independent, there is a perspective which is offered whereby this independence can be read as a kind of dependence. This will become more clear the further we investigation Levinas's claims.
5. This reference to a "universal history" is yet another example of Levinas's subtle critique of German Idealism. A clear reference to Hegel's claim that all occurrences in history are part of the universal self-realization of Spirit, Levinas's seems to suggest that within a Hegelian framework no real individuality can emerge. Hegel's system thus appears to be for him little more than an intellectualized pantheism. This seems to be a criticism that Levinas makes of Heidegger's notion of history of well, which should be of little surprise considering Heidegger's life long love affair with the German Idealists, as is readily apparent by even the most cursory survey of the titles in the *Gesamtausgabe*. Whether this a fair reading of the German Idealists in general, or Hegel in particular, or of Heidegger's appropriation of the German Idealists, is yet to be seen however.
6. Visker, *Truth and Singularity*, 265, n. 39; italics mine.
7. Note here the way that the infinite renames for Levinas an absence. The "trace of an absence" within human existence is manifest as a superlative, as an infinite which overflows the limits of its finite contained. In this quote we again see the collusion of emptiness and fullness manifest in human longing as explored throughout this text.
8. Richard Cohen has traced to great effect in a number of places Levinas's dependence upon Franz Rosenzweig but further shows how the basic message of Rosenzweig's work comes from Schelling, a connection which we will explore further in this chapter. For more on this

see Cohen, "Levinas, Rosenzweig and the Phenomenologies of Husserl and Heidegger."

9. Brown, *The Later Philosophy of Schelling*, 146.

10. Žižek, *The Indivisible Remainder*, 14 (cf. p. 13: "at the Beginning proper stands a resolution, an act of decision which, by differentiating between past and present, resolves the preceding unbearable tension of the rotary motion of drives").

11. See Norman, "The Logic of Longing," 96, 102.

12. Note the similarity here to the claim we observed Fichte to make in the last chapter: "No Thou, no I: no I, no Thou" (*SK* 172–73). The intimate tie between Fichte and Schelling's idealism is both revealed and dissolved in this line. For it is precisely in how they differ which makes their availability for integration into the Levinasian scheme and their relation to a creation account so different. For while Fichte's claim concerning the I-Thou relationship extends only to the intersubjective realm, Schelling's modification of it carries it into the heart of existence and grounds it in an decision not made by the I, but first made by God.

13. Norman, "The Logic of Longing," 91; italics mine.

14. To really get a feel for the power of Schelling's description of the creative act, one should attempt to hear it in the original German. God's *choice* for itself is an *Entscheidung*, it is the formation of a *boundary* a *Scheide*. It is a kind of *separation* and cutting free (*schneiden*). The root of decision (*Entscheidung*) *Scheide* is of course the same word that is used to demand a divorce in German (*Ich lass mich Scheiden!*). Creation, then, as a form of negation, is God's *divorce* from the superabundant presence of the *Ungrund*—it is his *separation* from being as such, as will become more clear shortly.

15. Žižek, *The Indivisible Remainder*, 21.

16. Ibid., 42.

17. Brown, *The Later Philosophy of Schelling*, 241.

18. The connection between Schelling's notion of love and Levinas's analysis of the erotic should be apparent here. For both, it seems erotic love expresses a curious movement beyond being which in some ways reflects the original creative act. Furthermore, it is interesting to note that Schelling's descriptions of the "supreme love," which he identifies with the existence of God, resembles remarkably his descriptions of the *Ungrund* in much the same way that Levinas's descriptions of the Infinite resemble his descriptions of the *il y a*. Still, for both, though similar to the point of possible confusion, these respective forces could not be more different and must be distinguished from one another for the function of consciousness to properly be understood. The nature and reason behind this possible confusion will be explored more fully in the next chapter.

19. White, *Schelling*, 177.

20. Žižek claims on p. 21 of his *The Indivisible Remainder* that this decision by man is a "repetition" in time of God's immemorial act. While we could concede that the human decision to be is certainly a *reflection* of God's primordial decision to not-be, given the profound and not at all insignificant difference in direction of these two movements, one must uphold that, in contrast to Žižek's proposition, the former can most certainly *not* be seen as a mere *repetition* of the latter though it still participates with it and remains inexorably tied to it.

21. As we sill see in more detail later, Schelling unites the function of reason with the function of longing. Together, he claims, they work to aid human beings to divide and separate the forces within nature and within themselves and in so doing maintain the legacy of the creative act.

22. White, *Schelling*, 129.

23. Ibid., 68, where White claims that for Schelling the time of Gods existence "has not yet begun; in that period the providence guiding history will be fully manifest to all. Then and only then will God exist for only then will the absolute know itself in and through finite individuals."

24. This is in fact what is implied by Schelling in his title *Ages of the World*. Explored more thoroughly in his work on mythology, Schelling seems to propose the possibility of a future age wherein God can finally move from possibility to actuality through the realization by human beings of this potentiality and their interconnectedness to it (see Žižek, *The Indivisible Remainder*, 5).

25. In this way Schelling's work foreshadows the work of Walter Benjamin on the nature of the messianic, a connection which has been little explored within contemporary scholarship. It also reflects Levinas's own reflections on the nature of the messianic (see *EI* 114).

26. Brown, *The Later Philosophy of Schelling*, 144.

27. See White, *Schelling*, 164.

28. Brown, "Resources in Schelling," 4 (cf. p. 14: "God is primarily the 'non-existent' ground of consciousness, and only secondarily and contingently its object.")

29. See Gibbs, "The Limits of Thought," 626, 628.

30. Cf. Žižek, *The Indivisible Remainder*, 21–22: "What is done eternally (in the sense of remaining, in its very withdrawal, the eternal foundation of the present, not just something disappearing in the recess of the past) must be eternally (at anytime always-already) done, and is therefore inherently past—that is, it has to belong to a past which was never present."

31. See Norman, "The Logic of Longing," 103.

32. Žižek, *The Indivisible Remainder*, 23.

33. The only other example I have seen of the attempt to read Levinas backward through the work of Schelling is Joseph P. Lawrence's essay "Schelling and Levinas: The Harrowing of Hell," *Levinas Studies: An Annual Review,* vol. 2, which correctly identifies the ground of Levinas's theological thinking on Schelling.

34. Steinkamp, "Eternity and Time," 207.

35. Ibid., 207.

36. Ibid., 208; italics mine.

37. While it is true that we ended chapter 2 by denoting Levinas's failure to fully grasp the depth of the Heideggerian insistence on ontological difference and the subsequent meaning of Being implied therein, it is by no means a concept which is absent in his thought, as Steinkamp seems to think. Levinas's work repeatedly draws upon the notion of ontological difference in his understanding of the procession of creation, he simple does not employ it as universally as Heidegger does nor does he seem to think that it designates a understanding of Being that goes *beyond being*. Ultimately for him, Being, though separate and distinct from beings still presences as a weight and burden that threatens to overwhelm singularity—whereas for Heidegger it appears to be a force which, precisely in its absence, precisely in its situatedness beyond beings, allows presence to emerge, much like Levinas and Schelling's God.

38. Steinkamp, "Eternity and Time," 208.

39. There is of course an ambiguity between the *il y a* and God which lends itself to this kind of confusion. But, it is not to this ambiguity that Steinkamp refers in her comparison of the two. This is an ambiguity which will be explored further in the next chapter.

40. Ibid., 209.

41. See ibid., 213 where Steinkamp explicitly links Levinas's descriptions of the *il y a* with Schelling's conception of God.

42. While it is true that God can be seen as somehow complicitous in the *Ungrund* as his potential to be is contained therein alongside our own, this complicity does not make God identifiable with the *Ungrund*, nor its author. To the contrary, God is precisely the one who destroys the *Ungrund* by canceling its own potentiality to be. Still God's initial connection with the *Ungrund* is such that some possible confusion can arise—a confusion which Levinas himself seems to recognize (see *BPW* 141). As mentioned before, this possible confusion will be explored in more detail in the next chapter.

43. Steinkamp, "Eternity and Time," 211.

44. Ibid., 214.

45. Ibid., 218.

46. Ibid., 219.

47. Of course, it is precisely this *neutrality* that marks it for Levinas as evil. For evil, he claims, is just such an indifference between forces. For Levinas, to be neutral between the good and the bad is already to be oriented toward the bad for these are forces which one cannot be neutral before. Before them one must make a choice and the attempt to hold them out as equal forces or not make a choice is already indicative of the fact that one has *not chosen* the good, and therefore for him, tacitly chosen the bad.

48. Cf. Visker, *The Inhuman Condition*, 155–56.

49. Cf. Brown, *The Later Philosophy of Schelling*, 127; Linker, "From Kant to Schelling," 359; Norman, "The Logic of Longing," 100.

50. See Norman, "The Logic of Longing," 95.

51. Longing thus always carries within it, thinks Schelling, the legacy of its sickly origin. Thus though it is itself something which resolves this sickness, it nevertheless caries the trace of the sickness present in the *Ungrund* within it. Longing is, in this sense, the antibody which arises from an infection. It is thus a redeemed expression of the offending virus which serves to protect the body. The way in which longing functions in this way will be explored at the end of the next chapter.

52. See Steinkamp, "Eternity and Time," 174. For Steinkamp longing expresses the fact that man too carries primal nature within himself, and thus, according to her read, "it is because we have the principle of primal nature within us that we are able to trace back to the beginning."

53. Judith Norman characterizes longing as the desire to stop desiring, the longing for stability which will only be accomplished when the unruly desire of God for self-realization will be satisfied ("The Logic of Longing," 98–99). Given God's infinite nature, however, this satisfaction, full self-actualization, is an endless task. Longing thus becomes an infinite activity and the promise for a future always just outside the horizon of realizable time.

54. Since longing is the power whereby one can distance oneself from being, it could also be tied to the work of ethics, which, as we have already seen, is for Schelling also opened up through this kind of division, the decision for the good and the possibility of being truly moral coming through the aperture one opens between themselves and his or her own being. This is a move, however, which Schelling, never explicitly makes. Nevertheless, it is one which would be consistent with his system and logic.

55. This further illuminates the seemingly inherent reference in longing to sickness, as we have seen throughout this text, a reference which will be explored in more detail in the following and final chapter.

NOTES TO CHAPTER FIVE

1. This reference to longing as "the feeling of a God *without being*," is a deliberate reference to the work of Jean-Luc Marion who, in keeping with Levinas and Schelling, has attempted to detail in his work a phenomenology of the holy. The reason I have not expressly interacted with the work of Marion in the body of this text, however, is due to the apparent lack of a concept of longing therein. Though he does detail very briefly in *God without Being* the concept of the desire/love of/for God, what he describes therein too easily falls into the category of nostalgia, as it was detailed earlier as a separate and distinct phenomenon from longing. This is also the case with his work *Le phénomène érotique* which, by my read, figures desire, in line with tradition, as a kind of loss. Because it fails to deal with a phenomenon akin to the one pursued in this thesis, Marion's work must remain somewhat marginal to the investigation under way. Nevertheless, it would be fruitful in later works to examine how a concept like longing could fit within Marion's conception of God as having passed from being.

2. Otto's suggestion that the holy should not be taken to primarily signify a power that is unambiguously morally good parallels Heidegger's reluctance, explored in chapter 2, to attribute moral value to the notion of the Platonic Good beyond being. It is also interesting to note that, like Heidegger, it is Otto's intention to overturn this evaluation of the holy as morally good precisely in order to further his analysis of it as a kind of overwhelming power. This clearly parallels Heidegger's attempt to overturn the moral evaluation of Plato's conception of the Good beyond being in favor of an understanding of it as the empowering of appearance.

3. This is a claim with which Levinas would perhaps take issue considering his expressed condemnations of the idea of the holy and his deliberate attempts to define the Good beyond being as something which is good precisely because it negates its attractive power as a mystery. Nevertheless, as we shall see in more detail shortly, there is just cause to claim that despite Levinas's attempt to define his conception of the beyond being as a metaphysical power without mystery, his work nevertheless contains, albeit perhaps inadvertently, some element of the holy as it is described by Otto.

4. On Heidegger, see Schalow, *Heidegger and the Quest for the Sacred*, 29–30; on Levinas see, Moyn, *Origins of the Other,* where Levinas's dependence upon the work of Protestant thinkers such as Otto and Kierkegaard is traced especially as it informs his enigmatic use of such concepts as the wholly other.

5. Blanchot, "The Absence of the Book." Mark C. Taylor also recognizes this connection in his article on Otto and Heidegger entitled "The Non-absent Absence of the Holy," where he claims that "The Holy is Other—Wholly Other—*'das ganz Andere.'* The failure of philosophy to think this Other is not an accident. To the contrary, philosophy constitutes itself by *not* thinking the Other. *Das ganz Andere* is not only unthought; it is, more importantly, *unthinkable*. In *Das Helige,* Otto undertakes the impossible task of thinking this unthinkable Other by developing a phenomenological description of the experience of that which escapes all phenomenological description. Never present, without ever being absent, the holy is, in Blanchot's apt phrase, a 'non absent absence'" (21–22).

6. As Rudi Visker notes in *Truth and Singularity* the word "*divine*" "is a word that [Levinas] could never accept" (238; cf. *OB* 162). Instead he almost always refers concretely to the concept of a *God,* who is a third, an *illeity*, a He. By contrast, the term divine seems to express for Levinas a kind of homogeneity and continuity. It expresses for him a kind of threat against the independence and separation which are for him the foundation of true identity and ethics. The reasons for this will become more clear momentarily. Otto does in fact appear to use the two terms, sacred and holy, interchangeably; see, for example, p. 113 of *The Idea of the Holy* where he writes, "we must no longer understand by 'the holy' or 'sacred' the merely numinous." Here we can see how for Otto the sacred and the holy appear to be synonymous (cf. *IH* 131).

7. This quotation comes from the group discussion held at the Facultés Universitaires Saint-Louis, Brussels in 1977. Though the paper he presented there, "*La Révélation dans la tradition juive*" is translated into English in the *Levinas Reader* the discussion is not. The translations given above are thus my own. In any case, the distinction between the sacred and the holy in Levinas is one that is well recognized and has been often discussed. See for instance: Wyschogrod, "From the Disaster to the Other," 71; or Visker, "Dispossessed: How to Remain Silent 'after' Levinas," in *Truth and Singularity,* 125–29.

8. This reference to Hegel, and this distinction between a bad infinite and a good infinite, comes both from the *Logic* (*Hegel's Logic,* 137–38) and the *Philosophy of Right* (*Elements of the Philosophy of Right,* 54). Therein Hegel distinguishes between a good, or true, infinite, which is for him the infinitude of the uncontained and is associated with reason, whereas the bad, or false, infinite expresses for him the infinitude of infinite regress or the divisibility of time, matter, and so on. In other words, the good infinite is for Hegel a qualitative function (i.e., infinitely different) whereas the bad infinite is nothing more than a quantitative measure.

Levinas's reading of Hegel on the distinction between the good infinite and the bad infinite and his reflections on the presentation of the idea of the infinite throughout the rest of the history of philosophy is most clearly presented in *Alterity and Transcendence,* 59–76.

9. This link between the sacred/numinous and the bad infinite is also recognized by Rudi Visker who writes that "the bad infinite, that is, allows for no relation with it: it is, as Levinas suggests in a later passage, 'numinous,' it 'annihilates'" (*Truth and Singularity,* 237).

10. This connection between the bad infinite and the *there is* is also expressed in *Otherwise Than Being* where Levinas writes "essence stretching on indefinitely, without any possible halt or interruption, the equality of essence not justifying, in all equity, any instant's halt, without respite, without any possible suspension, is the horrifying *there is* behind all finality proper to the thematizing ego" (*OB* 163).

11. Visker, *Truth and Singularity,* 126.

12. We should take caution to note that for Levinas "the Other is not the incarnation of God, but precisely by his face, in which he is *disincarnate,* is the manifestation of the height in which God is revealed" (*TI* 79; italics mine).

13. This is, to my knowledge, one of the few exceptional occasions in which Levinas refers to the transcendence present in the face of the other as divine ("*La dimension du divin s'ouvre à partir du visage humain*"). Generally, as noted before, this is a word that Levinas eschews and situates in contrast to the ethical encounter.

14. This idea of the holy as a protection is also brought out by Rudi Visker in his book *Truth and Singularity*. There he writes in regards to Levinas that "the holy is not the sacred, but the only thing that can prevent it from overwhelming us" (125).

15. This is not only the case with Levinas, as we shall see shortly, but also, and perhaps more significantly for the study at hand, with Schelling. It is this protective function of longing, which will become more apparent as this chapter goes on and which will be developed in the conclusion to this chapter.

16. See Caputo, "To the Point of a Possible Confusion"; Rudi Visker, "No Privacy?," in *Truth and Singularity,* 235–73.

17. Blanchot, "Our Clandestine Companion," 49.

18. It should be noted that since the being of God is actually presented in Schelling as the withdrawal from being, the withdrawal which opens a space for the emergence of free and independent beings, the way in which God is most present to humans is as the absence before them—as their freedom. The *revelation* that Schelling details here is not simply the

manifestation of this radical freedom to humans, though this too may be part of it. It is, more specifically, the appearance of the determinate possibility of God coming to being. Revelation is thus not felt as the emptiness of a universe without the divine, thinks Schelling, but, in stark contrast, is instead experienced as the appearance of the possibility of a God who *is* everything—who may come into being and, in doing so, cast away human freedom.

19. Heidegger further explores the conception of the look in his 1942 seminar on *Parmenides* written in 1942 where he defines the look as the clearing through which beings appear (see *GA* 54: 153–54 / 103). As such, for him there, the look of man expresses for him the Being of beings. But, this looking, he argues, does not belong to man, but rather belongs to Being itself. It is thus, in a sense, he claims, "the look of the god who stems from Being [and] can emerge 'in' man and can look out from the form of 'man' as gathered in the look" (161 / 109).

20. Note the way that Heidegger employs the words "craving" (*Sucht*) and "self-craving" (*Eigensucht*) in contradistinction to longing (*Sehnsucht*). As we will see shortly, it is this distinction which serves as the lynchpin uniting what we have seen above concerning Schelling's determination of the nature of evil and the nature of human longing.

21. This analysis of the relation between the proper/authentic treatment of longing, as an indeterminate drive toward the beyond, and human freedom resembles what we observed in chapter 2 in Heidegger's analysis of the function of authentic Eros (see, for example, the section entitled "The Internal Inherence of Having and Striving in the Erotic Phenomenon"). You will remember that there Heidegger claimed that authentic Eros, by relating to its object properly, protected true human freedom, whilst inauthentic Eros, as the desire to own and possess, though appearing initially as the elevation of freedom actually resulted in the loss of freedom.

22. Žižek, *The Indivisible Remainder,* 66.

BIBLIOGRAPHY

Primary Sources

WORKS BY FICHTE

Fichte, J. G. *Foundations of Natural Right, According to the Principles of the Wissenschaftslehre*. Translated by Michael Baur. Edited by Frederick Neuhauser. Cambridge: Cambridge University Press, 2000.

———. *Foundations of Transcendental Philosophy: (Wissenschaftslehre) nova methodo (1796/99)*. Translated and Edited by Daniel Breazeale. Ithaca: Cornell University Press, 1992.

———. *Science of Knowledge — with the First and Second Introductions*. Translated and edited by Peter Heath and John Lachs. Cambridge: Cambridge University Press, 1982.

WORKS BY HEIDEGGER

Heidegger, Martin. *An Introduction Metaphysics*. Translated by Ralph Manheim. New Haven: Yale University Press, 1987.

———. *Being and Time*. Translated by John Macquarie and Edward Robinson. New York: Harper and Row, 1962.

———. *Die Grundbegriffe der Metaphysik: Welt—Endlichkeit—Einsamkeit*. Frankfurt Am Main: Vittorio Klostermann, 1992. (*GA* 29/30).

―――. *Einführung in die Metaphysik*. Frankfurt Am Main: Vitorrio Klostermann, 1983. (*GA* 40).

―――. *The Essence of Truth: On Plato's Cave Allegory and Theaetetus*. Translated by Ted Sadler. London: Continuum, 2002.

―――. *The Fundamental Concepts of Metaphysics: World, Finitude, Solitude*. Translated by William McNeill and Nicholas Walker. Bloomington: Indiana University Press, 1995.

―――. *Hölderlin's Hymn "The Ister."* Translated by William McNeill and Julia Davis. Bloomington: Indiana University Press, 1996.

―――. *Hölderlins Hymne "Der Ister."* Frankfurt Am Main: Vittorio Klostermann, 1993. (*GA* 53).

―――. *Holzewege*. Frankfurt Am Main: Vittorio Kolstermann, 1994. (*GA* 5).

―――. *Identität und Differenz*. Frankfurt Am Main: Vittorio Klostermann, 2006. (*GA* 11).

―――. *Identity and Difference*. Translated by Joan Stambaugh. New York: Harper and Row Publishers, 1969.

―――. *Nietzsche*. 2 vols. Translated by David Farrell Krell. San Francisco: Harper Collins, 1979 and 1984.

―――. *Nietzsche*. Volume 1. Frankfurt Am Main: Vittorio Klostermann, 1996. (*GA* 6).

―――. *On Time and Being*. Translated by Joan Stambaugh. New York: Harper and Row Publishers, 1972.

―――. *Off the Beaten Track*. Edited and Translated by Julian Young and Kenneth Haynes. Cambridge: Cambridge University Press, 2002.

―――. *Parmenides*. Translated by André Schuwer and Richard Rojcewicz. Bloomington: Indiana University Press, 1992.

―――. *Parmenides*. Frankfurt Am Main: Vittorio Klostermann, 1992. (*GA* 54).

―――. *Pathmarks*. Edited by William McNeill. Cambridge: Cambridge University Press, 1998.

―――. *Plato's Sophist*. Translated by Richard Rojcewicz and André Schuwer. Bloomington: Indiana University Press, 1997.

―――. *Plato: Sophistes*. Frankfurt Am Main: Vittorio Klostermann, 1992. (*GA* 19).

―――. *Schelling's Treatise on the Essence of Human Freedom*. Translated by Joan Stambaugh. Athens: Ohio University Press, 1985.

―――. *Schelling: Vom das Wesen der menschlichen Freiheit (1809)*. Frankfurt Am Main: Vittorio Klostermann, 1988. (*GA* 42).

―――. *Sein und Zeit*. Tubingen: Maz Niemeyer Verlag, 1993. (*GA* 2).

―――. *Vom Wesen der Warheit*. Frankfurt Am Main: Vittorio Klostermann, 1988. (*GA* 34).

―――. *Wegmarken*. Frankfurt Am Main: Vittorio Klotsermann, 1976. (*GA* 9).

―――. *Zur Sache des Denkens*. Tübingen, Max Niemeyer, 1969. (*GA* 14).

WORKS BY LEVINAS

Levinas, Emmanuel. *Alterity and Transcendence*. Translated by Michael B. Smith. New York: Columbia University Press, 1999.

―――. *Basic Philosophical Writings*. Edited by Adriaan T. Peperzak, Simon Critchley, and Robert Bernasconi. Bloomington: Indiana University Press, 1996.

―――. *Collected Philosophical Papers*. Translated by Alphonso Lingis. Pittsburgh: Duquesne University Press, 1998.

―――. *Difficult Freedom: Essays on Judaism*. Translated by Sean Hand. Baltimore: The Johns Hopkins University Press, 1990.

―――. "Discussion d'ensemble." In *La Révélation*. Brussels: Facultés universitaires Saint-Louis, 1977.

―――. *Entre Nous: Thinking-of-the-Other*. Translated by Michael B. Smith and Barbara Harshav. New York: Columbia University Press, 1998.

―――. *Ethics and Infinity: Conversations with Philippe Nemo*. Translated by Richard A. Cohen. Pittsburgh: Duquesne University Press, 1985.

―――. *Existence and Existents*. Translated by Alphonso Lingis. Pittsburgh: Duquesne University Press, 2001.

―――. *God, Death and Time*. Translated by Bettina Bergo. Stanford: Stanford University Press, 1993.

———. "Martin Buber and the Theory of Knowledge." In *The Levinas Reader*, edited by Sean Hand, 59–74. Oxford: Blackwell, 1989.

———. *Nine Talmudic Readings*. Translated by Annette Aronowicz. Bloomington: Indiana University Press, 1994.

———. *On Escape*. Translated by. Bettina Bergo. Stanford: Stanford University Press, 2003.

———. *Otherwise Than Being or Beyond Essence*. Translated by Alphonso Lingis. Pittsburgh: Duquesne University Press, 1998.

———. "Revelation and the Jewish Tradition." In *The Levinas Reader*, edited by Sean Hand, 190–210. Oxford: Blackwell, 1989.

———. *Time and the Other*. Translated by Richard A. Cohen. Pittsburgh: Duquesne University Press, 1987.

———. *Totality and Infinity*. Translated by Alphonso Lingus. Pittsburgh: Duquesne University Press, 1969.

———. "The Trace of the Other." Translated by Alphonso Lingis. In *Deconstruction in Context*, edited by Mark C. Taylor, 345–59. Chicago: University of Chicago Press, 1986.

WORKS BY PLATO

Plato. "Cratylus." In *The Loeb Classical Library: Plato—Cratylus, Parmenides, Greater Hippias, Lesser Hippias*, translated by H. N. Fowler. Cambridge, Mass.: Harvard University Press, 1926.

———. "Meno." In *The Loeb Classical Library: Plato—Laches, Protagoras, Meno, Euthydemus*, translated by W. R. H. Lamb. Cambridge, Mass.: Harvard University Press, 1924.

———. "Parmenides." In *The Loeb Classical Library: Plato—Cratlyus, Parmenides, Greater Hippias, Lesser Hippias*, translated by H. N. Fowler. Cambridge, Mass.: Harvard University Press, 1926.

———. "Phaedrus." In *The Loeb Classical Library: Plato—Euthyphro, Apology, Crito, Phaedo, Phaedrus*, translated by W. R. H. Lamb. Cambridge, Mass.: Harvard University Press, 1914.

———. "Philebus." In *The Loeb Classical Library: Plato—Statesman, Philebus, Ion*, translated by W. R. H. Lamb. Cambridge, Mass.: Harvard University Press, 1925.

———. *The Republic of Plato*. Translated by Fancis MacDonald Cornford. Oxford: Oxford University Press, 1941.

———. "Symposium." In *The Loeb Classical Library: Plato—Lysis, Symposium, Gorgias,* translated by W. R. H. Lamb. Cambridge, Mass.: Harvard University Press, 1925.

———. "Theaetetus." In *The Loeb Classical Library: Plato—Theaetetus, Sophist,* translated by Harold North Fowler. Cambridge, Mass.: Harvard University Press, 1921.

WORKS BY SCHELLING

Schelling, F. W. J. *The Ages of the World (fragment): From the Handwritten Remains—Third Version (c. 1815).* Translated by Jason M. Wirth. Albany: State University of New York Press, 2000.

———. *Of Human Freedom.* Translated by James Gutman. Chicago: Open Court, 1936.

———. "Stuttgart Seminars." In *Idealism and the Endgame of Theory: Three Essays by F. W. J. Schelling,* translated and edited by Thomas Pfau, 197–244. Albany: State University of New York Press, 1944.

———. *Philosophische Untersuchungen über das Wesen der menschlichen Freiheit und die damit zusammenhängenden Gegenstände.* Edited by Thomas Buchheim. Hamburg: Feliz Meiner Verlang, 1997.

Other Significant Sources

Augustine. *Confessions.* Translated by William Watts. Cambridge, Mass.: Harvard University Press, 1912.

Blanchot, Maurice. "The Absence of the Book." In *The Gaze of Orpheus and Other Literary Essays,* translated by Lydia Davis, 145–52. New York: Station Hill Press, 1981.

———. "Our Clandestine Companion." In *Face to Face with Levinas,* edited by Richard A. Cohen, 41–50. Albany: State University of New York, 1986.

Derrida, Jacques. "Plato's Pharmacy." In *Dissemination,* translated by Barbara Johnson, 61–171. Chicago: University of Chicago Press, 1981.

———. "Violence and Metaphysics." In *Writing and Difference,* translated and edited by Alan Bass, 79–153. Chicago: University of Chicago Press, 1978.

Freud, Sigmund. *Three essays on the Theory of Sexuality.* Translated and edited by James Strachey. New York: Basic Books, 2000.

Gadamer, Hans-Georg. *Heidegger's Ways.* Translated by John W. Stanley. Albany: State University of New York Press, 1994.

Hegel, G. W. F. *Elements of the Philosophy of Right.* Edited by Allen W. Wood. Translated by H. B. Nisbet. Cambridge: Cambridge University Press, 1991.

———. *Hegel's Logic.* Translated by William Wallace. Oxford: Clarendon Press, 1975.

Marion, Jean-Luc. *God Without Being.* Translated by Thomas A. Carlson. Chicago: University of Chicago Press, 1991.

———. *Le phénomène érotique.* Paris: Bernard Grasset, 2003.

Nietzsche, Friedrich. "On the Uses and Disadvantages of History for Life." *Untimely Meditations,* translated by R. J. Hollingdale. Cambridge: Cambridge University Press, 1983.

Otto, Rudolf. *The Idea of the Holy: An Inquiry into the Non-Rational Factor in the Idea of the Divine and its Relation to the Rational.* Translated by John H. Harvey. Oxford: Oxford University Press, 1926.

Sartre, Jean-Paul. *Being and Nothingness.* Translated by Hazel E. Barnes. New York: Washington Square Press, 1956.

Spinoza, Benedict. *Ethics.* Translated by W. H. White. Revised by A. H. Stirling. Ware: Wordsworth Classics of World Literature, 2001.

Secondary Sources

Achentberg, Deborah. "The Eternal and the New: Socrates and Levinas on Desire and Need." In *Levinas and the Ancients,* edited by Brian Schroeder and Silvia Benso, 24–39. Bloomington: Indiana University Press, 2008.

Allen, Sarah. *The Philosophical Sense of Transcendence: Levinas and Plato on Loving Beyond Being.* Pittsburgh: Duquesne University Press, 2009.

Bergo, Bettina. "Ontology, Transcendence, and Immanence in Emmanuel Levinas's Philosophy." *Research in Phenomenology* 35 (2005): 141–77.

Bernasconi, Robert. "No Exit: Levinas's Aporetic Account of Transcendence." *Research in Phenomenology* 35 (2005): 101–17.

———. "Levinas Face to Face with Hegel." *British Society of Phenomenology* 13, no. 3 (October 1982): 267–76.

Bernet, Rudolf. "Heimwee en Nostalgie." *Tijdschrift voor Filosofie* 67 (2005): 635–54.

Brown, Robert F. *The Later Philosophy of Schelling: The Influence of Böehme on the works of 1809–1815.* London: Associated University Press, 1977.

———. "Resources in Schelling for New Directions in Theology." *Idealistic Studies* (January 1990): 1–17.

Caputo, John D. "To the Point of a Possible Confusion: God and il y a." In *Levinas: The Face of the Other,* 1–36. Pittsburgh: Simon Silverman Center, 1998.

Chanter, Tina. *Time, Death and the Feminine: Levinas with Heidegger.* Stanford: Stanford University Press, 2001.

Ciaramelli, Fabio. "The Posteriority of the Anterior." *Graduate Faculty Philosophy Journal* 20, no. 2, vol. 21, no. 1 (1997): 409–26.

Clark, David. "Heidegger's Craving Being-on-Schelling." *Diacritics* 27, no. 3 (1997): 8–33.

Cohen, Richard. "Levinas, Rosenzweig and the Phenomenologies of Husserl and Heidegger." *Philosophy Today* 32, no. 2 (1988): 165–78.

———. "Some Notes on the Title of Levinas's *Totality and Infinity* and Its First Sentence." *Studia Phaenomenologica* 6 (2006): 117–37.

———. "The Family and Ethics: The Metaphysics of Eros in Emmanuel Levinas's *Totality and Infinity.*" *Contemporary Philosophy* 15, no. 4 (1993): 1–7.

———. *The Height of the Good in Rosenzweig and Levinas.* Chicago: University of Chicago Press, 1994.

Critchley, Simon. *Infinitely Demanding: Ethics of Commitment, Politics of Resistance.* London: Verso, 2007.

Ganz, Steven. "Ethics or Ontology: Levinas and Heidegger." *Philosophy Today* 16 (1972): 117–21.

Gibbs, Robert. "The Limits of Thought: Rosenzwieg, Schelling, and Cohen." *Zeitschrift für philosophische Forschung* 43, no. 4 (1989): 618–40.

Gonzalez, Francisco J. "Levinas Questioning Plato on Eros and Maieutics." In *Levinas and the Ancients,* edited by Brian Schroeder and Silvia Benso, 40–61. Bloomington: Indiana University Press, 2008.

Hohler, T. P. *Imagination and Reflection: Intersubjectivity—Fichte's Grundlage of 1794.* The Hague: Martinus Nijhoff, 1982.

Houlgate, Stephen. "Hegel and Fichte: Recognition, Otherness, and Absolute Knowing." *The Owl of Minerva* 26, no. 1 (1999): 3–19.

Hyland, Drew A. *Finitude and Transcendence in the Platonic Dialogues.* Albany: State University of New York, 1995.

———. "Ἔρως, Ἐπιθυμία, and Φιλία in Plato." *Phronesis* 13 (1968): 32–47.

Irigaray, Luce. "The Fecundity of the Caress: A Reading of Levinas, section IV, B, 'The Phenomenology of Eros.'" In *Face to Face with Levinas*, edited by Richard A. Cohen, 231–356. Albany: State University of New York Press, 1986.

Jay, Martin. *Downcast Eyes: The Denigration of Vision in Twentieth-Century French Thought.* Berkeley and Los Angeles: University of California Press, 1994.

Keyes, C. D. "An Evaluation of Levinas's Critique of Heidegger." *Research in Phenomenology* 2 (1974): 121–42.

Kosky, Jeffery L. *Levinas and the Philosophy of Religion.* Bloomington: Indiana University Press, 2001.

Lawrence, Joseph P. "Schelling and Levinas: The Harrowing of Hell." In *Levinas Studies: An Annual Review,* vol. 2, edited by Jeffrey Bloechl. Pittsburgh: Duquesne University Press, 2007.

Linker, Damon. "From Kant to Schelling: Counter-Enlightenment in the Name of Reason." *Review of Metaphysics* 54 (December 2003): 337–77.

Lumsden, Simon. "Fichte's Striving Subject." *Inquiry* 47, no. 2 (2004): 123–42.

———. "Absolute Difference and Social Ontology: Levinas Face to Face with Buber and Fichte." *Human Studies* 23 (2000).

Manning, Robert John Sheffling. *Interpreting Otherwise Than Heidegger: Emmanuel Levinas's Ethics as First Philosophy*. Pittsburgh: Duquesne University Press, 1993.

Mitchell, Robert Lloyd. *The Hymn to Eros: A Reading of Plato's Symposium*. Lanham: University Press of America, 1993.

Moyaert, Paul. "The Phenomenology of Eros: A Reading of *Totality and Infinity*." In *The Face of the Other and the Trace of God*, edited by Jeffrey Bloechl, 30–42. New York: Fordham University Press, 2000.

Moyn, Samuel. *Origins of the Other: Emmanuel Levinas Between Revelation and Ethics*. Ithaca: Cornell University Press, 2005.

Neske, Guther and Emil Kettering. *Martin Heidegger and National Socialism: Questions and Answers*. Saint Paul: Paragon House, 1990.

Norman, Judith. "The Logic of Longing: Schelling's Philosophy of Will." *British Journal for the History of Philosophy* 10, no. 1 (2002): 89–107.

O'Connor, Noreen. "Being and the Good: Heidegger and Levinas." *Philosophical Studies* 27 (1980): 212–20.

Peperzak, Adriaan. *Beyond: The Philosophy of Emmanuel Levinas*. Evanston: Northwestern University Press, 1997.

———. *To the Other: An Introduction to the Philosophy of Emmanuel Levinas*. Lafayette: Purdue University Press, 1993.

———. "Phenomenology—Ontology—Metaphysics: Levinas's Perspective of Husserl and Heidegger." *Man and World* 16 (1983): 113–27.

———. "Some Remarks on Hegel, Kant and Levinas." In *Face to Face with Levinas,* edited by Richard A. Cohen, 205–17. Albany: State University of New York Press, 1986.

Purcell, Michael. *Levinas and Theology*. Cambridge: Cambridge University Press, 2006.

Raffoul, Farncois. *Heidegger and the Subject*. Translated by David Pettigrew and Gregory Recco. Atlantic Highlands: Humanities Press, 1998.

Rockmore, Tom. *On Heidegger's Nazism and Philosophy*. Berkley and Los Angeles: University of California Press, 1997.

Rosen, Stanley. "Heidegger's Interpretation of Plato." *Journal of Existentialism* 7 (1967): 477–504.

———. *Plato's Symposium*. New Haven: Yale University Press, 1968.

Sanford, Stella. "Plato and Levinas: The Same and the Other." *Journal of the British Society for Phenomenology* 35 (2005): 101–17.

Schalow, Frank. *Heidegger and the Quest for the Sacred: From Thought to the Sanctuary of Faith*. Dordrecht: Kluwer Academic, 2001.

Scribner, F. Scott. "Levinas Face to Face with Fichte." *Southwest Philosophy Review* 16, no. 1 (2000): 151–60.

Steinkamp, Fiona. "Eternity and Time: Levinas Returns to Schelling." In *Schelling Now: Contemporary Readings,* edited by Jason M. Wirth, 207–22. Bloomington: Indiana University Press, 2005.

Taminiaux, Jacques, "The Early Levinas's Reply to Heidegger's Fundamental Ontology." *Philosophy and Social Criticism* 23, no. 6 (1997): 29–49.

Taylor, Mark C. "The Non-Absence of the Holy." In *Phenomenology and the Numinous: The Fifth Annual Symposium of the Simon Silverman Phenomenology Center*. Pittsburgh: Simon Silverman Center, 1988.

Vedder, Ben. "Heidegger on Desire." *Continental Philosophy Review* 31 (1998): 353–68.

Visker, Rudi. *The Inhuman Condition: Looking for Difference after Levinas and Heidegger*. Pittsburgh: Duquesne University Press, 2008.

———. *Truth and Singularity: Taking Foucault into Phenomenology*. Dordrecht: Kluwer Academic, 1999.

———. "Is There Death after Life?" *Umbr(a): Incurable.* (2006): 101–18.

White, Alan. *Schelling: An Introduction to the System of Freedom*. New Haven: Yale University Press, 1983.

Williams, Robert R. *Recognition: Fichte and Hegel on the Other*. Albany: State University of New York Press, 1992.

Wyschogrod, Edith. "From the Disaster to the Other: Tracing the Name of God in Levinas." In *Phenomenology and the Numinous: The Fifth Annual Symposium of the Simon Silverman Phenomenology Center*, 67–86. Pittsburgh: Simon Silverman Center, 1988.

Zimmerman, Michael E. "Ontical Craving versus Ontological Desire." In *From Phenomenology to Thought, Errancy and Desire,* edited by Babette E. Babich. Dordrecht: Kluwer Academic, 1995.

Žižek, Slavoj. *The Indivisible Remainder: An Essay on Schelling and Related Matters*. London: Verso, 1996.

Zöeller, Gunter. *Fichte's Transcendental Philosophy: The Original Duplicity of Intelligence and Will*. Cambridge: Cambridge University Press, 1998.

Nonphilosophical Sources

Arnold, Matthew. "The Buried Life." In *The Poems of Matthew Arnold 1984–1867*, edited by A. T. Quiller-Couch. Oxford: Oxford University Press, 1909.

Deutsches Wörterbuch von Jacob Grimm und Wilhelm Grimm. Leipzig: Verlag von S. Hirzel, 1905.

Ende, Michael. *Die unendliche Geschichte*. Stuttgart: K. Thienemanns Verlang. 1979.

Goethe, Johann Wolfgang. "Selige Sehnsucht." In *Selected Verse: Dual Language Edition with Plain Language Translations of Each Poem*. London: Penguin Classics, 1964.

———. *Maxims and Reflections*. London: Penguin Books, 1998.

Hemingway, Ernest. *A Moveable Feast*. New York: Charles Scribner's and Sons, 1964.

Herbert, George. "The Temple." In *George Herbert: The Complete English Poems*. London: Penguin Classics, 2005.

Homer. *The Odyssey*. Translated by Robert Fitzgerald. New York: Farrar, Straus and Giroux, 1998.

Lewis, C. S. *Surprised by Joy: The Shape of my Early Life*. San Diego: Harcourt, 1995.

Liddell and Scott's Greek-English Lexicon. Oxford: Oxford University Press, 1984.

Shakespeare, William. "*Anthony and Cleopatra.*" In *The Complete Works of William Shakespeare,* edited by W. J. Craig. London: Oxford University Press, 1943.

———. "Sonnet 147." In *William Shakespeare: The Complete Sonnets and Poems,* edited by Colin Burrow. Oxford: Oxford University Press, 2002.

Tennyson, Alfred Lord. "Ulysses." In *Tennyson's Poetry*, edited by Robert W. Hill Jr., 82–84. New York: W. W. Norton, 1999.

The American Heritage Dictionary of the English Language, Fourth Edition. Boston: Houghton Mifflin, 2000.

The New American Standard Bible. Nashville: Broadman and Holman, 1960.

The Oxford English Dictionary, vol. 8, *Interval-Looie,* 2nd ed. Prepared by J. A. Simpson and E. S. C. Weiner. Oxford: Clarendon Press, 1989.

Wildhagen and Héraucourt German-English Dictionary. 2nd ed. Weisbaden: Brandstetter Verlag, 1972.

INDEX

Abraham, 23
alterity, 88, 106, 117, 155, 160–61, 243, 273n13
Anthony and Cleopatra (Shakespeare), 5–6
Aristophanes, 28, 34
Arnold, Matthew, 5, 276n27
atheism, 174–75, 186, 240
authenticity, 72–78, 80–93, 273n13
awakening, 41–42

beauty, 31, 47–48
Being: absence of, 193; anonymity of, 96; and being, 69, 98–101, 207, 277n35, 277n36, 286n37; empowerment of, 107; and evil, 247; and the Good, 25, 41, 95–98, 101–08, 241–43, 288n2–3; and *il y a,* 105; Levinas on, 41, 95–98, 104–08, 265n7, 271n2; and metaphysics, 103–04. *See also* Other, the
being: and Being, 69, 98–101, 207, 277n35, 277n36, 286n37; of God, 256; Heidegger on, 97–106, 277n35, 278n38, 286n37; history before, 169; and hypostasis, 183–87; tyranny of, 134; without beings, 207. *See also* beyond being
Being and Time (Heidegger), 74, 251
Bernasconi, Robert, 267n25, 271n2, 279n50, 280n8
beyond being: ambiguity in nature of, 244; and the Good, 95–98, 104–08; and Heidegger, 98–104; Levinas on, 271n2; and longing, 215–18, 228–35, 241–43, 258; and the numinous, 232; and responsibility to the Other, 134. *See also* being
Blanchot, Maurice, 243, 278n43
Böehme, Jacob, 196, 233
Brown, Robert, 193, 197, 203
Buber, Martin, 16, 159
"The Buried Life" (Arnold), 5

Chanter, Tina, 278n41
child, 56–57, 259, 270n51
cogito. *See* the I
Cohen, Richard, 57, 264n2, 270n47, 278n41, 284n8
coming-to-be-home, 90

conscience and the self, 120
consciousness: and creation, 200; Fichte on, 161; and freedom, 131; and the I, 115, 145–46; and shame, 128–33
consumption and longing, 226, 254, 260
contractio Dei, 171–79, 185–86, 196–97
contractio hominis, 182–87
Cratylus (Plato), 64, 269n40
craving, 85, 291n20. *See also* desire; longing
creation: and consciousness, 200; as *contractio Dei,* 171–79, 185–86, 196–97; as *contractio hominis,* 182–87; as the eternal beginning and eternally past, 204–05; and ethics, 212–15; and the face, 180–81; and God, 171–81; Levinas on, 169–79, 212–15; and longing, 181–82; and metaphysical desire, 178; and the Other, 169–71; passivity of, 175; preceded by *il y a,* 207–08; Schelling on, 187–92, 194–206, 212–15, 284n14; and shame, 181; and time, 204–05; and the trace, 178–82
Critchley, Simon, 267n31

daemon, 32
Dasein, 74–75, 82, 90
dependence, 173–77, 188–90, 200–06, 283n4. *See also* independence
Der Ister lectures (Heidegger), 89–90
Derrida, Jacques, 107, 265n8, 268n39

Descartes, René, 15, 115–16, 177
desire: erotic, 270n51; immanence of, 56; and metaphysical desire, 54–60; and need and nostalgia, 59–60; for the Other, 20; and pleasure, 51–53; and the self, 120; and shame, 137–38; as sickness, 266n13; versus longing, 219, 225–27, 253–57. *See also* craving; longing
Desire, desire, 54–56, 77–79; erotic, 56, 270n51
Diotima, 27, 34
divine, the, 63–65, 208, 210, 218–19, 239–40, 253, 255, 289n6, 290n13. *See also* God; the numinous; the Other

Eckhart, Meister, 233
ego: finite and infinite, 151–52; passivity of, 139–41; and the self, 131; and shame, 119–20; tyranny of, 116. *See also* I, the
egoism, 116, 281n10
emancipation, 41
empowerment, 102–03, 107
enjoyment, 58–59, 122–24, 173–77
epiphany, 136
epithumia (lust), 61–65
Eros: authenticity of, 72–78, 85–93; and beauty, 31, 47; as daemon, 32; and the divine, 63–65; and ethics, 266n17; Heidegger on, 70–72, 77, 79, 81, 272–73n11, 291n21; and homecoming and homelessness, 34–36; Levinas on, 27–29, 45–47, 52–54, 56; and longing, 155–56; and

metaphysical desire, 36–37, 60; and need, 32–33; and nostalgia, 46; passivity of, 48; Plato on, 27–33; and pleasure, 53, 61–63; and striving and having, 72, 79–85, 177; as "way out," 32–33, 267–68n32
Essence of Truth, The (Heidegger), 70–71
"Eternity and Time: Levinas Returns to Schelling" (Steinkamp), 206–12
eternity, 211
ethics, ethical: and creation, 212–15; and Eros, 266n17; and freedom, 134–36; and the holy, 239–41; and the I, 149–56; and longing, 156, 168; and metaphysical desire, 113–14, 156; and the Other, 179; as spiritual optics, 167; transcendence of, 267n25
Ethics (Spinoza), 23
evil, 95–96, 212–13, 238, 245–49, 260, 287n47
excess, 82
Existence and Existents (Levinas), 58
exteriority, 20–21, 46–47

face, the, 39–40, 136, 180–81
fecundity, 57, 259, 270n51
Fichte, Johann Gottlieb, 16, 115, 139–48, 150–64, 281n10, 281–82nn12–14
field of forces, 207–08
finitude, 145, 151–52. *See also* infinite, the
foreign, the, 90–91
freedom: of consciousness, 131; ethical, 134–36; in God, 191; of humans, 201–02; and the I, 115–18; Levinas on, 125; and shame, 134–36; summons to, 147
Freud, Sigmund, 267n28
Fundamental Concepts of Metaphysics (Heidegger), 91

Gadamer, Hans-Georg, 274n20
Ganz, Steven, 278n38, 279n51
God: actuality of, 285n24; as beyond being, 215–16, 222, 228, 235; and *contractio Dei,* 171–79, 185–86, 196–98; and creation, 180–81; as a determinate possibility, 198–99, 202–03; and evil, 248–49; Heidegger on, 251–52, 291n19; and the holy, 229–32; and longing, 215–20, 228–29; and relationship with another, 239–41; revelation of, 126–32, 250–53, 291n18; Schelling on, 245–57, 291n18; and time, 202–04, 210–11; and the *Ungrund,* 194–97, 286–87n42; and unity of forces, 209; will of, 250–53. *See also* longing; the divine; the Other
Goethe, Johann Wolfgang von, 9, 257, 264n24
Good, the: and beyond Being, 25, 41, 95–98, 101–08, 241–43, 288n2–3; and creation, 212; and evil, 249; Heidegger on, 101–08, 278n40, 288n2; and the holy, 230, 288–89nn2–3; as interruption, 266n22; and metaphysical desire, 37–38; and metaphysics, 107; and the Other, 38–40; and the other,

40–41; Plato and, 288n2; possession and, 44–45; transcendence and, 107–08
Grimm brothers, 8–9

having, 72, 77, 79–93, 97, 273n13. *See also* striving
Hegel, Georg Wilhelm Friedrich, 16, 139, 238, 283n5, 289–90n8
Heidegger, Martin: on art, 276n28; on being and beings, 96–106, 277n35, 278n38, 286n37; on empowerment, 102–03; on Eros, 70–72, 77, 79, 81, 272–73n11, 291n21; on evil, 246–49; on excess, 82; on the foreign, 90–91; on God, 251–52, 291n19; on the Good, 101–08, 278n40, 288n2; on homesickness, 91–92; and Levinas, 15, 67–69, 94–98; on longing, 87–98, 104–05, 109–10, 158, 253–54, 273n15; and metaphysics, 103–04; on need, 273n15; on nihilism, 69, 277–78n37; and Plato, 69–71, 271–72n3; on possession, 83–84; on restlessness, 91, 276n26; and Schelling, 274n20; on the soul, 277n34; on striving and having, 273n13, 277n34; and truth, 272n8; on the wholly other, 231–32; works of: *Being and Time,* 74, 251; *Der Ister* lectures, 89–90; *The Essence of Truth,* 70–71; *Fundamental Concepts of Metaphysics,* 91; *Introduction to Metaphysics* lectures, 100; "On the Essence of Truth," 101; *Schelling's Treatise* lectures, 87–88; "Time and Being" lectures, 99; "What Is Metaphysics?", 100, 272n4
Hemingway, Ernest, 5
Herbert, George, 7
Hero, 64, 269n40
Hestia, 35
himeros (love), 63–65
history, 169
Hohler, T. P., 146, 148
holy, the; holiness: and the ethical, 239–41; and God, 229–32; and the Good, 230, 288–89nn2–3; and the infinite, 240–41, 244; Levinas on, 239–41; and longing, 10; as protection, 290n14; and the sacred, 236–38, 242, 260
homecoming, 33–36
homelessness, 23, 28, 34–36
homesickness, 7, 91–92
Husserl, Edmund, 15
Hyland, Drew, 36, 62
hypostasis, 182–87. *See also* independence; self, the

I, the: and creation, 177; and the ethical, 149–56; as finite, 145; and freedom, 115–18; and hypostasis, 183–87; and idealism, 115, 117; Levinas on, 280n5; and otherness of the world, 122–25; and responsibility for the Other, 132–37; self-positing of, 141–48, 200, 281–82n13; and shame, 118–33; summoning of, 146–48; and the Thou, 146–48,

151, 158–60, 284n12. *See also* ego
idealism, 114–20, 138–40, 162, 280n4, 283n5, 284n12
Idea of the Holy, The (Otto), 229–36
illumination from the Other, 39, 126–28, 168–69, 258, 267n28
il y a, 95–97, 105, 183–87, 207–13, 243. *See also* there is
inauthenticity, 73–79, 84–85
independence, 173–77, 188–90, 200–06, 283n4. *See also* dependence; hypostasis
infinite: bad, 238, 242–44, 260, 276n31, 289–90n8, 290n10; and the ego, 151–52; and eternity, 211; exteriority of, 46–47; Fichte on, 157–58; and the holy, 240–41; idea of, 44; Levinas on, 157–58, 242–44, 260; and longing, 225, 244, 259–60; and metaphysical desire, 2–3; within oneself, 268n37; passivity of, 45; and the sacred, 237–38; striving for, 151–56; and the subject, 152. *See also* finitude
interiority, 44, 173
intersubjectivity, 158–60
Introduction to Metaphysics lectures (Heidegger), 100
Irigaray, Luce, 270n49

Kant, Immanuel, 116, 264n1
Kierkegaard, Søren, 15

law of identity, 188–90, 210, 212
Levinas, Emmanuel: on authenticity, 76; on Being, 41, 95–98, 104–08, 265n7, 271n2; on creation, 169–79, 212–15; on Desire and desire, 77–79; on the divine, 239–40, 289n6, 290n13; on Eros, 27–29, 45–47, 52–54, 78; on erotic love, 269n45–46; and Fichte, 139–48, 150, 157–64; and field of forces, 207–08; on freedom, 125; and Heidegger, 67–69, 94–98; on the holy, 239–41; on hypostasis, 182–87; on the I, 280n5; and *il y a,* 95–97, 105, 183–87, 207–13; on the infinite, 157–58, 242–44, 260; influences on, 15–16; on longing, 94–98, 104–05, 109–10, 167–68, 257–61; on metaphysical desire, 19–24; on the mythical, 238; on the numinous, 236–38; on the Other, 290n12; and Plato, 15, 25–29, 265nn7–8, 271–72n3; on pleasure, 50–52; and Schelling, 206–22; on shame, 168–69; and *there is,* 95, 184, 237–38, 243, 277n36, 290n10; on time, 177–78; on Western philosophy, 114–20, 139; on the wholly other, 231; works of: *Existence and Existents,* 58; *On Escape,* 60, 281n11; *Totality and Infinity,* 20, 36, 56, 68, 131, 281n11
Lewis, C. S., 5, 8, 257
longing: and beyond Being, 215–16, 218, 228–35, 241–43, 258; and consumption, 226, 254, 260; and creation, 181–82; definition of, 4–10, 257; and Eros, 155–56; and ethics and the ethical, 156,

168; etymology of, 6–10; and evil, 260; and God, 215–20, 228–29; grammar of, 11–14; Heidegger on, 87–98, 104–05, 109–10, 158, 253–54, 273n15; and holiness, 10; and identity, 4; as indeterminate, 226–67; and the infinite, 225, 244, 259–60; insatiability of, 22–24, 44, 66, 226; Levinas on, 94–98, 104–05, 109–10, 157–58, 162, 167–68, 257–61; manifestations of, 221; and meaning, 258; as metaphysical desire, 3, 155, 167–68, 227–28; metaphysical grounding of, 162–63; and the numinous, 235–36, 244; for the Other, 113–14, 218–19; passivity of, 6, 13–14, 222, 259; as phenomenon, 261; as protection, 241, 257–58; and reason, 220; and revelation of God, 252–53; Schelling on, 215–20, 253–57; and self, 157; semantics and etymology of, 6–10; and shame, 137–38; as sickness, 7–9, 266n13, 287n51; and striving and having, 97, 153–56, 268n39; and the trace, 179; transcendence of, 258; versus desire, 219, 225–27, 253–57; versus need, 155, 222; versus nostalgia, 218, 259. *See also* craving; God; having; striving

love, 63–65, 198; erotic, 56–58, 269n45–46, 284n18

Lumsden, Simon, 150–51

lust, 61–65

madness, 47–48

Marion, Jean-Luc, 288n1

meaning, 230–32, 258

memory, 28

metaphysical desire: as awakening, 41–42; and beyond being, 95–96; and creation, 178; definition of, 2–3, 19–24; and desire, 54–60; and Eros, 36–37, 60; and erotic desire, 270n51; as ethical movement, 113–14, 156; and exteriority, 20–21; and the Good, 37–38, 95; and the infinite, 2–3; insatiability of, 23–24; longing as, 155, 167–68, 227–28; origins of, 43; as phenomenon, 25; as protection, 241; transascendence of, 21, 42, 114; transcendence of, 20–21, 56

metaphysics, 103–04, 107, 162–63

Milton, John, 5

Moveable Feast, A (Hemingway), 5

mysterium, 231

mysticism, 232–36

myth, 115, 117

namelessness, 93, 276nn27–28

need: and desire, 59–60; Eros as, 32–33; Heidegger on, 273n15; and Plato, 26–28; and possession, 84; and the self, 21–23; versus longing, 155, 222

Nemo, Philippe, 67

Nietzsche, Friedrich, 13, 277–78n37

Norman, Judith, 195, 287n53

nostalgia: definition of, 265n5;

and desire, 59–60; and Eros, 46; and Plato, 26–28; and the self, 21–23; versus longing, 218, 259
not-being-at-home, 90–91, 275n25
numinous, the, 232–36, 244–45. *See also* divine, the

Odysseus, 22–23, 26, 251, 264–65n3, 280n7
Of Human Freedom (Schelling), 187, 210, 244–45
On Escape (Levinas), 60, 281n11
"On the Essence of Truth" (Heidegger), 101
Other, the: and alterity, 160–61; and creation, 169–71; desire for, 20; and emancipation, 41; and enjoyment, 58–59; ethical encounter with, 179; and the face, 180–81; and the Good, 38–40; illuminative power of, 39, 126–28, 168–69, 267n28; Levinas on, 290n12; and longing, 113–14; and responsibility, 132–37; and shame, 119–20, 122–25, 129–30. *See also* Being; God
otherwise than being, 243
Otto, Rudolf, 16, 229–36, 288–89nn2–3

pain and pleasure, 53–54
Parmenides (Plato), 269n43
passivity: of atheism, 175; of creation, 175; and the ego, 139–41; of Eros, 48; of human existence, 225; and the infinite, 45; of longing, 6, 13–14, 222, 259; and philosophy, 269n43;

of shame, 118–20; and striving, 80–82; and suffering, 140
Peperzak, Adriaan, 36, 42, 54, 264n1, 266n17
Phaedrus (Plato), 27, 34–35, 45, 48, 53, 60–65
phenomenon, 25, 234–35, 248, 261
Plato: and desire, 26–29; on Eros, 27–33; and the Good, 288n2; and Heidegger, 69–71, 271–72n3; and Levinas, 15, 25–29, 265nn7–8, 271–72n3; on need, 26–28; works of: *Cratylus,* 64; *Parmenides,* 269n43; *Phaedrus,* 27, 34–35, 45, 48, 53, 60–65; *The Republic,* 27; *Symposium,* 27–28, 30–32, 61; *Theaetetus,* 48–49, 269n40, 269n42
pleasure, 50–54, 61–63
Poros (way) and *Penia* (lack), 32, 156, 266n14
possession, 44–45, 83–84, 268n36
posteriority of the anterior, 42, 170–71
Purcell, Michael, 36

Republic, The (Plato), 27
responsibility, 40–41, 132–37
restlessness, 91, 276n26
revelation, 126–33, 250–53, 291n18
Rosen, Stanley, 36, 106
Rosenzweig, Franz, 15, 284n8

sacred, the, and the holy, 236–38, 242, 260
Sartre, Jean-Paul, 270n52

Schelling, Friedrich Wilhelm Joseph, 16; on, 284n14; compared to Levinas, 206–22; on creation, 187–92, 194–206, 212–15, 284n14; on evil, 245–57; on God, 245–57, 291n18; and Heidegger, 274n20; on human freedom, 201–02; and identity, 188–90; on longing, 215–20, 253–57; on love, 198; on the *Ungrund*, 192–97, 210–11, 213, 286–87n42; works of: *Of Human Freedom,* 187, 210, 244–45

Schelling's Treatise lectures (Heidegger), 87–88

Scribner, F. Scott, 150, 161

Sehnsucht. See longing

self, the, 21–22, 120, 131, 134–36, 144, 157. *See also* hypostasis

self-consciousness, 128–33, 145–46

self-identification, 177

self-positing: of the I, 117, 141–48, 200, 281–82n13; of the *Ungrund,* 195

"Selige Sehnsucht" (Goethe), 9

Shakespeare, William, 5–6, 8, 257

shame: as beyond being, 168–69; and creation, 181; and desire, 137–38; and ego, 119–20; and freedom, 134–36; and the I, 118–33; and longing, 137–38; and the Other, 114–20, 122–25, 129–30; passivity of, 118–20; and responsibility, 132–37; and revelation, 126–33; and the trace, 179

sickness, 7–9, 266n13, 268n39, 287n51

Socrates, 30–31, 34, 47–49, 60–65, 97, 271n59

Spinoza, Baruch, 15, 23

Steinkamp, Fiona, 206–12

stirring, 92–93

striving: and authenticity, 85–93; and Eros, 72, 77, 79–85; erotic, 81–82; Heidegger on, 277n34; and inauthenticity, 84–85; for the infinite, 151–56; and longing, 97, 153–56; and passivity, 80–82. *See also* having; longing

subject. *See* I, the

Surprised by Joy (Lewis), 5

Symposium (Plato), 27–28, 30–32, 61

Theaetetus (Plato), 48–49, 269n40, 269n42

there is, 95, 184, 237–38, 243, 277n36, 290n10. *See also il y a*

Thou, the, 146–47, 151, 158–60, 284n12

time, 177–78, 202–05, 210–11

"Time and Being" lecture (Heidegger), 99

Totality and Infinity (Levinas), 20, 36, 56, 68, 131

trace, the, 40, 178–82, 211

transascendence, 21, 42, 114

transcendence: erotic, 27–28, 35, 53–54, 63, 77, 82, 86–87, 274n16; and ethics, 267n25; and the Good, 107–08; of longing, 258; of metaphysical desire, 20–21, 56; and the numinous, 235–36; temporary, 22–23

truth, 70, 74, 272n8

Ungrund, 192–97, 210–11, 213, 286–87n42

Vedder, Ben, 71, 87
vision, 38–39
Visker, Rudi, 168, 239, 266n22, 290nn9, 290n14

"What Is Metaphysics?" (Heidegger), 100, 272n4

wholly other, 231–32
Williams, Robert R., 149–50, 282n27
Wissenschaftslehre (Fichte), 139–48, 281n12
world, 122–25

Žižek, Slavoj, 195, 206, 256, 285n20
Zöller, Gunter, 146, 160